W9-BAV-669

OXFORD READINGS IN POLITICS
AND GOVERNMENT

JUSTICE

OXFORD READINGS IN POLITICS
AND GOVERNMENT

General Editors: Vernon Bogdanor and Geoffrey Marshall

The readings in this series are chosen from a variety of journals and other sources to cover major areas or issues in the study of politics, government, and political theory. Each volume contains an introductory essay by the editor and a select guide to further reading.

ALSO PUBLISHED IN THIS SERIES

Communitarianism and Individualism
Edited by Shlomo Avineri and Avner de-Shalit

Marxist Theory
Edited by Alex Callinicos

Parliamentary versus Presidential Government
Edited by Arend Lijphart

The West European Party System
Edited by Peter Mair

Ministerial Responsibility
Edited by Geoffrey Marshall

Liberty
Edited by David Miller

Legislatures
Edited by Philip Norton

Pressure Groups
Edited by Jeremy J. Richardson

JUSTICE

EDITED BY

ALAN RYAN

OXFORD UNIVERSITY PRESS

1993

4-21-94 dmi

Oxford University Press, Walton Street, Oxford OX2 6DP
Oxford New York Toronto
Delhi Bombay Calcutta Madras Karachi
Kuala Lumpur Singapore Hong Kong Tokyo
Nairobi Dar es Salaam Cape Town
Melbourne Auckland Madrid
and associated companies in
Berlin Ibadan

Oxford is a trade mark of Oxford University Press

Published in the United States
by Oxford University Press Inc., New York

This selection and editorial matter © Alan Ryan 1993

All rights reserved. No part of this publication may be reproduced,
stored in a retrieval system, or transmitted, in any form or by any means,
without the prior permission in writing of Oxford University Press.
Within the UK, exceptions are allowed in respect of any fair dealing for the
purpose of research or private study, or criticism or review, as permitted
under the Copyright, Designs and Patents Act, 1988, or in the case of
reprographic reproduction in accordance with the terms of the licences
issued by the Copyright Licensing Agency. Enquiries concerning
reproduction outside these terms and in other countries should be
sent to the Rights Department, Oxford University Press,
at the address above.

The paperback edition of this book is sold subject to the condition that it
shall not, by way of trade or otherwise, be lent, re-sold, hired out or otherwise
circulated without the publisher's prior consent in any form of binding or cover
other than that in which it is published and without a similar condition including
this condition being imposed on the subsequent purchaser

British Library Cataloguing in Publication Data
Data available

Library of Congress Cataloging in Publication Data
Justice/edited by Alan Ryan.
p. cm. — (Oxford readings in politics and government)
Collection of previously published articles.
Includes bibliographical references.
1. Justice. I. Ryan, Alan. II. Series.
JC578.J863 1993 320'.01'1–dc20 92–35200
ISBN 0–19–878037–0
ISBN 0–19–878038–9 (Pbk.)

Typeset by Pentacor PLC, High Wycombe, Bucks
Printed in Great Britain
on acid-free paper by
Bookcraft (Bath) Ltd., Midsomer Norton, Avon

JC
578
.J863
1993

CANISIUS COLLEGE LIBRARY
BUFFALO, N.Y.

CONTENTS

INTRODUCTION

ALAN RYAN

JUSTICE IN GENERAL

Mankind has always argued about justice and injustice, while social scientists and politicians have endlessly discussed the conditions which make justice more or less attainable. These essays discuss a more philosophical issue—what justice *is* and why it matters. Although their authors were philosophers, few of them were 'professional' philosophers; Plato may have played an active part in Athenian politics, Cicero was certainly an important Roman politician, David Hume was a partisan historian, sometime diplomat, and man of letters, while John Stuart Mill earned his living by managing the East India Company's political relations with the Indian princely states.

This is appropriate. Justice is the most 'political' or institutional of the virtues.[1] The legitimacy of a state rests upon its claim to do justice. 'Take away justice', said St Augustine, 'and what is a state but a large robber band?'[2] All enterprises ought to be conducted justly, but the state especially must police other institutions and itself. Doing justice is not the primary purpose of the family, the classroom, the small business, even though a father, teacher, or employer ought to behave justly towards children, pupils, or employees when rearing them, teaching them, and employing them.[3] This introduction discusses several differences in the ways the authors of the essays collected here understood justice and its demands, but I begin with the peculiarly institutional or political quality of justice, and what follows from that.

Justice is peculiarly stringent. Its demands may not be modified. Judges and rulers must 'do justice though the heavens fall', not allow family connections, friendship, or even personal worth to turn them aside. The court in Shakespeare's Venice could have turned

---

[1] See David Hume, below, pp. 49–50; John Rawls, *A Theory of Justice* (Clarendon Press: Oxford, 1972), 3 ff.

[2] St Augustine, *The City of God*, Bk. IV (Penguin: Harmondsworth, 1984), 139.

[3] Though I do not mean to deny Susan Okin's claim that recent writers have excessively neglected justice within the family, and have ignored the questions that the division of labour in the family poses for a theory of justice. Indeed, I take it for granted that she is quite right. See her *Justice, Gender and the Family* (Basic Books: New York, 1990).

down Shylock's demand for a pound of flesh if it was sufficient that
he was ill-natured, nobody's friend, and a grasping Jew. It was not.
He demanded justice, not friendship or approval. He had a valid
contract,[4] and until Portia came up with a device for invalidating it,
he could stand on his rights, even the right to a pound of someone
else's flesh.[5]

Stringency involves consistency. Shylock insisted that contracts
must be kept, not to suit the friends of the rulers of Venice, but
contracts as such. The rest of life is more flexible. A man who drinks
tea at breakfast is not condemned for drinking coffee at dinner or at
breakfast the following day.[6] The judge who gives one burglar
eighteen months at ten in the morning and an identical burglar five
years at four in the afternoon will have the longer sentence appealed:
just punishment cannot be both eighteen months and five years, the
same offence must attract the same treatment. This has to be taken
with qualifications: the judge might have found mitigating
circumstances in the first case. Qualifications themselves must be
qualified; mercy must not be capricious. Immanuel Kant, indeed,
claimed that courts could not let criminals off the full rigour of the
law's demands, an opinion summarized in the chilling view that a
society which knew it was to perish from the face of the earth in the
morning must leave none of its condemned murderers unhanged.[7]
Few writers go so far. Most think justice sets a limit to what the law
can demand, not that the law must demand all it can.

Justice is closely connected to respect for rights. Modern writers
discuss both subjects together with no suggestion that one might
discuss one with the other.[8] It was not always so. Greek political
theory and Roman Law had sophisticated ideas about justice in its
various aspects, but did not embrace *our* conception of individual
rights. This may seem counter-intuitive. How could a society
recognize someone as the owner of a piece of property without
acknowledging an individual right? How does legitimate one-man-
rule, monarchy, differ from its illegitimate parody, tyranny, unless
the lawful king has a right to the authority he exercises that the
tyrant does not?

The answer is that property and authority were defined by law
rather than our notion of individual rights. To own property was to

---

[4] In fact, the English common law would have invalidated it as one which it
would be contrary to the public interest to enforce.

[5] *The Merchant of Venice*, IV. i.

[6] Cf. the plea of the defendant in Gilbert and Sullivan's *Trial by Jury*, who observes
that it is no crime to turn from roast beef to mutton.

[7] H. B. Reiss (ed.) *Kant's Political Writings* (Cambridge University Press:
Cambridge, 1992), 156.

[8] Rawls, *A Theory of Justice*, is the paradigm.

be the person to whom the law accorded the privileges and immunities that locally defined ownership. To be a legitimate ruler was to be the person the law designated to rule. It is a commonplace that ancient notions of law accorded far more power over property to the family and other groups than modern notions of private property do.[9] Even under the Roman Law, where ownership had an 'absolute' and sovereign character, property was not understood in the modern way; when the law told the judge to give a man his *ius*, this primarily meant that he should be treated as the law required. The 'subjective' understanding of rights, whereby the right-holder may stand on his rights or not as he chooses, was not a Roman notion.[10]

Neither Plato nor Aristotle held that justice was a matter of individual rights. Plato's confiding power to the Guardians and Auxiliaries, and his insistence on an aristocratic form of government may seem to imply that only philosophers are *entitled* to rule, or have a *right* to govern. But this is not the argument. The setting is that of building a state on rational principles; the standpoint is not that of individuals claiming rights, but that of a builder placing human material in its proper place in the fabric. States need good rulers, and that is what the Guardians are. Aristotle's discussion of a state that achieves freedom and justice in a stable setting does not treat this as a question of rights—unlike Locke's treatment of the same question. Locke's state is the result of a contract between the holders of prior rights; Aristotle's allocates authority to classes and individuals according to a rational and morally acceptable scheme—according to justice—but not to protect or recognize individual rights.[11]

There is a last point to be made about the connection between justice and rights. Hume and Mill discuss them together, not raising the question whether one is logically or morally prior to the other. They write as naturalists, explaining morality as a system of rules of conduct accepted to promote human welfare. For anti-utilitarian, non-naturalistic writers such as John Rawls and Robert Nozick, either rights or justice have to bear the heaviest argumentative weight. For Rawls, the principles of justice are fundamental, and the rights we have are those justice dictates; for Nozick, we begin with 'entitlements' that we are born with or acquire, and justice exists

---

[9] Sir Alfred Zimmern, *The Greek Commonwealth* (Clarendon Press: Oxford, 1935), 133.
[10] Richard Tuck, *Natural Law Theories* (Cambridge University Press: Cambridge, 1979), 7–13.
[11] Aristotle, *Politics*, trans. and ed. E. Barker (Clarendon Press: Oxford, 1969), III, ss. 12–13, pp. 129–36.

when people have what they are entitled to.[12] Understanding our basic entitlements is the foundation of all else.

Justice is a virtue, but not one that makes people lovable. 'Hard but just' is a common appraisal of judges, employers, teachers, and others; those who are 'hard but just' will not wrong us, but they are not attractive figures.[13] For justice is not always what we seek. The visitor to an invalid who comes because he has visited six persons already and thinks it would be unfair to leave out the seventh is less welcome than the visitor who calls out of a selfish desire to enjoy the invalid's company. The parent who apportions his affections so as not to treat his children unjustly will be less loved than a more capricious but more spontaneous parent. Justice is a political or institutional virtue more aptly practised by people who do not have warm ties to one another. We do not want the judge to allow natural feeling to swamp his desire to do justice to the plaintiff before him, but we do want intimate relationships to be sustained by natural feeling. A person who practised only what justice demanded would be an odd fish and a cold one.

These considerations suggest another feature of justice, which is its *basicness*. John Rawls says that justice is the 'first virtue' of social institutions, meaning that it is more fundamental than any other, and that we cannot expect individuals to accept social regulation, and engage in social co-operation unless the terms on which society operates are seen as reasonably just.[14] To talk as though Plato and Aristotle saw justice as a matter of the terms of social and political co-operation may suggest a modern and individualist perspective foreign to both. Yet it is not wholly misleading.[15] They thought that justice was a matter of the allocation of fundamental tasks, of putting people in the social roles they had to fulfil, and that catches the thought that justice is concerned with the terms of social life. Over the content of the terms, there is no agreement. Aristotle devoted a lot of space to the principle of allocating advantages according to desert or merit, while John Rawls leaves out desert entirely.[16]

Justice stands in an awkward relationship with utility. The general practice of justice conduces to human welfare, probably more than anything else. The old tag sums up justice as 'honeste vivere, neminem laedere, suum cuique tribuere'; the usefulness of

[12] Below, pp. 96–102.
[13] Hume, below, p. 47.
[14] *A Theory of Justice*, 3–14.
[15] Especially in the light of *Republic*, II, ss. 358–9, which comes very close to a theory of social contract, as Cornford points out in his edition, pp. 53–4.
[16] Cf. *A Theory of Justice*, 310–15 with Aristotle, below, pp. 36–9.

rules which enforce honesty, prevent harm, and secure each person his own is too obvious to bear mentioning. Kindness we can do without; if we are fortunate, we can look after ourselves on our own resources. But we cannot survive without the security that comes from other people neither lying to us, injuring us, nor stealing from us. Such considerations figure largely in justice as explained by Hume and Mill.[17]

Yet, justice seems also to conflict with utility and even with the *general* welfare, let alone the welfare of particular people. Consider the reflections of a few paragraphs back; a judge has punished half a dozen offenders with the full rigour of the law. He now thinks enough has been done to deter future offenders and ensure the law is taken seriously, so gives very light sentences to the next three offenders. In utilitarian terms, this is a good idea; he has done all he can do for public security, and further penalties would be unkind. Has he acted justly? Cannot the first half dozen offenders ask why they have been punished and the equally wicked let off lightly? Has the judge not acted capriciously by punishing some and excusing others? He may have increased the sum of human welfare, but has he not acted less than justly?

Many contexts provoke the same question. I lend you twenty pounds; the time comes to repay, and you reflect that I am miserable, a person of bad taste, and have less use for the money than many other people to whom you might give it. I insist only that the money is *mine*. Again, we seek to appoint a new professor. My brother is an adequate teacher and scholar and the students he teaches will not know there were better candidates. I will be happy if he is appointed; he will be happy; the whole of my family will be happy. But all this is nothing at all in face of the principle that we act unjustly if we do not appoint the best candidate. We shall soon see some answers to the question, what good is justice if it does not advance the general welfare? Here it is enough to notice that it is as hard to believe that justice is wholly explained by utility as that it has nothing to do with utility at all.

ACCOUNTS OF JUSTICE

Plato's *Republic* is a treatise on justice, written as a dialogue between Socrates and some of his upper-class Athenian friends. Socrates was impressed by the way decent and upright fathers were disgraced by the pride and ambition of their sons. The fathers must have known

[17] Below, pp. 62–3.

what justice is—they had practised it in their own lives and had tried to bring up their sons to love justice and practise it also. Why had they been unsuccessful? Socrates thought that contrary to appearances, they did not know what justice was; that ignorance explained their failure to teach their children justice. Real teaching demanded real knowledge. That meant knowledge of the essence of justice, the ability to give its *definition*.

Socrates' friends are not unable to behave decently and justly. But they suffer from an inability to ascend from particular cases of just behaviour to a definition that will pick out what it is that makes them just. Watching Socrates tormenting his friends, twentieth-century readers often feel that he takes advantage of his interlocutors' lack of philosophical skill. Yet this is beside the point. Socrates seeks an answer to two questions. One is the place of justice in the pantheon of virtues. The other, and more striking, is, what good does it do us to be just? Many readers think this a curious question. They think that justice often requires us to sacrifice our own interests. How can this be good for us?

Socrates starts from a commonplace of Greek ethical thinking. Ethics was about living well, and a theory of justice that represented it as a bad bargain would have been unacceptable. Among his first interlocutors, Thrasymachus takes the line that justice is not a good at all; it is a bad because it does its possessors no good. Thrasymachus' view was that the good life meant getting our way whenever and however possible. Restraint and self-abnegation—beyond a limited amount of tactical self-control—is absurd. Socrates offers to show that it is always better to practise justice than injustice, better to suffer injustice than to practise it. Socrates' argument with Thrasymachus is not printed here; but Glaucon takes up Thrasymachus' case in more moderate terms and provides Socrates' target in the remainder of the *Republic*. Glaucon offers a social contract theory. We would like to do wrong, but not to suffer it. So we agree to forgo injustice so long as others do so; backed up by his brother Adeimantus, he claims that if we could behave badly with impunity, we would be foolish not to. Socrates sets out to show how justice is good in itself, and that doing evil is a bad bargain.

To see how he does this, we must turn to his other question. Plato wishes to discover the place of justice among the other virtues of individuals and societies. Socrates persuades his hearers that justice is more visible in large entities than small ones, and more easily seen in the city (or *polis*) than in the individual. He constructs a model of an ideal city, composed of three social classes, the plebeian producers engaged in economic life whose specific virtue is temperance, the courageous 'auxiliaries', and the élite 'guardians', or philosopher-kings. Socrates announces that since the virtues of self-control, courage, and wisdom have been appropriated, justice must be inherent in the organization of the whole. It consists in everyone doing his proper task; the wise rule, the courageous enforce what the wise decree, and the producers concentrate on economic activity without succumbing to over-indulgence.

In the next passage printed here, he concludes that the soul mirrors the society, and the just man's character displays the same order as the just city. To act unjustly is to act in a disturbed fashion. Few readers have been persuaded. The person who seeks to behave badly on every occasion will find himself leading a very odd life, but this is far from showing that it never profits him to behave badly. It is one thing to show that a compulsive thief will do badly, another to show that someone who steals only when it is sensible will do worse than if he never stole at all. It is harder still to argue that the person who is robbed is better off than the robber. Plato later supports his case by two dubious arguments. The first invokes the philosopher's unconcern with the things of this world; the philosopher has seen through earthly illusion and has contemplated the realm of the true, the good and the beautiful, and takes no interest in worldly matters. If his contemplation of these absolutes is not touched, no earthly misfortune can damage him. A few pages of this argument are printed here.[18]

This argument can be apt. Some people's interests lie so much in the things of the mind that we find it plausible to say that they are undamaged by earthly ill-treatment. But such people are few in number, and even they would in the ordinary sense 'do better' by being the beneficiaries of injustice rather than its victims. As for everyone else, whose worldly interests exhaust their welfare, the argument cannot touch them. Plato was conscious of this; his second line of defence resorts to the myth of an after life in which we get what we deserve, and the imbalance between desert and outcome so visible in this life is finally rectified.

Plato certainly shows something significant. It is *on average* better to be just. The unjust man must always fear that others will discover his injustices and defend themselves against him, and is exposed to anxieties the just man escapes. Plato's picture of the man who climbs to power over the wreckage of his relationships with those he has betrayed is a powerful one. His 'success' is bought at an appalling price, for he will have never an easy moment. Stalin offers a striking example of the truth of this; when he died, it emerged that he had spent his last years in a state of terror, living in a set of rooms

[18] Below, pp. 29–33.

deep in the Kremlin, as much a prisoner of his fears as his victims were of his secret police.

Socrates and Plato had no time for Athenian democracy, and wanted a revived aristocratic government for their city. But both were moral radicals; they thought ordinary morality was radically misguided, and that public opinion should be ignored when it was at odds with one's conscience or reason. Things are very different in Aristotle. Plato's concern for the balance of the soul was shared by Aristotle, but not his ethical radicalism. Aristotle held that in ethics mankind knew what was to be known, and the imprecision of its knowledge reflected an imprecise subject-matter. In any case, the point of ethical enquiry was good behaviour; for that, good training in morally upright habits will do more than any amount of philosophy.[19]

Aristotle did not try to show that justice is invariably better for us than injustice. He was anxious only to provide an orderly account of the varieties of justice that we in fact try to practise. So well did he perform this task that writers still start from his framework. None the less, the modern reader may find some of Aristotle's concerns baffling. This is to be expected from a writer whose aim was to spell out the assumptions about 'living well' that all well-brought-up Greeks would accept. Thus, it seems odd to say that a man who demands less than his due treats himself unjustly. We sometimes say that someone has been 'less than fair to himself'; we do not think this is an act of injustice. Aristotle treats it as 'one of the questions in doubt' whether a man can treat himself unjustly; when he comes to decide the issue he never relies on the modern idea that we have a perfect right to forgo just treatment. The modern reader is likely to hold that we have a right to accept less than our due, and that that ends the matter.

The *Nicomachean Ethics* spells out the virtues a man needs to lead a good life. A good life is happy (or fulfilled), and fulfilled by doing good things—displaying virtue. Aristotle frequently associates the virtues with finding a mean between extremes; for example, courage is the mean between the vices of rashness and cowardice. Not all virtues can be so treated; a murderer cannot say that he has killed neither too many victims nor too few. Considered as a virtue of character, however, justice is rather plausibly represented as the disposition to give and receive neither too much nor too little. Aristotle first distinguishes justice as a special virtue from justice considered as the sum of all virtues. Aristotle sees we sometimes

[19] Aristotle, *Nicomachean Ethics*, trans. and ed. W. D. Ross (Oxford University Press, 1925), II, ss. i–ii, pp. 28–30.

think a 'just man' does everything he ought while at other times we distinguish being just from being merciful, courageous, prudent, and so on. Aristotle's contribution is the analysis of justice as a specific virtue; here I have selected some portions of Book Five of the *Ethics* that further this analysis.

Justice is of two kinds, justice in distribution and justice in rectification. 'Rectificatory' justice marks a contrast between our world and Aristotle's. Modern writers distinguish distributive justice from criminal justice, or the distributive from the retributive. Rectification is not the modern notion of retribution. Aristotle thinks primarily of setting things straight, and denies that rectificatory justice contains an element of 'tit for tat'. The criminal who wounds another should not *only* be wounded himself; something more should be done to him by way of punishment, to wipe out any gain from his crime. The notion of wiping out the advantage gained by the wrongdoer is more salient than requiting evil with evil.

Though Aristotle discusses distributive justice with his characteristic passion for detailed distinctions and fine shadings, the fundamental thought is that justice is proportionate equality. Persons ought to receive goods in proportion to their merits. A just world is one in which the best do best, and the less good do less well. It is what Robert Nozick calls a 'patterned' conception of justice, distributing benefits according to a dimension along which individuals can be ranked.[20] In the *Magna moralia* and the *Eudemian Ethics*, Aristotle explains further what aspects of a man—he is almost exclusively concerned with men—constitute the merits according to which he ought to do well. It is striking how many are not within our control. We associate deserving with doing, in a way Aristotle did not. Aristotelian justice allocates good results to good persons without enquiring how much they can do about their goodness. We do not always differ from Aristotle. Justice is done if the best runner wins the race, even if the best runner has spectacular natural capacities and trains rather little.

Cicero's *De officiis*, or 'The Duties', is written as a letter to his son, and its tone is that of a man of practical wisdom and some philosophical erudition explaining the moral decencies to a young man. Cicero discusses justice as the second of the four cardinal virtues (wisdom, justice, courage, and temperance) whose presence constitutes moral goodness. Justice is the virtue that holds society together and allows us to pursue the common good for whose sake society exists. Cicero's discussion is so orderly and straightforward that it needs no summary. One interesting feature is his concern

[20] Below, pp. 100–2.

with *in*justice. The practical bent of *De officiis* (even more apparent in Books II and III) leads Cicero to emphasize the ways in which greed, and the lust for power lead to injustice. His political rival Julius Caesar was the specific target of the discussion of ambition's role in unjust action, but the argument is universal. Cicero also wants to show what virtues justice needs to complement it—especially generosity, because without it justice would be cold and limited. Society must be permeated by kinder and warmer virtues, although justice retains its priority: we may not be generous with what is not ours.

Cicero holds that we must treat others justly even if they have not so treated us. We often think of justice as 'tit-for-tat', returning good for good and evil for evil, and often think a person who has behaved unjustly to us has forfeited the right to just treatment. 'You cheated first' is heard as commonly around the international negotiating table as in the nursery. The Stoic view that morality promotes the common good implies that we must try to restore the social relationship that has been violated. Victors in war must bring their opponents round to their way of thinking, not wreak whatever vengeance they could colourably take. It is no wonder that Cicero was one of the pagan authors popular with Christian philosophers.

Hume's account of justice is part of a larger account of the moral and political virtues generally. Hume wrote as a philosophical anthropologist, not as a reformer, unlike Bentham and Mill who set out to reform our moral outlook rather than merely to explain it. He starts from the thought that moral judgements are logically distinctive. They are neither statements of fact nor statements of logical connection. For Hume, this means they must express a certain kind of sentiment, and it is always possible (though very unlikely) that people's sentiments will be differently aroused by the same states of affairs. Hume summarized this view in two famous remarks, the first that 'reason is and ought only to be the slave of the passions', the other that ''tis not contrary to reason to prefer the destruction of the whole world to the scratching of my finger'.[21] Action requires a motive, and this must in the last resort be supplied by our wanting or not wanting the states of affairs the action realizes or prevents. The man who prefers the destruction of the whole world to the scratching of his little finger is defective in his desires, not in his perceptual or logical skills.

Moral assessment considers the character displayed in action; we disapprove the cruel character displayed in cruel action, and the unjust character displayed in unjust action. Some reactions are

---

[21] David Hume, *A Treatise on Human Nature* (Clarendon Press: Oxford, 2nd edn., 1978), Bk. II, pp. 415–16.

natural and simple; we naturally find some aspects of human nature agreeable and attractive, and our moral judgements express this feeling. Justice is different. We may approve of the hard but just judge, but we do not find his character likeable. Justice draws our approval by a more elaborate route. We perceive that rules that confer rights, and protect property are indispensable to the general welfare, and become attached to them. Hume linked justice to property; where there is no property, there is no justice. Critics have thought this far-fetched; there are ways of behaving unjustly that have nothing to do with property. I promise to take you and your brother to the cinema, then rat on you, and still take him. This is unfair, and if I make a habit of it, I treat you unjustly. Yet there is no violation of property rights; property has nothing to do with it.

Two responses may reduce the oddness of the claim. The first is to place Hume's claim in context. Hume held that only when human existence became more than a search for food and drink, sexual pleasure, and shelter did mankind need justice. All human society needs rules against violence and sexual violation; rules against theft, and in favour of the sanctity of contract have no place before there is something to steal and something to exchange. Once this stage is reached, the rules of justice are more important than any others. Without property, they have no place. The second is to observe that all rights have elements of proprietorship in them. When I promise to take you to the cinema, I give you something—my claim to my time—and make it yours.

Mill's discussion of justice is like and unlike Hume's. Like Hume, Mill was an ethical naturalist, looking to the function of the rules of justice in social life. Unlike Hume, Mill went beyond an analysis of the emotions expressed in judgements of justice. Critics of utilitarianism had argued that utility was not a stringent moral guide. Would not people be tempted to make exceptions in the name of utility, would they not make exceptions in their own favour; could they treat rules as obligatory if rules were only means to utilitarian goals? Mill tried to show how a utilitarian account of justice dealt with every consideration his critics came up with. Justice was universally acknowledged to make the most stringent demands of all the moral virtues, its observance was agreed to be basic to social life; Mill had to show how utilitarianism could incorporate these points.

The importance he attached to this is revealed by the fact that this last chapter of *Utilitarianism* is much the longest of the essay. Yet, the basic argument is simple. Justice is distinguished from the rest of morality by its stringency. It is good to be charitable, but we can *demand* the payment of a debt. Mill explicates justice in terms of doing what people have a right to. Rights he explains, not very satisfactorily, in terms of the way rights-violations involve harm to 'assignable' individuals. It is simple to construct counter-examples. If I am a beggar, and you do not give me food, I shall suffer; I am an assignable individual, and the connection between your action and my suffering is direct. Still, I had no *right* to the food; you have been unkind but you did not violate my rights.

None the less, the main outlines of Mill's claims are plausible. We have rules conferring rights, and treat them with peculiar strictness because they give us security. Security matters more than anything else; we can do without most goods, or can find substitutes for them, but security nobody can do without. It has a peculiarly urgent and important utility that explains the strictness with which we regard the rules of justice. Whether this does justice to such concepts as fairness or desert may be doubted; that it does a good job of accounting for the importance of rights is less easily denied.

Mill's attempt to explain justice in utilitarian terms confronts a problem that twentieth-century writers have made much of although it seems to have attracted little attention earlier. Utilitarianism is a maximizing doctrine, that is, it holds that the justification of rights and of the rules of justice has to lie in the way they promote the greatest possible quantity of happiness (or well-being). Justice, on the other hand, is distributive and individualizing; it denies that we may maximize well-being if in the process we violate someone's rights. We may not sacrifice individuals to the general welfare. Mill and Hume both held that in extreme cases we rightly make such sacrifices, that 'fiat justitia et pereat mundus' is not a maxim we follow when the world really will perish. When starvation threatens, we break open the granaries, and the property rights of the owners go for nothing. Even then, we try to paper over the conflict between utility and justice, saying that in a case like this it is just to override the rights of the grain owners.

The most famous modern assertion of the conflict between utilitarian and justice-based considerations is contained in John Rawls's masterpiece, *A Theory of Justice*. Rawls builds his account of justice around the principle of the 'separateness of persons'; each individual is a separate life, and a separate centre of moral value. The apparent rationality of aggregating the welfare of each individual in order to define the social welfare is illusory. There is no such entity as society to experience this well-being. The happiness of two people is simply two people being happy, and the compellingness of utilitarian calculation therefore much less great than it looks at first sight.

Rawls's work has been the subject of so much commentary that it is otiose to do more than sketch the basic structure that emerges in the essay below. Rawls begins from Hume's and Mill's premises, but reaches very different conclusions. Like them, he sees justice as regulating the results of social co-operation; unlike Plato, he does not think of justice as operating 'within the soul'. Justice is institutional and political; we co-operate with one another within an institutional framework, and that framework dictates the broad outlines of the results. His large book, as well as his shorter essays, considers justice in the context of establishing the constitution of a society—its abstract political and economic framework. He is therefore not concerned with the justice and injustice of every particular outcome, but of the mechanisms through which they are achieved.

The theory aims to rationalize our existing thoughts about justice, so that when we have brought our ideas into order, we can reject views that we once held but now seem inconsistent with the rest of the fabric of our ideas, and can more confidently hold ideas that are now seen to be deeply entrenched. As to the fundamentals of our conception of justice Rawls suggests two principles. The first is that each person is entitled to the maximum liberty consistent with a like liberty for all; the second that the benefits of co-operation should be distributed in such a way that the least advantaged person does as well as the least advantaged person can do. In effect. equality is a baseline, and departures from equality justified to the extent that they benefit the least favoured. Needless to say, these principles have been disputed. It is more interesting that they have been disputed in tones that suggest that they do catch something important about our current notions of justice even if it is hard to say what that is.

Rawls's theory belongs to a class of theories that explain 'social justice', that is, the justice of the way the benefits of social and economic co-operation are allocated. One popular objection to this whole class of theories is that there can be no such thing as social justice. This view is represented by two of the chapters that follow. Professor von Hayek's account of 'the myth' of social justice is so limpidly formulated that it needs only sufficient introduction to distinguish it from Professor Nozick's. Briefly, Hayek and Nozick both think that talk of distributive justice is misleading, because it suggests the presence of a distributing person or mechanism; in a developed economy there is no such thing, and in a free society, the attempt to institute such a thing would destroy all freedom. Hayek, however, supports this view with an account of the computational impossibility of deciding what to produce and distribute in order to achieve justice, while Nozick is more concerned to emphasize that the state has *no right* to seize the resources of individuals in order to distribute them according to any principle whatever. It is worth noticing, however, that Hayek does not deny that the state ought to do something to assure the least favoured of an adequate living; Rawls's principles are persuasive—but not as principles of *justice*.

Rawls's theory starts from a world in which there are no rights. Rawls treats resources as 'common assets', whose allocation it is the task of the theory of justice to decide. In so doing it rules out alternatives, but not always explicitly. Distribution according to desert, or moral merit, is explicitly ruled out.[22] 'Natural aristocracy', which is what Aristotle favoured, is explicitly ruled out, too. The thought that we come into the world with natural rights in ourselves and our capacities is not argued against, so much as ruled out by the starting-point. But natural proprietorship of oneself is what Nozick favours as the foundation of any theory of justice. As the extract from *Anarchy, State and Utopia* below suggests, it is not entirely clear, to Nozick himself or to his readers, whether this starting-point yields a theory of distributive justice or not. In one sense, it must. People should have what they have a title to; people who take what others have a title to, without their permission, must be made to give it back; people who do not have a title to something can acquire it in one legitimate way, and that is by free transfer from its lawful owner, gratuitously or in exchange for something of value. A state exists in order to ensure that these are the only transfers that take place, and to make sure that nobody violates anyone else's ownership of their person and possessions.

But this theory is silent on the form of the resulting distribution. If a theory of distributive justice is meant to pronounce on the merits of some distributions as against others, or to advise some person or organ whose task it is to make such distributions, Nozick does not offer a theory of distributive justice at all. Any distribution that comes about through the right procedures is fine, and any that does not is unjust. Similarly, if each person is sovereign over himself and his possessions, there can be nobody and no institution which is entitled to bring about distributions that owners do not assent to, and therefore there is no need for a theory advising them what principles to operate by.

DOUBTS ABOUT JUSTICE

We have seen that justice is not a lovable virtue. It is also a defensive one; we are concerned to be secure against theft and fraud, we have rights in order not to depend on the unpredictable good or ill will of

[22] *A Theory of Justice*, 310 ff.

others. These considerations raise the question whether we cannot create a world in which justice would have no place. Such a question makes no sense addressed to Plato or Aristotle; Plato's vision of justice as what held all the other virtues in place makes justice and reason mirror images of each other, while Aristotle's discussion of the way the better sort of person merits a better sort of life could hardly be translated to a different context. But Hume and Mill and Rawls agree that justice is a virtue only because our wants cannot all be satisfied, and because we have only limited benevolence. Were we wholly altruistic and scarcity non-existent, justice would not be needed. We could rely on the lovable virtues.

Marxists have always treated justice with some disdain. Because they have thought that most accounts of what is 'natural' merely reflect the political prejudices and the economic needs of ruling classes intent on preserving their social and political position, they have refused to see either scarcity or limited altruism as dictates of nature. Altruism is limited in capitalist societies because the altruist makes himself the prey of his competitors, and scarcity is a cultural construct equally dependent on the kind of society one lives in. Competitive societies feel the pinch of scarcity because what people are after is not 'enough' but 'more than everyone else'. There logically cannot be more than one person at the peak of the competition to do better than everyone else, and the more competitive the society the more intense the sense of scarcity. There is plainly a good deal to this observation. It is certainly true that there is little correlation between high incomes and a sense of having enough.

Steven Lukes's essay is part of an enquiry into Marx's complaints against capitalism and the values that underlie his socialism. Lukes's question is whether Marx thought capitalist exploitation was deplorable—which he plainly did think—because it was unjust, or for some other reason. Lukes's answer is difficult to summarize, but amounts to the claim that Marx did not concern himself with rights and justice, but with an ethics of emancipation. In this light, capitalist exploitation, like the exploitation of other epochs, is not interesting in virtue of being unjust but in virtue of being yet another form of servitude that awaits the final liberation of mankind for its destruction.

Marx objected to two features of talk about justice, one that it was associated with a rhetoric of 'eternal' principles, the other that 'equal right' must in practice mean unequal results; the small farmer and John D. Rockefeller have 'equal right' to their property, but the small farmer owns five acres and Rockefeller Standard Oil. As the short passage from the *Critique of the Gotha Programme* illustrates,

Marx thought a concern with rights and with distributive justice might lead us to a 'lower' form of socialism, but that beyond it there lay a higher form of society where such notions were obsolete, and that in general a concern with forms of distribution was 'unscientific', since what determined possible forms of distribution was the mode of production.

Although not represented here, the Marxist criticisms of liberal accounts of justice have their non-Marxist counterparts in communitarianism.[23] Justice is a chilly virtue, appropriate to the dealings of those who are strangers to each other, and who look to each other neither for intimacy nor for unrequited assistance. Can justice really be the 'first virtue' of social institutions? Can a society survive on justice alone; would it not need warmer and closer virtues to cement it? It is not surprising that Marxist and communitarian critics converge, and that their target is liberal theories of justice. Marxism is a communitarian creed, differing from most forms of communitarianism in being resolutely unnostalgic and hard-nosed about the material underpinnings of community and its loss. Liberals determined to make the best of the here and now, and to take individuals as they find them in the modern Western world, are undaunted. Society would be impossible if it relied on justice alone, and intolerably bleak if *per impossibile* it tried to rely on justice alone. None the less, justice is the foundation of everything else. The question turns on how important and justice is in what respects as compared with the warmer and more personal, 'natural' virtues described by Hume, and admits of no simple answer.

CONCLUSION

The bibliography at the end of this collection lists a good deal of work that has not been mentioned here at all. In particular, there has grown up an intriguing semi-technical literature tying theories of justice to such disciplines as game theory and theories of rational choice. Of theories mentioned here, John Rawls's has obvious connections with welfare economics, and many writers have discussed his 'minimax' arguments for the difference principle in the context of traditional welfare economics. Paradoxically, Rawls himself has moved away from such arguments in the past decade and has stressed the extent to which his account of justice aims to mirror an existing public outlook, and to be politically rather than

[23] Michael Sandel, *Liberalism and the Limits of Justice* (Cambridge University Press: Cambridge, 1982).

technically acceptable. The one thing we can say is that if Socrates really expected to get a definitive answer to his question, 'What is justice?' when talking to his friends on their way back to the Piraeus, he has been disappointed. It remains a contentious and disputed subject.

THE REPUBLIC

PLATO

I thought that, with these words, I was quit of the discussion; but it seems this was only a prelude. Glaucon, undaunted as ever, was not content to let Thrasymachus abandon the field.

Socrates, he broke out, you have made a show of proving that justice is better than injustice in every way. Is that enough, or do you want us to be really convinced?

Certainly I do, if it rests with me.

Then you are not going the right way about it. I want to know how you classify the things we call good. Are there not some which we should wish to have, not for their consequences, but just for their own sake, such as harmless pleasures and enjoyments that have no further result beyond the satisfaction of the moment?

Yes, I think there are good things of that description.

And also some that we value both for their own sake and for their consequences—things like knowledge and health and the use of our eyes?

Yes.

And a third class which would include physical training, medical treatment, earning one's bread as a doctor or otherwise—useful, but burdensome things, which we want only for the sake of the profit or other benefit they bring.

Yes, there is that third class. What then?

In which class do you place justice?

I should say, in the highest, as a thing which anyone who is to gain happiness must value both for itself and for its results.

Well, that is not the common opinion. Most people would say it was one of those things, tiresome and disagreeable in themselves, which we cannot avoid practising for the sake of reward or a good reputation.

I know, said I; that is why Thrasymachus has been finding fault

From Plato, *The Republic*, Bks II, ss. 357–67, IV, ss. 441–5, IX, ss. 588–92, trans. F. M. Cornford (1941). Reprinted by permission of Oxford University Press.

with it all this time and praising injustice. But I seem to be slow in seeing his point.

Listen to me, then, and see if you agree with mine. There was no need, I think, for Thrasymachus to yield so readily, like a snake you had charmed into submission; and nothing so far said about justice and injustice has been established to my satisfaction. I want to be told what each of them really is, and what effect each has, in itself, on the soul that harbours it, when all rewards and consequences are left out of account. So here is my plan, if you approve. I shall revive Thrasymachus' theory. First, I will state what is commonly held about the nature of justice and its origin; secondly, I shall maintain that it is always practised with reluctance, not as good in itself, but as a thing one cannot do without; and thirdly, that this reluctance is reasonable, because the life of injustice is much the better life of the two—so people say. That is not what I think myself, Socrates; only I am bewildered by all that Thrasymachus and ever so many others have dinned into my ears; and I have never yet heard the case for justice stated as I wish to hear it. You, I believe, if anyone, can tell me what is to be said in praise of justice in and for itself; that is what I want. Accordingly, I shall set you an example by glorifying the life of injustice with all the energy that I hope you will show later in denouncing it and exalting justice in its stead. Will that plan suit you?

Nothing could be better, I replied. Of all subjects this is one on which a sensible man must always be glad to exchange ideas.

Good, said Glaucon. Listen then, and I will begin with my first point: the nature and origin of justice.

What people say is that to do wrong is, in itself, a desirable thing; on the other hand, it is not at all desirable to suffer wrong, and the harm to the sufferer outweighs the advantage to the doer. Consequently, when men have had a taste of both, those who have not the power to seize the advantage and escape the harm decide that they would be better off if they made a compact neither to do wrong nor to suffer it. Hence they began to make laws and covenants with one another; and whatever the law prescribed they called lawful and right. That is what right or justice is and how it came into existence; it stands half-way between the best thing of all—to do wrong with impunity—and the worst, which is to suffer wrong without the power to retaliate. So justice is accepted as a compromise, and valued, not as good in itself, but for lack of power to do wrong; no man worthy of the name, who had that power, would ever enter into such a compact with anyone; he would be mad if he did. That, Socrates, is the nature of justice according to this account, and such the circumstances in which it arose.

The next point is that men practise it against the grain, for lack of power to do wrong. How true that is, we shall best see if we imagine two men, one just, the other unjust, given full licence to do whatever they like, and then follow them to observe where each will be led by his desires. We shall catch the just man taking the same road as the unjust; he will be moved by self-interest, the end which it is natural to every creature to pursue as good, until forcibly turned aside by law and custom to respect the principle of equality.

Now, the easiest way to give them that complete liberty of action would be to imagine them possessed of the talisman found by Gyges, the ancestor of the famous Lydian. The story tells how he was a shepherd in the King's service. One day there was a great storm, and the ground where his flock was feeding was rent by an earthquake. Astonished at the sight, he went down into the chasm and saw, among other wonders of which the story tells, a brazen horse, hollow, with windows in its sides. Peering in, he saw a dead body, which seemed to be of more than human size. It was naked save for a gold ring, which he took from the finger and made his way out. When the shepherds met, as they did every month, to send an account to the King of the state of his flocks, Gyges came wearing the ring. As he was sitting with the others, he happened to turn the bezel of the ring inside his hand. At once he became invisible, and his companions, to his surprise, began to speak of him as if he had left them. Then, as he was fingering the ring, he turned the bezel outwards and became visible again. With that, he set about testing the ring to see if it really had this power, and always with the same result: according as he turned the bezel inside or out he vanished and reappeared. After this discovery he contrived to be one of the messengers sent to the court. There he seduced the Queen, and with her help murdered the King and seized the throne.

Now suppose there were two such magic rings, and one were given to the just man, the other to the unjust. No one, it is commonly believed, would have such iron strength of mind as to stand fast in doing right or keep his hands off other men's goods, when he could go to the market-place and fearlessly help himself to anything he wanted, enter houses and sleep with any woman he chose, set prisoners free and kill men at his pleasure, and in a word go about among men with the powers of a god. He would behave no better than the other; both would take the same course. Surely this would be strong proof that men do right only under compulsion; no individual thinks of it as good for him personally, since he does

wrong whenever he finds he has the power. Every man believes that
wrongdoing pays him personally much better, and, according to this
theory, that is the truth. Granted full licence to do as he liked, people
would think him a miserable fool if they found him refusing to wrong
his neighbours or to touch their belongings, though in public they
would keep up a pretence of praising his conduct, for fear of being
wronged themselves. So much for that.

Finally, if we are really to judge between the two lives, the only
way is to contrast the extremes of justice and injustice. We can best
do that by imagining our two men to be perfect types, and crediting
both to the full with the qualities they need for their respective ways
of life. To begin with the unjust man: he must be like any
consummate master of a craft, a physician or a captain who,
knowing just what his art can do, never tries to do more, and can
always retrieve a false step. The unjust man, if he is to reach
perfection, must be equally discreet in his criminal attempts, and he
must not be found out, or we shall think him a bungler; for the
highest pitch of injustice is to seem just when you are not. So we
must endow our man with the full complement of injustice; we must
allow him to have secured a spotless reputation for virtue while
committing the blackest crimes; he must be able to retrieve any
mistake, to defend himself with convincing eloquence if his misdeeds
are denounced, and, when force is required, to bear down all
opposition by his courage and strength and by his command of
friends and money.

Now set beside this paragon the just man in his simplicity and
nobleness, one who, in Aeschylus' words, 'would be, not seem, the
best'. There must, indeed, be so such seeming; for if his character
were apparent, his reputation would bring him honours and
rewards, and then we should not know whether it was for their sake
that he was just or for justice's sake alone. He must be stripped of
everything but justice, and denied every advantage the other
enjoyed. Doing no wrong, he must have the worst reputation for
wrongdoing, to test whether his virtue is proof against all that comes
of having a bad name; and under this lifelong imputation of
wickedness, let him hold on his course of justice unwavering to the
point of death. And so, when the two men have carried their justice
and injustice to the last extreme, we may judge which is the happier.

My dear Glaucon, I exclaimed, how vigorously you scour these
two characters clean for inspection, as if you were burnishing a
couple of statues!

I am doing my best, he answered. Well, given two such
characters, it is not hard, I fancy, to describe the sort of life that each
of them may expect; and if the description sounds rather coarse, take

it as coming from those who cry up the merits of injustice rather than from me. They will tell you that our just man will be thrown into prison, scourged and racked, will have his eyes burnt out, and after every kind of torment, be impaled. That will teach him how much better it is to seem virtuous than to be so. In fact those lines of Aeschylus I quoted are more fitly applied to the unjust man, who, they say, is a realist and does not live for appearances: 'he would be, not seem' unjust,

> reaping the harvest sown
> In those deep furrows of the thoughtful heart
> Whence wisdom springs.

With his reputation for virtue, he will hold offices of state, ally himself by marriage to any family he may choose, become a partner in any business, and, having no scruples about being dishonest, turn all these advantages to profit. If he is involved in a lawsuit, public or private, he will get the better of his opponents, grow rich on the proceeds, and be able to help his friends and harm his enemies. Finally, he can make sacrifices to the gods and dedicate offerings with due magnificence, and, being in a much better position than the just man to serve the gods as well as his chosen friends, he may reasonably hope to stand higher in the favour of heaven. So much better, they say, Socrates, is the life prepared for the unjust by gods and men.

Here Glaucon ended, and I was meditating a reply, when his brother Adeimantus exclaimed:

Surely, Socrates, you cannot suppose that that is all there is to be said.

Why, isn't it? said I.

The most essential part of the case has not been mentioned, he replied.

Well, I answered, there is a proverb about a brother's aid. If Glaucon has failed, it is for you to make good his shortcomings; though, so far as I am concerned, he has said quite enough to put me out of the running and leave me powerless to rescue the cause of justice.

Nonsense, said Adeimantus; there is more to be said, and you must listen to me. If we want a clear view of what I take to be Glaucon's meaning, we must study the opposite side of the case, the arguments used when justice is praised and injustice condemned. When children are told by their fathers and all their pastors and masters that it is a good thing to be just, what is commended is not justice in itself but the respectability it brings. They are to let men see how just they are, in order to gain high positions and marry well and win all the other advantages which Glaucon mentioned, since the just man owes all these to his good reputation.

In this matter of having a good name, they go farther still: they throw in the favourable opinion of heaven, and can tell us of no end of good things with which they say the gods reward piety. There is the good old Hesiod, who says the gods make the just man's oak-trees 'bear acorns at the top and bees in the middle; and their sheep's fleeces are heavy with wool,' and a great many other blessings of that sort. And Homer speaks in the same strain:

As when a blameless king fears the gods and upholds right judgement; then the dark earth yields wheat and barley, and the trees are laden with fruit; the young of his flocks are strong, and the sea gives abundance of fish.

Musaeus and his son Eumolpus enlarge in still more spirited terms upon the rewards from heaven they promise to the righteous. They take them to the other world and provide them with a banquet of the Blest, where they sit for all time carousing with garlands on their heads, as if virtue could not be more nobly recompensed than by an eternity of intoxication. Others, again, carry the rewards of heaven yet a stage farther: the pious man who keeps his oaths is to have children's children and to leave a posterity after him. When they have sung the praises of justice in that strain, with more to same effect, they proceed to plunge the sinners and unrighteous men into a pool of mud in the world below, and set them to fetch water in a sieve. Even in this life, too, they give them a bad name, and make out that the unjust suffer all those penalties which Glaucon described as falling upon the good man who has a bad reputation: they can think of no others. That is how justice is recommended and injustice denounced.

Besides all this, think of the way in which justice and injustice are spoken of, not only in ordinary life, but by the poets. All with one voice reiterate that self-control and justice, admirable as they may be, are difficult and irksome, whereas vice and injustice are pleasant and very easily to be had; it is mere convention to regard them as discreditable. They tell us that dishonesty generally pays better than honesty. They will cheerfully speak of a bad man as happy and load him with honours and social esteem, provided he be rich and otherwise powerful; while they despise and disregard one who has neither power nor wealth, though all the while they acknowledge that he is the better man of the two.

Most surprising of all is what they say about the gods and virtue: that heaven itself often allots misfortunes and a hard life to the good man, and gives prosperity to the wicked. Mendicant priests and soothsayers come to the rich man's door with a story of a power they

possess by the gift of heaven to atone for any offence that he or his
ancestors have committed with incantations and sacrifice agreeably
accompanied by feasting. If he wishes to injure an enemy, he can, at
a trifling expense, do him a hurt with equal ease, whether he be an
honest man or not, by means of certain invocations and spells which,
as they profess, prevail upon the gods to do their bidding. In support
of all these claims they call the poets to witness. Some, by way of
advertising the easiness of vice, quote the words: 'Unto wickedness
men attain easily and in multitudes; smooth is the way and her
dwelling is very near at hand. But the gods have ordained much
sweat upon the path to virtue' and a long road that is rough and
steep.

Others, to show that men can turn the gods from their purpose,
cite Homer: 'Even the gods themselves listen to entreaty. Their
hearts are turned by the entreaties of men with sacrifice and humble
prayers and libation and burnt offering, whensoever anyone
transgresses and does amiss.' They produce a whole farrago of books
in which Musaeus and Orpheus, described as descendants of the
Muses and the Moon, prescribe their ritual; and they persuade
entire communities, as well as individuals, that, both in this life and
after death, wrongdoing may be absolved and purged away by
means of sacrifices and agreeable performances which they are
pleased to call rites of initiation. These deliver us from punishment
in the other world, where awful things are in store for all who neglect
to sacrifice.

Now, my dear Socrates, when all this stuff is talked about the
estimation in which virtue and vice are held by heaven and by
mankind, what effect can we suppose it has upon the mind of a
young man quick-witted enough to gather honey from all these
flowers of popular wisdom and to draw his own conclusions as to the
sort of person he should be and the way he should go in order to lead
the best possible life? In all likelihood he would ask himself, in
Pindar's words: 'Will the way of right or the by-paths of deceit lead
me to the higher fortress,' where I may entrench myself for the rest
of my life? For, according to what they tell me, I have nothing to
gain but trouble and manifest loss from being honest, unless I also
get a name for being so; whereas, if I am dishonest and provide
myself with a reputation for honesty, they promise me a marvellous
career. Very well, then; since 'outward seeming', as wise men inform
me, 'overpowers the truth' and decides the question of happiness, I
had better go in for appearances wholeheartedly. I must ensconce
myself behind an imposing façade designed to look like virtue, and
trail the fox behind me, 'the cunning shifty fox'—Archilochus knew
the world as well as any man. You may say it is not so easy to be

wicked without ever being found out. Perhaps not; but great things are never easy. Anyhow, if we are to reach happiness, everything we have been told points to this as the road to be followed. We will form secret societies to save us from exposure; besides, there are men who teach the art of winning over popular assemblies and courts of law; so that, one way or another, by persuasion or violence, we shall get the better of our neighbours without being punished. You might object that the gods are not to be deceived and are beyond the reach of violence. But suppose that there are no gods, or that they do not concern themselves with the doings of men; when should we concern ourselves to deceive them? Or, if the gods do exist and care for mankind, all we know or have ever heard about them comes from current tradition and from the poets who recount their family history, and these same authorities also assure us that they can be won over and turned from their purpose 'by sacrifice and humble prayers' and votive offerings. We must either accept both these statements or neither. If we are to accept both, we had better do wrong and use part of the proceeds to offer sacrifice. By being just we may escape the punishment of heaven, but we shall be renouncing the profits of injustice; whereas by doing wrong we shall make our profit and escape punishment into the bargain, by means of those entreaties which win over the gods when we transgress and do amiss. But then, you will say, in the other world the penalty for our misdeeds on earth will fall either upon us or upon our children's children. We can counter that objection by reckoning on the great efficacy of mystic rites and the divinities of absolution, vouched for by the most advanced societies and by the descendants of the gods who have appeared as poets and spokesmen of heavenly inspiration.

What reason, then, remains for preferring justice to the extreme of injustice, when common belief and the best authorities promise us the fulfilment of our desires in this life and the next, if only we conceal our ill-doing under a veneer of decent behaviour? The upshot is, Socrates, that no man possessed of superior powers of mind or person or rank or wealth will set any value on justice; he is more likely to laugh when he hears it praised. So, even one who could prove my case false and were quite sure that justice is best, far from being indignant with the unjust, will be very ready to excuse them. He will know that, here and there, a man may refrain from wrong because it revolts some instinct he is graced with or because he has come to know the truth; no one else is virtuous of his own will; it is only lack of spirit or the infirmity of age or some other weakness that makes men condemn the iniquities they have not the strength to practise. This is easily seen: give such a man the power, and he will be the first to use it to the utmost.

What lies at the bottom of all this is nothing but the fact from which Glaucon, as well as I, started upon this long discourse. We put it to you, Socrates, with all respect, in this way. All you who profess to sing the praises of right conduct, from the ancient heroes whose legends have survived down to the men of the present day, have never denounced injustice or praised justice apart from the reputation, honours, and rewards they bring; but what effect either of them in itself has upon its possessor when it dwells in his soul unseen of gods or men, no poet or ordinary man has ever yet explained. No one has proved that a soul can harbour no worse evil than injustice, no greater good than justice. Had all of you said that from the first and tried to convince us from our youth up, we should not be keeping watch upon our neighbours to prevent them from doing wrong to us, but everyone would keep a far more effectual watch over himself, for fear lest by wronging others he should open his doors to the worst of all evils.

That, Socrates, is the view of justice and injustice which Thrasymachus and, no doubt, others would state, perhaps in even stronger words. For myself, I believe it to be a gross perversion of their true worth and effect; but, as I must frankly confess, I have put the case with all the force I could muster because I want to hear the other side from you. You must not be content with proving that justice is superior to injustice; you must make clear what good or what harm each of them does to its possessor, taking it simply in itself and, as Glaucon required, leaving out of account the reputation it bears. For unless you deprive each of its true reputation and attach to it the false one, we shall say that you are praising or denouncing nothing more than the appearances in either case, and recommending us to do wrong without being found out; and that you hold with Thrasymachus that right means what is good for someone else, being the interest of the stronger, and wrong is what really pays, serving one's own interest at the expense of the weaker. You have agreed that justice belongs to that highest class of good things which are worth having not only for their consequences, but much more for their own sakes—things like sight and hearing, knowledge, and health, whose value is genuine and intrinsic, not dependent on opinion. So I want you, in commending justice, to consider only how justice, in itself, benefits a man who has it in him, and how injustice harms him, leaving rewards and reputation out of account. I might put up with others dwelling on those outward effects as a reason for praising the one and condemning the other; but from you, who have spent your life in the study of this question, I must beg leave to demand something better. You must not be content merely to prove that justice is superior to injustice, but explain how one is good, the other evil, in virtue of the intrinsic effect each has on its possessor, whether gods or men see it or not. . . .

And so, after a stormy passage, we have reached the land. We are fairly agreed that the same three elements exist alike in the state and in the individual soul.

That is so.

Does it not follow at once that state and individual will be wise or brave by virtue of the same element in each and in the same way? Both will possess in the same manner any quality that makes for excellence.

That must be true.

Then it applies to justice: we shall conclude that a man is just in the same way that a state was just. And we have surely not forgotten that justice in the state meant that each of the three orders in it was doing its own proper work. So we may henceforth bear in mind that each one of us likewise will be a just person, fulfilling his proper function, only if the several parts of our nature fulfil theirs.

Certainly.

And it will be the business of reason to rule with wisdom and forethought on behalf of the entire soul; while the spirited element ought to act as its subordinate and ally. The two will be brought into accord, as we said earlier, by that combination of mental and bodily training which will tune up one string of the instrument and relax the other, nourishing the reasoning part on the study of noble literature and allaying the other's wildness by harmony and rhythm. When both have been thus nurtured and trained to know their own true functions, they must be set in command over the appetites, which form the greater part of each man's soul and are by nature insatiably covetous. They must keep watch lest this part, by battening on the pleasures that are called bodily, should grow so great and powerful that it will no longer keep to its own work, but will try to enslave the others and usurp a dominion to which it has no right, thus turning the whole of life upside down. At the same time, those two together will be the best of guardians for the entire soul and for the body against all enemies from without: the one will take counsel, while the other will do battle, following its ruler's commands and by its own bravery giving effect to the ruler's designs.

Yes, that is all true.

And so we call an individual brave in virtue of this spirited part of his nature, when, in spite of pain or pleasure, it holds fast to the injunctions of reason about what he ought or ought not to be afraid of.

True.

And wise in virtue of that small part which rules and issues these injunctions, possessing as it does the knowledge of what is good for each of the three elements and for all of them in common.

Certainly.

And, again, temperate by reason of the unanimity and concord of all three, when there is no internal conflict between the ruling element and its two subjects, but all are agreed that reason should be ruler.

Yes, that is an exact account of temperance, whether in the state or in the individual.

Finally, a man will be just by observing the principle we have so often stated.

Necessarily.

Now is there any indistinctness in our vision of justice, that might make it seem somehow different from what we found it to be in the state?

I don't think so.

Because, if we have any lingering doubt, we might make sure by comparing it with some commonplace notions. Suppose, for instance, that a sum of money were entrusted to our state or to an individual of corresponding character and training, would anyone imagine that such a person would be specially likely to embezzle it?

No.

And would he not be incapable of sacrilege and theft, or of treachery to friend or country; never false to an oath or any other compact; the last to be guilty of adultery or of neglecting parents or the due service of the gods?

Yes.

And the reason for all this is that each part of his nature is exercising its proper function, of ruling or of being ruled.

Yes, exactly.

Are you satisfied, then, that justice is the power which produces states or individuals of whom that is true, or must we look further?

There is no need; I am quite satisfied.

And so our dream has come true—I mean the inkling we had that, by some happy chance, we had lighted upon a rudimentary form of justice from the very moment when we set about founding our commonwealth. Our principle that the born shoemaker or carpenter had better stick to his trade turns out to have been an adumbration of justice; and that it why it has helped us. But in reality justice, though evidently analogous to this principle, is not a matter of external behaviour, but of the inward self and of attending to all that is, in the fullest sense, a man's proper concern. The just man does not allow the several elements in his soul to usurp one another's functions; he is indeed one who sets his house in order, by self-mastery and discipline coming to be at peace with himself, and bringing into tune those three parts, like the terms in the proportion of a musical scale, the highest and lowest notes and the mean between them, with all the intermediate intervals. Only when he has linked these parts together in well-tempered harmony and has made himself one man instead of many, will he be ready to go about whatever he may have to do, whether it be making money and satisfying bodily wants, or business transactions, or the affairs of state. In all these fields when he speaks of just and honourable conduct, he will mean the behaviour that helps to produce and to preserve this habit of mind; and by wisdom he will mean the knowledge which presides over such conduct. Any action which tends to break down this habit will be for him unjust; and the notions governing it he will call ignorance and folly.

That is perfectly true, Socrates.

Good, said I. I believe we should not be thought altogether mistaken, if we claimed to have discovered the just man and the just state, and wherein their justice consists.

Indeed we should not.

Shall we make that claim, then?

Yes, we will.

So be it, said I. Next, I suppose, we have to consider injustice.

Evidently.

This must surely be a sort of civil strife among the three elements, whereby they usurp and encroach upon one another's functions and some one part of the soul rises up in rebellion against the whole, claiming a supremacy to which it has no right because its nature fits it only to be the servant of the ruling principle. Such turmoil and aberration we shall, I think, identify with injustice, intemperance, cowardice, ignorance, and in a word with all wickedness.

Exactly.

And now that we know the nature of justice and injustice, we can be equally clear about what is meant by acting justly and again by unjust action and wrongdoing.

How do you mean?

Plainly, they are exactly analogous to those wholesome and unwholesome activities which respectively produce a healthy or unhealthy condition in the body; in the same way just and unjust conduct produce a just or unjust character. Justice is produced in the soul, like health in the body, by establishing the elements concerned in their natural relations of control and subordination, whereas injustice is like disease and means that this natural order is inverted.

Quite so.

It appears, then, that virtue is as it were the health and comeliness and well-being of the soul, as wickedness is disease, deformity, and weakness.

True.

And also that virtue and wickedness are brought about by one's way of life, honourable or disgraceful.

That follows.

So now it only remains to consider which is the more profitable course: to do right and live honourably and be just, whether or not anyone knows what manner of man you are, or to do wrong and be unjust, provided that you can escape the chastisement which might make you a better man.

But really, Socrates, it seems to me ridiculous to ask that question now that the nature of justice and injustice has been brought to light. People think that all the luxury and wealth and power in the world cannot make life worth living when the bodily constitution is going to rack and ruin; and are we to believe that, when the very principle whereby we live is deranged and corrupted, life will be worth living so long as a man can do as he will, and wills to do anything rather than to free himself from vice and wrongdoing and to win justice and virtue?

Yes, I replied, it is a ridiculous question. . . .

Good, said I. And now that the argument has brought us to this point, let us recall something that was said at the outset, namely, if I remember aright, that wrongdoing is profitable when a man is completely unjust but has a reputation for justice.

Yes, that position was stated.

Well, we are now agreed about the real meaning and consequences of doing wrong as well as of doing right, and the time has come to point out to anyone who maintains that position what his statement implies. We may do so by likening the soul to one of those many fabulous monsters said to have existed long ago, such as the Chimaera or Scylla or Cerberus, which combined the forms of several creatures in one. Imagine, to begin with, the figure of a multifarious and many-headed beast, girt round with heads of animals, tame and wild, which it can grow out of itself and transform at will.

That would tax the skill of a sculptor; but luckily the stuff of imagination is easier to mould than wax.

Now add two other forms, a lion and a man. The many-headed beast is to be the largest by far, and the lion next to it in size. Then join them in such a way that the three somehow grow together into one. Lastly, mould the outside into the likeness of one of them, the man, so that, to eyes which cannot see inside the outward sheath, the whole may look like a single creature, a human being.

Very well. What then?

We can now reply to anyone who says that for this human creature wrongdoing pays and there is nothing to be gained by doing right. This simply means, we shall tell him, that it pays to feed up and strengthen the composite beast and all that belongs to the lion, and to starve the man till he is so enfeebled that the other two can drag him whither they will, and he cannot bring them to live together in peace, but must leave them to bite and struggle and devour one another. On the other hand, to declare that justice pays is to assert that all our words and actions should tend towards giving the man within us complete mastery over the whole human creature, and letting him take the many-headed beast under his care and tame its wildness, like the gardener who trains his cherished plants while he checks the growth of weeds. He should enlist the lion as his ally, and caring for all alike, should foster their growth by first reconciling them to one another and to himself.

Yes, such are the implications when justice or injustice is commended.

From every point of view, then, whether of pleasure or reputation or advantage, one who praises justice speaks the truth; he who disparages it does not know what it is that he idly condemns.

I agree; he has no conception.

But his error is not wilful; so let us reason with him gently. We will ask him on what grounds conduct has come to be approved or disapproved by law and custom. Is it not according as conduct tends to subdue the brutish parts of our nature to the human—perhaps I should rather say to the divine in us—or to enslave our humanity to the savagery of the beast? Will he agree?

Yes, if he has any regard for my opinion.

On that showing, then, can it profit a man to take money unjustly, if he is thereby enslaving the best part of his nature to the vilest? No amount of money could make it worth his while to sell a son or daughter as slaves into the hands of cruel and evil men; and when it is a matter of ruthlessly subjugating all that is most godlike in himself to whatsoever is most ungodly and despicable, is not the wretch taking a bribe far more disastrous than the necklace Eriphyle took as the price of her husband's life?

Far more, said Glaucon, if I may answer on his behalf.

You will agree, too, with the reasons why certain faults have always been condemned: profligacy, because it gives too much licence to the multiform monster; self-will and ill temper, when the lion and serpent part of us is strengthened till its sinews are overstrung: luxury and effeminacy, because they relax those sinews till the heart grows faint; flattery and meanness, in that the heart's high spirit is subordinated to the turbulent beast, and for the sake of money to gratify the creature's insatiable greed the lion is brow-beaten and schooled from youth up to become an ape. Why, again, is mechanical toil discredited as debasing? Is it not simply when the highest thing in a man's nature is naturally so weak that it cannot control the animal parts but can only learn how to pamper them?

I suppose so.

Then, if we say that people of this sort ought to be subject to the highest type of man, we intend that the subject should be governed, not, as Thrasymachus thought, to his own detriment, but on the same principle as his superior, who is himself governed by the divine element within him. It is better for everyone, we believe, to be subject to a power of godlike wisdom residing within himself, or, failing that, imposed from without, in order that all of us, being under one guidance, may be so far as possible equal and united. This, moreover, is plainly the intention of the law in lending its support to every member of the community, and also of the government of children; for we allow them to go free only when we have established in each one of them as it were a constitutional ruler, whom we have trained to take over the guardianship from the same principle in ourselves.

True.

On what ground, then, can we say that it is profitable for a man to be unjust or self-indulgent or to do any disgraceful act which will make him a worse man, though he may gain money and power? Or how can it profit the wrongdoer to escape detection and punishment? He will only grow still worse; whereas if he is found out, chastisement will tame the brute in him and lay it to rest, while the gentler part is set free; and thus the entire soul, restored to its native soundness, will gain, in the temperance and righteousness which wisdom brings, a condition more precious than the strength and beauty which health brings to the body, in proportion as the soul itself surpasses the body in worth. To this end the man of understanding will bend all his powers through life, prizing in the first place those studies only which will fashion these qualities in his soul; and, so far from abandoning the care of his bodily condition to the irrational pleasures of the brute and setting his face in that direction, he will not even make health his chief object. Health, strength, and beauty he will value only in so far as they bring soundness of mind, and you will find him keeping his bodily frame in tune always for the sake of the resulting concord in the soul.

Yes, if he is to have true music in him.

And in the matter of acquiring wealth he will order his life in harmony with the same purpose. He will not be carried away by the vulgar notion of happiness into heaping up an unbounded store which would bring him endless troubles. Rather, in adding to or spending his substance, he will, to the best of his power, be guided by watchful care that neither want nor abundance may unsettle the constitution set up in his soul. Again, in accepting power and honours he will keep the same end in view, ready to enjoy any position in public or private life which he thinks will make him a better man, and avoiding any that would break down the established order within him.

Then, if that is his chief concern, he will have no wish to take part in politics.

Indeed he will, in the politics of his own commonwealth, though not perhaps in those of his country, unless some miraculous chance should come about.

I understand, said Glaucon: you mean this commonwealth we have been founding in the realm of discourse; for I think it nowhere exists on earth.

No, I replied; but perhaps there is a pattern set up in the heavens for one who desires to see it and, seeing it, to found one in himself. But whether it exists anywhere or ever will exist is no matter; for this is the only commonwealth in whose politics he can ever take part.

I suspect you are right.

NICOMACHEAN ETHICS

ARISTOTLE

2

. . . what we are investigating is the justice which is *part* of virtue; for there is a justice of this kind, as we maintain. Similarly it is with injustice in the particular sense that we are concerned.

That there is such a thing is indicated by the fact that while the man who exhibits in action the other forms of wickedness acts wrongly indeed, but not graspingly (e.g. the man who throws away his shield through cowardice or speaks harshly through bad temper or fails to help a friend with money through meanness), when a man acts graspingly he often exhibits none of these vices—no, nor all together, but certainly wickedness of some kind (for we blame him) and injustice. There is, then, another kind of injustice which is a part of injustice in the wide sense, and a use of the word 'unjust' which answers to a part of what is unjust in the wide sense of 'contrary to the law'. Again, if one man commits adultery for the sake of gain and makes money by it, while another does so at the bidding of appetite though he loses money and is penalized for it, the latter would be held to be self-indulgent rather than grasping, but the former is unjust, but not self-indulgent; evidently, therefore, he is unjust by reason of his making gain by his act. Again, all other unjust acts are ascribed invariably to some particular kind of wickedness, e.g. adultery to self-indulgence, the desertion of a comrade in battle to cowardice, physical violence to anger; but if a man makes gain, his action is ascribed to no form of wickedness but injustice. Evidently, therefore, there is apart from injustice in the wide sense another, 'particular', injustice which shares the name and nature of the first, because its definition falls within the same genus; for the significance of both consists in a relation to one's neighbour, but the one is concerned with honour or money or safety—or that which includes

From Aristotle, *Nicomachean Ethics*, Bk. v, ss. 2–7, omitting part of 1130b, part of 1132b, 1133a, 1133b, part of 1134a, and the end of s. 7; trans. W. D. Ross (1925). Reprinted by permission of Oxford University Press.

pleasure that arises from gain; while the other is concerned with all the objects with which the good man is concerned.

It is clear, then, that there is more than one kind of justice, and that there is one which is distinct from virtue entire; we must try to grasp its genus and differentia. . . .

Of particular justice and that which is just in the corresponding sense, (A) one kind is that which is manifested in distributions of honour or money or the other things that fall to be divided among those who have a share in the constitution (for in these it is possible for one man to have a share either unequal or equal to that of another), and (B) one is that which plays a rectifying part in transactions between man and man. Of this there are two divisions; of transactions (1) some are voluntary and (2) others involuntary—voluntary such transactions as sale, purchase, loan for consumption, pledging, loan for use, depositing, letting (they are called voluntary because the origin of these transactions is voluntary), while of the involuntary (a) some are clandestine, such as theft, adultery, poisoning, procuring, enticement of slaves, assassination, false witness, and (b) others are violent, such as assault, imprisonment, murder, robbery with violence, mutilation, abuse, insult.

3

(A) We have shown that both the unjust man and the unjust act are unfair or unequal; now it is clear that there is also an intermediate between the two unequals involved in either case. And this is the equal; for in any kind of action in which there is a more and a less there is also what is equal. If, then, the unjust is unequal, the just is equal, as all men suppose it to be, even apart from argument. And since the equal is intermediate, the just will be an intermediate. Now equality implies at least two things. The just, then, must be both intermediate and equal and relative (i.e. for certain persons). And *qua* intermediate it must be between certain things (which are respectively greater and less); *qua* equal, it involves *two* things; *qua* just, it is for certain people. The just, therefore, involves at least four terms; for the persons for whom it is in fact just are two, and the things in which it is manifested, the objects distributed, are two. And the same equality will exist between the persons and between the things concerned; for as the latter—the things concerned—are related, so are the former; if they are not equal, they will not have what is equal, but this is the origin of quarrels and complaints—when either equals have and are awarded unequal shares, or unequals equal shares. Further, this is plain from the fact that awards should be 'according to merit'; for all men agree that what is just in distribution must be according to merit in some sense, though they do not all specify the same sort of merit, but democrats identify it with the status of freeman, supporters of oligarchy with wealth (or with noble birth), and supporters of aristocracy with excellence.

The just, then, is a species of the proportionate (proportion being not a property only of the kind of number which consists of abstract units, but of number in general). For proportion is equality of ratios, and involves four terms at least (that discrete proportion involves four terms is plain, but so does continuous proportion, for it uses one term as two and mentions it twice; e.g. 'as the line A is to the line B, so is the line B to the line C'; the line B, then, has been mentioned twice, so that if the line B be assumed twice, the proportional terms will be four); and the just, too, involves at least four terms, and the ratio between one pair is the same as that between the other pair; for there is a similar distinction between the persons and between the things. As the term A, then, is to B, so will C be to D, and therefore, *alternando*, as A is to C, B will be to D. Therefore also the whole is in the same ratio to the whole; and this coupling the distribution effects, and, if the terms are so combined, effects justly. The conjunction, then, of the term A with C and of B with D is what is just in distribution, and this species of the just is intermediate, and the unjust is what violates the proportion; for the proportional is intermediate, and the just is proportional. (Mathematicians call this kind of proportion geometrical; for it is in geometrical proportion that it follows that the whole is to be the whole as either part is to the corresponding part.) This proportion is not continuous; for we cannot get a single term standing for a person and a thing.

This, then, is what the just is—the proportional; the unjust is what violates the proportion. Hence one term becomes too great, the other too small, as indeed happens in practice; for the man who acts unjustly has too much, and the man who is unjustly treated too little, of what is good. In the case of evil the reverse is true; for the lesser evil is reckoned a good in comparison with the greater evil, since the lesser evil is rather to be chosen than the greater, and what is worthy of choice is good, and what is worthier of choice a greater good.

This, then, is one species of the just.

4

(B) The remaining one is the rectificatory, which arises in connection with transactions both voluntary and involuntary. This form of the just has a different specific character from the former. For the justice which distributes common possessions is always in accordance with the kind of proportion mentioned above (for in the case also in which the distribution is made from the common funds of a partnership it will be according to the same ratio which the funds put into the business by the partners bear to one another); and the injustice opposed to this kind of justice is that which violates the proportion. But the justice in transactions between man and man is a sort of equality indeed, and the injustice a sort of inequality; not according to that kind of proportion, however, but according to arithmetical proportion. For it makes no difference whether a good man has defrauded a bad man or a bad man a good one, nor whether it is a good or a bad man that has committed adultery; the law looks only to the distinctive character of the injury, and treats the parties as equal, if one is in the wrong and the other is being wronged, and if one inflicted injury and the other has received it. Therefore, this kind of injustice being an inequality, the judge tries to equalize it; for in the case also in which one has received and the other has inflicted a wound, or one has slain and the other been slain, the suffering and the action have been unequally distributed; but the judge tries to equalize things by means of the penalty, taking away from the gain of the assailant. For the term 'gain' is applied generally to such cases, even if it be not a term appropriate to certain cases, e.g. to the person who inflicts a wound—and 'loss' to the sufferer; at all events when the suffering has been estimated, the one is called loss and the other gain. Therefore the equal is intermediate between the greater and the less, but the gain and the loss are respectively greater and less in contrary ways; more of the good and less of the evil are gain, and the contrary is loss; intermediate between them is, as we saw, the equal, which we say is just; therefore corrective justice will be the intermediate between loss and gain. This is why, when people dispute, they take refuge in the judge; and to go to the judge is to go to justice; for the nature of the judge is to be a sort of animate justice; and they seek the judge as an intermediate, and in some states they call judges mediators, on the assumption that if they get what is intermediate they will get what is just. The just, then, is an intermediate, since the judge is so. Now the judge restores equality; it is as though there were a line divided into unequal parts, and he took away that by which the greater segment exceeds the half, and added it to the smaller segment. And when the whole has been equally divided, then they say they have 'their own'—i.e. when they have got what is equal. The equal is intermediate between the greater and the lesser line according to arithmetical proportion. It is for this reason also that it is called just (δίκαιον), because it is a division into two equal parts (δίχα), just as if one were to call it δίχαιον; and the judge (δικαστής) is one who bisects (διχαστής). For when something is subtracted from one of two equals and added to the other, the other is in excess by these two; since if what was taken from the one had not been added to the other, the latter would have been in excess by one only. It therefore exceeds the intermediate by one, and the intermediate exceeds by one that from which something was taken. By this, then, we shall recognize both what we must subtract from that which has more, and what we must add to that which has less; we must add to the latter that by which the intermediate exceeds it, and subtract from the greatest that by which it exceeds the intermediate. Let the lines AA', BB', CC' be equal to one another; from the line AA' let the segment AE have been subtracted, and to the line CC' let the segment CD have been added, so that the whole line DCC' exceeds the line EA' by the segment CD and the segment CF; therefore it exceeds the line BB' by the segment CD.

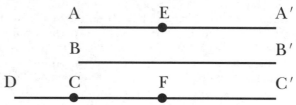

These names, both loss and gain, have come from voluntary exchange; for to have more than one's own is called gaining, and to have less than one's original share is called losing, e.g. in buying and selling and in all other matters in which the law has left people free to make their own terms; but when they get neither more nor less but just what belongs to themselves, they say that they have their own and that they neither lose nor gain.

Therefore the just is intermediate between a sort of gain and a sort of loss, viz. those which are involuntary; it consists in having an equal amount before and after the transaction. . . .

6

. . . we must not forget that what we are looking for is not only what is just without qualification but also political justice. This is found among men who share their life with a view to self-sufficiency, men who are free and either proportionately or arithmetically equal, so that between those who do not fulfil this condition there is no political justice but justice in a special sense and by analogy. For justice exists only between men whose mutual relations are governed by law; and law exists for men between whom there is injustice; for legal justice is the discrimination of the just and the unjust. And between men between whom there is injustice there is also unjust action (though there is not injustice between all between whom there is unjust action), and this is assigning too much to oneself of things good in themselves and too little of things evil in themselves. This is why we do not allow a *man* to rule, but *rational principle*, because a man behaves thus in his own interests and becomes a tyrant. The magistrate on the other hand is the guardian of justice, and, if of justice, then of equality also. And since he is assumed to have no more than his share, if he is just (for he does not assign to himself more of what is good in itself, unless such a share is proportional to his merits—so that it is for others that he labours, and it is for this reason that men, as we stated previously, say that justice is 'another's good'), therefore a reward must be given him, and this is honour and privilege; but those for whom such things are not enough become tyrants.

The justice of a master and that of a father are not the same as the justice of citizens, though they are like it; for there can be no injustice in the unqualified sense towards things that are one's own, but a man's chattel, and his child until it reaches a certain age and sets up for itself, are as it were part of himself, and no one chooses to hurt himself (for which reason there can be no injustice towards oneself). Therefore the justice or injustice of citizens is not manifested in these relations; for it was as we saw according to law, and between people naturally subject to law, and these as we saw are people who have an equal share in ruling and being ruled. Hence justice can more truly be manifested towards a wife than towards children and chattels, for the former is household justice; but even this is different from political justice.

7

Of political justice part is natural, part legal—natural, that which everywhere has the same force and does not exist by people's thinking this or that; legal, that which is originally indifferent, but when it has been laid down is not indifferent, e.g. that a prisoner's ransom shall be a mina, or that a goat and not two sheep shall be sacrificed, and again all the laws that are passed for particular cases, e.g. that sacrifice shall be made in honour of Brasidas, and the provisions of decrees. Now some think that all justice is of this sort, because that which is by nature is unchangeable and has everywhere the same force (as fire burns both here and in Persia), while they see change in the things recognized as just. This, however, is not true in this unqualified way, but is true in a sense; or rather, with the gods it is perhaps not true at all, while with us there is something that is just even by nature, yet all of it is changeable; but still some is by nature, some not by nature. It is evident which sort of thing, among things capable of being otherwise, is by nature, and which is not but is legal and conventional, assuming that both are equally changeable. And in all other things the same distinction will apply; by nature the right hand is stronger, yet it is possible that all men should come to be ambidextrous. The things which are just by virtue of convention and expediency are like measures; for wine and corn measures are not everywhere equal, but larger in wholesale and smaller in retail markets. Similarly, the things which are just not by nature but by human enactment are not everywhere the same, since constitutions also are not the same, though there is but one which is everywhere by nature the best.

3

DE OFFICIIS

CICERO

7. Justice

Of the three remaining divisions, the most extensive in its application is the principle by which society and what we may call its 'common bonds' are maintained. Of this again there are two divisions—justice, in which is the crowning glory of the virtues and on the basis of which men are called 'good men'; and, close akin to justice, charity, which may also be called kindness or generosity.

The first office of justice is to keep one man from doing harm to another, unless provoked by wrong; and the next is to lead men to use common possessions for the common interests, private property for their own.

There is, however, no such thing as private ownership established by nature, but property becomes private either through long occupancy (as in the case of those who long ago settled in unoccupied territory) or through conquest (as in the case of those who took it in war) or by due process of law, bargain, or purchase, or by allotment. On this principle the lands of Arpinum are said to belong to the Arpinates, the Tusculan lands to the Tusculans; and similar is the assignment of private property. Therefore, inasmuch as in each case some of those things which by nature had been common property became the property of individuals, each one should retain possession of that which has fallen to his lot; and if anyone appropriates to himself anything beyond that, he will be violating the laws of human society.

But since, as Plato has admirably expressed it, we are not born for ourselves alone, but our country claims a share of our being, and our friends a share; and since, as the Stoics hold, everything that the earth produces is created for man's use; and as men, too, are born for the sake of men, that they may be able mutually to help one another; in this direction we ought to follow Nature as our guide, to

From Cicero, *De officiis*, Bk. I, ss. 7–13, omitting matters of recent Roman history; from the Loeb parallel text translation (Harvard University Press: Cambridge, Mass., 1930). Reprinted by permission of the publishers and Loeb Classical Library.

contribute to the general good by an interchange of acts of kindness, by giving and receiving, and thus by our skill, our industry, and our talents to cement human society more closely together, man to man.

The foundation of justice, moreover, is good faith—that is, truth and fidelity to promises and agreements. And therefore we may follow the Stoics, who diligently investigate the etymology of words; and we may accept their statement that 'good faith' is so called because what is promised is 'made good', although some may find this derivation rather far-fetched.

There are, on the other hand, two kinds of injustice—the one, on the part of those who inflict wrong, the other on the part of those who, when they can, do not shield from wrong those upon whom it is being inflicted. For he who, under the influence of anger or some other passion, wrongfully assaults another seems, as it were, to be laying violent hands upon a comrade; but he who does not prevent or oppose wrong, if he can, is just as guilty of wrong as if he deserted his parents or his friends or his country. Then, too, those very wrongs which people try to inflict on purpose to injure are often the result of fear: that is, he who premeditates injuring another is afraid that, if he does not do so, he may himself be made to suffer some hurt. But, for the most part, people are led to wrongdoing in order to secure some personal end; in this vice, avarice is generally the controlling motive.

8. The Dangers of Ambition

Again, men seek riches partly to supply the needs of life, partly to secure the enjoyment of pleasure. With those who cherish higher ambitions, the desire for wealth is entertained with a view to power and influence and the means of bestowing favours; Marcus Crassus, for example, not long since declared that no amount of wealth was enough for the man who aspired to be the foremost citizen of the state, unless with the income from it he could maintain an army. Fine establishments and the comforts of life in elegance and abundance also afford pleasure, and the desire to secure it gives rise to the insatiable thirst for wealth. Still, I do not mean to find fault with the accumulation of property, provided it hurts nobody, but unjust acquisition of it is always to be avoided. . . .

The Motives to Wrong

But in any case of injustice it makes a vast deal of difference whether the wrong is done as a result of some impulse of passion, which is usually brief and transient, or whether it is committed wilfully and with premeditation; for offences that come through some sudden impulse are less culpable than those committed designedly and with malice aforethought.

But enough has been said on the subject of inflicting injury.

9. Motives to Passive Injustice

The motives for failure to prevent injury and so for slighting duty are likely to be various: people either are reluctant to incur enmity or trouble or expense; or through indifference, indolence, or incompetence, or through some preoccupation or self-interest they are so absorbed that they suffer those to be neglected whom it is their duty to protect. And so there is reason to fear that what Plato declares of the philosophers may be inadequate, when he says that they are just because they are busied with the pursuit of truth and because they despise and count as naught that which most men eagerly seek and for which they are prone to do battle against each other to the death. For they secure one sort of justice, to be sure, in that they do no positive wrong to anyone, but they fall into the opposite injustice; for hampered by their pursuit of learning they leave to their fate those whom they ought to defend. And so, Plato thinks, they will not even assume their civic duties except under compulsion. But in fact it were better that they should assume them of their own accord; for an action intrinsically right is just only on condition that it is voluntary.

There are some also who, either from zeal in attending to their own business or through some sort of aversion to their fellow-men, claim that they are occupied solely with their own affairs, without seeming to themselves to be doing anyone any injury. But while they steer clear of the one kind of injustice, they fall into the other: they are traitors to social life, for they contribute to it none of their interest, none of their effort, none of their means. . . .

10. Change of Duty in Change of Circumstances

. . . occasions often arise, when those duties which seem most becoming to the just man and to the 'good man', as we call him, undergo a change and take on a contrary aspect. It may, for example, not be a duty to restore a trust or to fulfil a promise, and it may become right and proper sometimes to evade and not to observe what truth and honour would usually demand. For we may well be guided by those fundamental principles of justice which I laid down at the outset: first, that no harm be done to anyone; second, that the common interests be conserved. When these are modified under changed circumstances, moral duty also undergoes a change, and it does not always remain the same. For a given promise or agreement may turn out in such a way that its performance will prove detrimental either to the one to whom the promise has been made or to the one who has made it. If, for example, Neptune, in the drama, had not carried out his promise to Theseus, Theseus would not have lost his son Hippolytus; for, as the story runs, of the three wishes that Neptune had promised to grant him the third was this: in a fit of anger he prayed for the death of Hippolytus, and the granting of this prayer plunged him into unspeakable grief. Promises are, therefore, not to be kept, if the keeping of them is to prove harmful to those to whom you have made them; and, if the fulfilment of a promise should do more harm to you than good to him to whom you have made it, it is no violation of moral duty to give the greater good precedence over the lesser good. For example, if you have made an appointment with anyone to appear as his advocate in court, and if in the meantime your son should fall dangerously ill, it would be no breach of your moral duty to fail in what you agreed to do; nay, rather, he to whom your promise was given would have a false conception of duty, if he should complain that he had been deserted in his time of need. Further than this, who fails to see that those promises are not binding which are extorted by intimidation or which we make when misled by false pretences? Such obligations are annulled in most cases by the praetor's edict in equity, in some cases by the laws. . . .

11. *Our Duty to Those Who Have Wronged Us*

Again, there are certain duties that we owe even to those who have wronged us. For there is a limit to retribution and to punishment; or rather, I am inclined to think, it is sufficient that the aggressor should be brought to repent of his wrongdoing, in order that he may not repeat the offence and that others may be deterred from doing wrong.

Then, too, in the case of a state in its external relations, the rights of war must be strictly observed. For since there are two ways of settling a dispute: first, by discussion; second, by physical force; and since the former is characteristic of man, the latter of the brute, we must resort to force only in case we may not avail ourselves of discussion. The only excuse, therefore, for going to war is that we may live in peace unharmed; and when the victory is won, we should spare those who have not been blood-thirsty and barbarous in their warfare.

. . . Not only must we show consideration for those whom we have conquered by force of arms but we must also ensure protection to those who lay down their arms and throw themselves upon the mercy of our generals, even though the battering-ram has hammered at their walls. And among our countrymen justice has been observed so conscientiously in this direction, that those who have given promise of protection to states or nations subdued in war become, after the custom of our forefathers, the patrons of those states. . . .

13. Fidelity to a Promise

Again, if under stress of circumstances individuals have made any promise to the enemy, they are bound to keep their word even then. For instance, in the First Punic War, when Regulus was taken prisoner by the Carthaginians, he was sent to Rome on parole to negotiate an exchange of prisoners; he came and, in the first place, it was he that made the motion in the Senate that the prisoners should not be restored; and in the second place, when his relatives and friends would have kept him back, he chose to return to a death by torture rather than prove false to his promise, though given to an enemy.

And again in the Second Punic War, after the Battle of Cannae, Hannibal sent to Rome ten Roman captives bound by an oath to return to him, if they did not succeed in ransoming his prisoners; and as long as any one of them lived, the censors kept them all degraded and disfranchised, because they were guilty of perjury in not returning. And they punished in like manner the one who had incurred guilt by an evasion of his oath: with Hannibal's permission this man left the camp and returned a little later on the pretext that he had forgotten something or other; and then, when he left the camp the second time, he claimed that he was released from the obligation of his oath; and so he was, according to the letter of it, but not according to the spirit. In the matter of a promise one must always consider the meaning and not the mere words. . . .

. . . We must have regard for justice even towards the humblest. Now the humblest station and the poorest fortune are those of slaves; and they give us no bad rule who bid us treat our slaves as we should our employees: they must be required to work; they must be given their dues.

While wrong may be done, then, in either of two ways, that is, by force or by fraud, both are bestial: fraud seems to belong to the cunning fox, force to the lion; both are wholly unworthy of man, but fraud is the more contemptible.

4

AN ENQUIRY CONCERNING THE PRINCIPLES OF MORALS

DAVID HUME

. . . The social virtues of humanity and benevolence exert their influence immediately by a direct tendency or instinct, which chiefly keeps in view the simple object, moving the affections, and comprehends not any scheme or system, nor the consequences resulting from the concurrence, imitation, or example of others. A parent flies to the relief of his child; transported by that natural sympathy which actuates him, and which affords no leisure to reflect on the sentiments or conduct of the rest of mankind in like circumstances. A generous man cheerfully embraces an opportunity of serving his friend; because he then feels himself under the dominion of the beneficent affections, nor is he concerned whether any other person in the universe were ever before actuated by such noble motives, or will ever afterwards prove their influence. In all these cases the social passions have in view a single individual object, and pursue the safety or happiness alone of the person loved and esteemed. With this they are satisfied: in this they acquiesce. And as the good, resulting from their benign influence, is in itself complete and entire, it also excites the moral sentiment of approbation, without any reflection on farther consequences, and without any more enlarged views of the concurrence or imitation of the other members of society. On the contrary, were the generous friend or disinterested patriot to stand alone in the practice of beneficence, this would rather enhance his value in our eyes, and join the praise of rarity and novelty to his other more exalted merits.

The case is not the same with the social virtues of justice and fidelity. They are highly useful, or indeed absolutely necessary to the well-being of mankind: but the benefit resulting from them is not the consequence of every individual single act; but arises from the whole scheme or system concurred in by the whole, or the greater part of

From David Hume, *Enquiries Concerning Human Understanding and Concerning the Principles of Morals*, Appendix III, omitting first paragraph and footnotes; ed. L. A. Selby-Bigge, revised by P. H. Nidditch (3rd edn., 1975), © OUP 1975. Reprinted by permission of Oxford University Press.

the society. General peace and order are the attendants of justice or a general abstinence from the possessions of others; but a particular regard to the particular right of one individual citizen may frequently, considered in itself, be productive of pernicious consequences. The result of the individual acts is here, in many instances, directly opposite to that of the whole system of actions; and the former may be extremely hurtful, while the latter is, to the highest degree, advantageous. Riches, inherited from a parent, are, in a bad man's hand, the instrument of mischief. The right of succession may, in one instance, be hurtful. Its benefit arises only from the observance of the general rule; and it is sufficient, if compensation be thereby made for all the ills and inconveniences which flow from particular characters and situations.

Cyrus, young and inexperienced, considered only the individual case before him, and reflected on a limited fitness and convenience, when he assigned the long coat to the tall boy, and the short coat to the other of smaller size. His governor instructed him better, while he pointed out more enlarged views and consequences, and informed his pupil of the general, inflexible rules, necessary to support general peace and order in society.

The happiness and prosperity of mankind, arising from the social virtue of benevolence and its subdivisions, may be compared to a wall, built by many hands, which still rises by each stone that is heaped upon it, and receives increase proportional to the diligence and care of each workman. The same happiness, raised by the social virtue of justice and its subdivisions, may be compared to the building of a vault, where each individual stone would, of itself, fall to the ground; nor is the whole fabric supported but by the mutual assistance and combination of its corresponding parts.

All the laws of nature, which regulate property, as well as all civil laws, are general, and regard alone some essential circumstances of the case, without taking into consideration the characters, situations, and connections of the person concerned, or any particular consequences which may result from the determination of these laws in any particular case which offers. They deprive, without scruple, a beneficent man of all his possessions, if acquired by mistake, without a good title; in order to bestow them on a selfish miser, who has already heaped up immense stores of superfluous riches. Public utility requires that property should be regulated by general inflexible rules; and though such rules are adopted as best serve the same end of public utility, it is impossible for them to prevent all particular hardships, or make beneficial consequences result from every individual case. It is sufficient, if the whole plan or scheme be necessary to the support of civil society, and if the balance of good, in the main, do thereby preponderate much above that of evil. Even the general laws of the universe, though planned by infinite wisdom, cannot exclude all evil or inconvenience in every particular operation.

It has been asserted by some, that justice arises from Human Conventions, and proceeds from the voluntary choice, consent, or combination of mankind. If by *convention* be meant a *promise* (which is the most usual sense of the word) nothing can be more absurd than this position. The observance of promises is itself one of the most considerable parts of justice, and we are not surely bound to keep our word because we have given our word to keep it. But if by convention be meant a sense of common interest; which sense each man feels in his own breast, which he remarks in his fellows, and which carries him, in concurrence with others, into a general plan or system of actions, which tends to public utility; it must be owned, that, in this sense, justice arises from human conventions. For if it be allowed (what is, indeed, evident) that the particular consequences of a particular act of justice may be hurtful to the public as well as to individuals; it follows that every man, in embracing that virtue, must have an eye to the whole plan or system, and must expect the concurrence of his fellows in the same conduct and behaviour. Did all his views terminate in the consequences of each act of his own, his benevolence and humanity, as well as his self-love, might often prescribe to him measures of conduct very different from those which are agreeable to the strict rules of right and justice.

Thus, two men pull the oars of a boat by common convention for common interest, without any promise or contract: thus gold and silver are made the measures of exchange; thus speech and words and language are fixed by human convention and agreement. Whatever is advantageous to two or more persons, if all perform their part; but what loses all advantage if only one perform, can arise from no other principle. There would otherwise be no motive for any one of them to enter into that scheme of conduct.

The word *natural* is commonly taken in so many senses and is of so loose a signification, that it seems vain to dispute whether justice be natural or not. If self-love, if benevolence be natural to man; if reason and forethought be also natural; then may the same epithet be applied to justice, order, fidelity, property, society. Men's inclination, their necessities, lead them to combine; their understanding and experience tell them that this combination is impossible where each governs himself by no rule, and pays no regard to the possessions of others: and from these passions and reflections conjoined, as soon as we observe like passions and reflections in others, the sentiment of justice, throughout all ages, has infallibly and certainly had place to some degree or other in every individual of the human species. In so sagacious an animal, what necessarily arises from the exertion of his intellectual faculties may justly be esteemed natural.

Among all civilized nations it has been the constant endeavour to remove everything arbitrary and partial from the decision of property, and to fix the sentence of judges by such general views and considerations as may be equal to every member of the society. For besides, that nothing could be more dangerous than to accustom the bench, even in the smallest instance, to regard private friendship or enmity; it is certain, that men, where they imagine that there was no other reason for the preference of their adversary but personal favour, are apt to entertain the strongest ill-will against the magistrates and judges. When natural reason, therefore, points out no fixed view of public utility by which a controversy of property can be decided, positive laws are often framed to supply its place, and direct the procedure of all courts of judicature. Where these too fail, as often happens, precedents are called for; and a former decision, though given itself without any sufficient reason, justly becomes a sufficient reason for a new decision. If direct laws and precedents be wanting, imperfect and indirect ones are brought in aid; and the controverted case is ranged under them by analogical reasonings and comparisons, and similitudes, and correspondencies, which are often more fanciful than real. In general, it may safely be affirmed that jurisprudence is, in this respect, different from all the sciences; and that in many of its nicer questions, there cannot properly be said to be truth or falsehood on either side. If one pleader bring the case under any former law or precedent, by a refined analogy or comparison; the opposite pleader is not at a loss to find an opposite analogy or comparison: and the preference given by the judge is often founded more on taste and imagination than on any solid argument. Public utility is the general object of all courts of judicature; and this utility too requires a stable rule in all controversies: but where several rules, nearly equal and indifferent, present themselves, it is a very slight turn of thought which fixes the decision in favour of either party.

We may just observe, before we conclude this subject, that after the laws of justice are fixed by views of general utility, the injury, the hardship, the harm, which result to any individual from a violation of them, enter very much into consideration, and are a great source of that universal blame which attends every wrong or iniquity. By the laws of society, this coat, this horse is mine, and *ought* to remain perpetually in my possession: I reckon on the secure enjoyment of it: by depriving me of it, you disappoint my expectations, and doubly displease me, and offend every bystander. It is a public wrong, so far as the rules of equity are violated: it is a private harm, so far as an individual is injured. And though the second consideration could have no place, were not the former previously established: for otherwise the distinction of *mine* and *thine* would be unknown in society: yet there is no question but the regard to general good is much enforced by the respect to particular. What injures the community, without hurting any individual, is often more lightly thought of. But where the greatest public wrong is also conjoined with a considerable private one, no wonder the highest disapprobation attends so iniquitous a behaviour.

5

ON THE CONNECTION BETWEEN JUSTICE AND UTILITY

J. S. MILL

In all ages of speculation, one of the strongest obstacles to the reception of the doctrine that Utility or Happiness is the criterion of right and wrong, has been drawn from the idea of Justice. The powerful sentiment, and apparently clear perception, which that word recalls with a rapidity and certainty resembling an instinct, have seemed to the majority of thinkers to point to an inherent quality in things; to show that the Just must have an existence in Nature as something absolute—generically distinct from every variety of the Expedient, and, in idea, opposed to it, though (as is commonly acknowledged) never, in the long run, disjoined from it in fact.

In the case of this, as of our other moral sentiments, there is no necessary connection between the question of its origin, and that of its binding force. That a feeling is bestowed on us by Nature, does not necessarily legitimate all its promptings. The feeling of justice might be a peculiar instinct, and might yet require, like our other instincts, to be controlled and enlightened by a higher reason. If we have intellectual instincts, leading us to judge in a particular way, as well as animal instincts that prompt us to act in a particular way, there is no necessity that the former should be more infallible in their sphere than the latter in theirs: it may as well happen that wrong judgements are occasionally suggested by those, as wrong actions by these. But though it is one thing to believe that we have natural feelings of justice, and another to acknowledge them as an ultimate criterion of conduct, these two opinions are very closely connected in point of fact. Mankind are always predisposed to believe that any subjective feeling, not otherwise accounted for, is a revelation of

J. S. Mill, 'On the Connection between Justice and Utility', chap. 5 of *Utilitarianism*, ed. A. Ryan (Penguin, Harmondsworth, 1987). Reprinted by permission of the publishers.

CANISIUS COLLEGE LIBRARY
BUFFALO, N.Y.

some objective reality. Our present object is to determine whether the reality, to which the feeling of justice corresponds, is one which needs any such special revelation; whether the justice or injustice of an action is a thing intrinsically peculiar, and distinct from all its other qualities, or only a combination of certain of those qualities, presented under a peculiar aspect. For the purpose of the enquiry, it is practically important to consider whether the feeling itself, of justice and injustice, is *sui generis* like our sensations of colour and taste, or a derivative feeling, formed by a combination of others. And this it is the more essential to examine, as people are in general willing enough to allow, that objectively the dictates of justice coincide with a part of the field of General Expediency; but inasmuch as the subjective mental feeling of Justice is different from that which commonly attaches to simple expediency, and, except in extreme cases of the latter, is far more imperative in its demands, people find it difficult to see, in Justice, only a particular kind or branch of general utility, and think that its superior binding force requires a totally different origin.

To throw light upon this question, it is necessary to attempt to ascertain what is the distinguishing character of justice, or of injustice: what is the quality, or whether there is any quality, attributed in common to all modes of conduct designated as unjust (for justice, like many other moral attributes, is best defined by its opposite), and distinguishing them from such modes of conduct as are disapproved, but without having that particular epithet of disapprobation applied to them. If, in everything which men are accustomed to characterize as just or unjust, some one common attribute or collection of attributes is always present, we may judge whether this particular attribute or combination of attributes would be capable of gathering round it a sentiment of that peculiar character and intensity by virtue of the general laws of our emotional constitution, or whether the sentiment is inexplicable, and requires to be regarded as a special provision of Nature. If we find the former to be the case, we shall, in resolving this question, have resolved also the main problem: if the latter, we shall have to seek for some other mode of investigating it.

To find the common attributes of a variety of objects, it is necessary to begin by surveying the objects themselves in the concrete. Let us therefore advert successively to the various modes of action, and arrangements of human affairs, which are classed, by universal or widely spread opinion, as Just or as Unjust. The things well known to excite the sentiments associated with those names, are of a very multifarious character. I shall pass them rapidly in review, without studying any particular arrangement.

In the first place, it is mostly considered unjust to deprive any one of his personal liberty, his property, or any other thing which belongs to him by law. Here, therefore, is one instance of the application of the terms just and unjust in a perfectly definite sense, namely, that it is just to respect, unjust to violate, the *legal rights* of anyone. But this judgement admits of several exceptions, arising from the other forms in which the notions of justice and injustice present themselves. For example, the person who suffers the deprivation may (as the phrase is) have *forfeited* the rights which he is so deprived of: a case to which we shall return presently. But also,

Secondly; the legal rights of which he is deprived, may be rights which *ought* not to have belonged to him; in other words, the law which confers on him these rights, may be a bad law. When it is so, or when (which is the same thing for our purpose) it is supposed to be so, opinions will differ as to the justice or injustice of infringing it. Some maintain that no law, however bad, ought to be disobeyed by an individual citizen; that his opposition to it, if shown at all, should only be shown in endeavouring to get it altered by competent authority. This opinion (which condemns many of the most illustrious benefactors of mankind, and would often protect pernicious institutions against the only weapons which, in the state of things existing at the time, have any chance of succeeding against them) is defended, by those who hold it, on grounds of expediency; principally on that of the importance, to the common interest of mankind, of maintaining inviolate the sentiment of submission to law. Other persons, again, hold the directly contrary opinion, that any law, judged to be bad, may blamelessly be disobeyed, even though it be not judged to be unjust, but only inexpedient; while others would confine the licence of disobedience to the case of unjust laws: but again, some say, that all laws which are inexpedient are unjust; since every law imposes some restriction on the natural liberty of mankind, which restriction is an injustice, unless legitimated by tending to their good. Among these diversities of opinion, it seems to be universally admitted that there may be unjust laws, and that law, consequently, is not the ultimate criterion of justice, but may give to one person a benefit, or impose on another an evil, which justice condemns. When, however, a law is thought to be unjust, it seems always to be regarded as being so in the same way in which a breach of law is unjust, namely, by infringing somebody's right; which, as it cannot in this case be a legal right, receives a different appellation, and is called a moral right. We may say, therefore, that a second case of injustice consists in taking or withholding from any person that to which he has a *moral right*.

Thirdly, it is universally considered just that each person should obtain that (whether good or evil) which he *deserves*; and unjust that he should obtain a good, or be made to undergo an evil, which he does not deserve. This is, perhaps, the clearest and most emphatic form in which the idea of justice is conceived by the general mind. As it involves the notion of desert, the question arises, what constitutes desert? Speaking in a general way, a person is understood to deserve good if he does right, evil if he does wrong; and in a more particular sense, to deserve good from those to whom he does or has done good, and evil from those to whom he does or has done evil. The precept of returning good for evil has never been regarded as a case of the fulfilment of justice, but as one in which the claims of justice are waived, in obedience to other considerations.

Fourthly, it is confessedly unjust to *break faith* with any one: to violate an engagement, either express or implied, or disappoint expectations raised by our own conduct, at least if we have raised those expectations knowingly and voluntarily. Like the other obligations of justice already spoken of, this one is not regarded as absolute, but as capable of being overruled by a stronger obligation of justice on the other side; or by such conduct on the part of the person concerned as is deemed to absolve us from our obligation to him, and to constitute a *forfeiture* of the benefit which he has been led to expect.

Fifthly, it is, by universal admission, inconsistent with justice to be *partial*; to show favour or preference to one person over another, in matters to which favour and preference do not properly apply. Impartiality, however, does not seem to be regarded as a duty in itself, but rather as instrumental to some other duty; for it is admitted that favour and preference are not always censurable, and indeed the cases in which they are condemned are rather the exception than the rule. A person would be more likely to be blamed than applauded for giving his family or friends no superiority in good offices over strangers, when he could do so without violating any other duty; and no one thinks it unjust to seek one person in preference to another as a friend, connection, or companion. Impartiality where rights are concerned is of course obligatory, but this is involved in the more general obligation of giving to everyone his right. A tribunal, for example, must be impartial, because it is bound to award, without regard to any other consideration, a disputed object to the one of two parties who has the right to it. There are other cases in which impartiality means being solely influenced by desert; as with those who, in the capacity of judges, preceptors, or parents, administer reward and punishment as such. There are cases, again, in which it means being solely influenced by consideration for the public interest; as in making a selection among candidates for a government employment. Impartiality, in short, as an obligation of justice, may be said to mean, being exclusively influenced by the considerations which it is supposed ought to influence the particular case in hand; and resisting the solicitation of any motives which prompt to conduct different from what those considerations would dictate.

Nearly allied to the idea of impartiality, is that of *equality*; which often enters as a component part both into the conception of justice and into the practice of it, and, in the eyes of many persons, constitutes its essence. But in this, still more than in any other case, the notion of justice varies in different persons, and always conforms in its variations to their notion of utility. Each person maintains that equality is the dictate of justice, except where he thinks that expediency requires inequality. The justice of giving equal protection to the rights of all, is maintained by those who support the most outrageous inequality in the rights themselves. Even in slave countries it is theoretically admitted that the rights of the slave, such as they are, ought to be as sacred as those of the master; and that a tribunal which fails to enforce them with equal strictness is wanting in justice; while, at the same time, institutions which leave to the slave scarcely any rights to enforce, are not deemed unjust, because they are not deemed inexpedient. Those who think that utility requires distinctions of rank, do not consider it unjust that riches and social privileges should be unequally dispensed; but those who think this inequality inexpedient, think it unjust also. Whoever thinks that government is necessary, sees no injustice in as much inequality as is constituted by giving to the magistrate powers not granted to other people. Even among those who hold levelling doctrines, there are as many questions of justice as there are differences of opinion about expediency. Some Communists consider it unjust that the produce of the labour of the community should be shared on any other principle than that of exact equality; others think it just that those should receive most whose needs are greatest; while others hold that those who work harder, or who produce more, or whose services are more valuable to the community, may justly claim a larger quota in the division of the produce. And the sense of natural justice may be plausibly appealed to in behalf of every one of these opinions.

Among so many diverse applications of the term Justice, which yet is not regarded as ambiguous, it is a matter of some difficulty to seize the mental link which holds them together, and on which the moral sentiment adhering to the term essentially depends. Perhaps, in this embarrassment, some help may be derived from the history of the word, as indicated by its etymology.

In most, if not in all, languages, the etymology of the word which corresponds to Just, points to an origin connected either with positive law, or with that which was in most cases the primitive form of law—authoritative custom. *Justum* is a form of *jussum*, that which has been ordered. *Jus* is of the same origin. Δίκαιον comes from δίκη, of which the principal meaning, at least in the historical ages of Greece, was a suit at law. Originally, indeed, it meant only the mode or *manner* of doing things, but it early came to mean the *prescribed* manner; that which the recognized authorities, patriarchal, judicial, or political, would enforce. *Recht*, from which came *right* and *righteous*, is synonymous with law. The original meaning indeed of *recht* did not point to law, but to physical straightness; as *wrong* and its Latin equivalents meant twisted or *tortuous*; and from this it is argued that right did not originally mean law, but on the contrary law meant right. But however this may be, the fact that *recht* and *droit* became restricted in their meaning to positive law, although much which is not required by law is equally necessary to moral straightness or rectitude, is as significant of the original character of moral ideas as if the derivation had been the reverse way. The courts of justice, the administration of justice, are the courts and the administration of law. *La justice*, in French, is the established term for judicature. There can, I think, be no doubt that the *idée mère*, the primitive element, in the formation of the notion of justice, was conformity to law. It constituted the entire idea among the Hebrews, up to the birth of Christianity; as might be expected in the case of a people whose laws attempted to embrace all subjects on which precepts were required, and who believed those laws to be a direct emanation from the Supreme Being. But other nations, and in particular the Greeks and Romans, who knew that their laws had been made originally, and still continued to be made, by men, were not afraid to admit that those men might make bad laws; might do, by law, the same things, and from the same motives, which, if done by individuals without the sanction of law, would be called unjust. And hence the sentiment of injustice came to be attached, not to all violations of law, but only to violations of such laws as *ought* to exist, including such as ought to exist but do not; and to laws themselves, if supposed to be contrary to what ought to be law. In this manner the idea of law and of its injunctions was still predominant in the notion of justice, even when the laws actually in force ceased to be accepted as the standard of it.

It is true that mankind consider the idea of justice and its obligations as applicable to many things which neither are, nor is it desired that they should be, regulated by law. Nobody desires that laws should interfere with the whole detail of private life; yet everyone allows that in all daily conduct a person may and does show himself to be either just or unjust. But even here, the idea of the breach of what ought to be law, still lingers in a modified shape. It would always give us pleasure, and chime in with our feelings of fitness, that acts which we deem unjust should be punished, though we do not always think it expedient that this should be done by the tribunals. We forgo that gratification on account of incidental inconveniences. We should be glad to see just conduct enforced and injustice repressed, even in the minutest details, if we were not, with reason, afraid of trusting the magistrate with so unlimited an amount of power over individuals. When we think that a person is bound in justice to do a thing, it is an ordinary form of language to say, that he ought to be compelled to do it. We should be gratified to see the obligation enforced by anybody who had the power. If we see that its enforcement by law would be inexpedient, we lament the impossibility, we consider the impunity given to injustice as an evil, and strive to make amends for it by bringing a strong expression of our own and the public disapprobation to bear upon the offender. Thus the idea of legal constraint is still the generating idea of the notion of justice, though undergoing several transformations before that notion, as it exists in an advanced state of society, becomes complete.

The above is, I think, a true account, as far as it goes, of the origin and progressive growth of the idea of justice. But we must observe, that it contains, as yet, nothing to distinguish that obligation from moral obligation in general. For the truth is, that the idea of penal sanction, which is the essence of law, enters not only into the conception of injustice, but into that of any kind of wrong. We do not call anything wrong, unless we mean to imply that a person ought to be punished in some way or other for doing it; if not by law, by the opinion of his fellow creatures; if not by opinion, by the reproaches of his own conscience. This seems the real turning point of the distinction between morality and simple expediency. It is a part of the notion of Duty in every one of its forms, that a person may rightfully be compelled to fulfil it. Duty is a thing which may be *exacted* from a person, as one exacts a debt. Unless we think that it might be exacted from him, we do not call it his duty. Reasons of prudence, or the interest of other people, may militate against actually exacting it; but the person himself, it is clearly understood, would not be entitled to complain. There are other things, on the contrary, which we wish that people should do, which we like or admire them for doing, perhaps dislike or despise them for not doing, but yet admit that they are not bound to do; it is not a case of moral obligation; we do not blame them, that is, we do not think that they are proper objects of punishment. How we come by these ideas of deserving and not deserving punishment, will appear, perhaps, in the sequel; but I think there is no doubt that this distinction lies at the bottom of the notions of right and wrong; that we call any conduct wrong, or employ, instead, some other term of dislike or disparagement, according as we think that the person ought, or ought not, to be punished for it; and we say that it would be right to do so and so, or merely that it would be desirable or laudable, according as we would wish to see the person whom it concerns, compelled, or only persuaded and exhorted, to act in that manner.

This, therefore, being the characteristic difference which marks off, not justice, but morality in general, from the remaining provinces of Expediency and Worthiness; the character is still to be sought which distinguishes justice from other branches of morality.

Now it is known that ethical writers divide moral duties into two classes, denoted by the ill-chosen expressions, duties of perfect and of imperfect obligation; the latter being those in which, though the act is obligatory, the particular occasions of performing it are left to our choice; as in the case of charity or beneficence, which we are indeed bound to practise, but not towards any definite person, nor at any prescribed time. In the more precise language of philosophic jurists, duties of perfect obligation are those duties in virtue of which a correlative *right* resides in some person or persons; duties of imperfect obligation are those moral obligations which do not give birth to any right. I think it will be found that this distinction exactly coincides with that which exists between justice and the other obligations* of morality. In our survey of the various popular acceptations of justice, the term appeared generally to involve the idea of a personal right—a claim on the part of one or more individuals, like that which the law gives when it confers a proprietary or other legal right. Whether the injustice consists in depriving a person of a possession, or in breaking faith with him, or in treating him worse than he deserves, or worse than other people who have no greater claims, in each case the supposition implies two things—a wrong done, and some assignable person who is wronged. Injustice may also be done by treating a person better than others; but the wrong in this case is to his competitors, who are also assignable persons. It seems to me that this feature in the case—a right in some person, correlative to the moral obligation—constitutes the specific difference between justice and generosity or beneficence. Justice implies something which it is not only right to do, and wrong not to do, but which some individual person can claim from us as his moral right. No one has a moral right to our generosity or beneficence, because we are not morally bound to practise those virtues towards any given individual. And it will be found with respect to this as with respect to every correct definition, that the instances which seem to conflict with it are those which most confirm it. For if a moralist attempts, as some have done, to make out that mankind generally, though not any given individual, have a right to all the good we can do them, he at once, by that thesis, includes generosity and beneficence within the category of justice. He is obliged to say, that our utmost exertions are *due* to our fellow creatures, thus assimilating them to a debt; or that nothing less can be a sufficient *return* for what society does for us, thus classing the case as one of gratitude; both of which are acknowledged cases of justice. Wherever there is a right, the case is one of justice, and not of the virtue of beneficence: and whoever does

not place the distinction between justice and morality in general
where we have now placed it, will be found to make no distinction
between them at all, but to merge all morality in justice.

Having thus endeavoured to determine the distinctive elements
which enter into the composition of the idea of justice, we are ready
to enter the enquiry, whether the feeling, which accompanies the
idea, is attached to it by a special dispensation of nature, or whether
it could have grown up, by any known laws, out of the idea itself;
and in particular, whether it can have originated in considerations of
general expediency.

I conceive that the sentiment itself does not arise from anything
which would commonly, or correctly, be termed an idea of
expediency, but that though the sentiment does not, whatever is
moral in it does.

We have seen that the two essential ingredients in the sentiment of
justice are, the desire to punish a person who has done harm, and
the knowledge or belief that there is some definite individual or
individuals to whom harm has been done.

Now it appears to me, that the desire to punish a person who has
done harm to some individual, is a spontaneous outgrowth from two
sentiments, both in the highest degree natural, and which either are
or resemble instincts; the impulse of self-defence, and the feeling of
sympathy.

It is natural to resent, and to repel or retaliate, any harm done or
attempted against ourselves, or against those with whom we
sympathize. The origin of this sentiment it is not necessary here to
discuss. Whether it be an instinct or a result of intelligence, it is, we
know, common to all animal nature; for every animal tries to hurt
those who have hurt, or who it thinks are about to hurt, itself or its
young. Human beings, on this point, only differ from other animals
in two particulars. First, in being capable of sympathizing, not solely
with their offspring, or, like some of the more noble animals, with
some superior animal who is kind to them, but with all human, and
even with all sentient, beings. Secondly, in having a more developed
intelligence, which gives a wider range to the whole of their
sentiments, whether self-regarding or sympathetic. By virtue of his
superior intelligence, even apart from his superior range of
sympathy, a human being is capable of apprehending a community
of interest between himself and the human society of which he forms
a part, such that any conduct which threatens the security of the
society generally, is threatening to his own, and calls forth his
instinct (if instinct it be) of self-defence. The same superiority of
intelligence, joined to the power of sympathizing with human beings

generally, enables him to attach himself to the collective idea of his tribe, his country, or mankind, in such a manner that any act hurtful to them rouses his instinct of sympathy, and urges him to resistance.

The sentiment of justice, in that one of its elements which consists of the desire to punish, is this, I conceive, the natural feeling of retaliation or vengeance, rendered by intellect and sympathy applicable to those injuries, that is, to those hurts, which wound us through, or in common with, society at large. This sentiment, in itself, has nothing moral in it; what is moral is, the exclusive subordination of it to the social sympathies, so as to wait on and obey their call. For the natural feeling tends to make us resent indiscriminately whatever any one does that is disagreeable to us; but when moralized by the social feeling, it only acts in the directions conformable to the general good: just persons resenting a hurt to society, though not otherwise a hurt to themselves, and not resenting a hurt to themselves, however painful, unless it be of the kind which society has a common interest with them in the repression of.

It is no objection against this doctrine to say, that when we feel our sentiment of justice outraged, we are not thinking of society at large, or of any collective interest, but only of the individual case. It is common enough certainly, though the reverse of commendable, to feel resentment merely because we have suffered pain; but a person whose resentment is really a moral feeling, that is, who considers whether an act is blameable before he allows himself to resent it—such a person, though he may not say expressly to himself that he is standing up for the interest of society, certainly does feel that he is asserting a rule which is for the benefit of others as well as for his own. If he is not feeling this—if he is regarding the act solely as it affects him individually—he is not consciously just; he is not concerning himself about the justice of his actions. This is admitted even by anti-utilitarian moralists. When Kant (as before remarked) propounds as the fundamental principle of morals, 'So act, that thy rule of conduct might be adopted as a law by all rational beings,' he virtually acknowledges that the interest of mankind collectively, or at least of mankind indiscriminately, must be in the mind of the agent when conscientiously deciding on the morality of the act. Otherwise he uses words without a meaning: for, that a rule even of utter selfishness could not *possibly* be adopted by all rational beings—that there is any insuperable obstacle in the nature of things to its adoption—cannot be even plausibly maintained. To give any meaning to Kant's principle, the sense put upon it must be, that we ought to shape our conduct by a rule which all rational beings might adopt *with benefit to their collective interest*.

To recapitulate: the idea of justice supposes two things; a rule of conduct, and a sentiment which sanctions the rule. The first must be supposed common to all mankind, and intended for their good. The other (the sentiment) is a desire that punishment may be suffered by those who infringe the rule. There is involved, in addition, the conception of some definite person who suffers by the infringement; whose rights (to use the expression appropriated to the case) are violated by it. And the sentiment of justice appears to me to be the animal desire to repel or retaliate a hurt or damage to oneself, or to those with whom one sympathizes, widened so as to include all persons, by the human capacity of enlarged sympathy, and the human conception of intelligent self-interest. From the latter elements, the feeling derives its morality; from the former, its peculiar impressiveness, and energy of self-assertion.

I have, throughout, treated the idea of a *right* residing in the injured person, and violated by the injury, not as a separate element in the composition of the idea and sentiment, but as one of the forms in which the other two elements clothe themselves. These elements are, a hurt to some assignable person or persons on the one hand, and a demand for punishment on the other. An examination of our own minds, I think, will show, that these two things include all that we mean when we speak of violation of a right. When we call anything a person's right, we mean that he has a valid claim on society to protect him in the possession of it, either by the force of law, or by that of education and opinion. If he has what we consider a sufficient claim, on whatever account, to have something guaranteed to him by society, we say that he has a right to it. If we desire to prove that anything does not belong to him by right, we think this done as soon as it is admitted that society ought not to take measures for securing it to him, but should leave it to chance, or to his own exertions. Thus, a person is said to have a right to what he can earn in fair professional competition; because society ought not to allow any other person to hinder him from endeavouring to earn in that manner as much as he can. But he has not a right to three hundred a year, though he may happen to be earning it; because society is not called on to provide that he shall earn that sum. On the contrary, if he owns ten thousand pounds three per cent stock, he *has* a right to three hundred a year; because society has come under an obligation to provide him with an income of that amount.

To have a right, then, is, I conceive, to have something which society ought to defend me in the possession of. If the objector goes on to ask why it ought, I can give him no other reason than general utility. If that expression does not seem to convey a sufficient feeling of the strength of the obligation, nor to account for the peculiar energy of the feeling, it is because there goes to the composition of the sentiment, not a rational only but also an animal element, the thirst for retaliation; and this thirst derives its intensity, as well as its moral justification, from the extraordinarily important and impressive kind of utility which is concerned. The interest involved is that of security, to every one's feelings the most vital of all interests. Nearly all other earthly benefits are needed by one person, not needed by another; and many of them can, if necessary, be cheerfully forgone, or replaced by something else; but security no human being can possibly do without; on it we depend for all our immunity from evil, and for the whole value of all and every good, beyond the passing moment; since nothing but the gratification of the instant could be of any worth to us, if we could be deprived of everything the next instant by whoever was momentarily stronger than ourselves. Now this most indispensable of all necessaries, after physical nutriment, cannot be had, unless the machinery for providing it is kept unintermittedly in active play. Our notion, therefore, of the claim we have on our fellow creatures to join in making safe for us the very groundwork of our existence, gathers feelings round it so much more intense than those concerned in any of the more common cases of utility, that the difference in degree (as is often the case in psychology) becomes a real difference in kind. The claim assumes that character of absoluteness, that apparent infinity, and incommensurability with all other considerations, which constitute the distinction between the feeling of right and wrong and that of ordinary expediency and inexpediency. The feelings concerned are so powerful, and we count so positively on finding a responsive feeling in others (all being alike interested), that *ought* and *should* grow into *must*, and recognized indispensability becomes a moral necessity, analogous to physical, and often not inferior to it in binding force.

If the preceding analysis, or something resembling it, be not the correct account of the notion of justice; if justice be totally independent of utility, and be a standard *per se*, which the mind can recognize by simple introspection of itself; it is hard to understand why that internal oracle is so ambiguous, and why so many things appear either just or unjust, according to the light in which they are regarded.

We are continually informed that Utility is an uncertain standard, which every different person interprets differently, and that there is no safety but in the immutable, ineffaceable, and unmistakable dictates of Justice, which carry their evidence in themselves, and are independent of the fluctuations of opinion. One would suppose from

this that on questions of justice there could be no controversy; that if
we take that for our rule, its application to any given case could
leave us in as little doubt as a mathematical demonstration. So far is
this from being the fact, that there is as much difference of opinion,
and as fierce discussion, about what is just, as about what is useful to
society. Not only have different nations and individuals different
notions of justice, but, in the mind of one and the same individual,
justice is not some one rule, principle, or maxim, but many, which
do not always coincide in their dictates, and in choosing between
which, he is guided either by some extraneous standard, or by his
own personal predilections.

For instance, there are some who say, that it is unjust to punish
anyone for the sake of example to others; that punishment is just,
only when intended for the good of the sufferer himself. Others
maintain the extreme reverse, contending that to punish persons
who have attained years of discretion, for their own benefit, is
despotism and injustice, since if the matter at issue is solely their own
good, no one has a right to control their own judgement of it; but
that they may justly be punished to prevent evil to others, this being
an exercise of the legitimate right of self-defence. Mr Owen, again,
affirms that it is unjust to punish at all; for the criminal did not make
his own character; his education, and the circumstances which
surround him, have made him a criminal, and for these he is not
responsible. All these opinions are extremely plausible; and so long
as the question is argued as one of justice simply, without going
down to the principles which lie under justice and are the source of
its authority, I am unable to see how any of these reasoners can be
refuted. For, in truth, every one of the three builds upon rules of
justice confessedly true. The first appeals to the acknowledged
injustice of singling out an individual, and making him a sacrifice,
without his consent, for other people's benefit. The second relies on
the acknowledged justice of self-defence, and the admitted injustice
of forcing one person to conform to another's notions of what
constitutes his good. The Owenite invokes the admitted principle,
that it is unjust to punish anyone for what he cannot help. Each is
triumphant so long as he is not compelled to take into consideration
any other maxims of justice than the one he has selected; but as soon
as their several maxims are brought face to face, each disputant
seems to have exactly as much to say for himself as the others. No
one of them can carry out his own notion of justice without
trampling upon another equally binding. These are difficulties; they
have always been felt to be such; and many devices have been
invented to turn rather than to overcome them. As a refuge from the
last of the three, men imagined what they called the freedom of the

will; fancying that they could not justify punishing a man whose will is in a thoroughly hateful state, unless it be supposed to have come into that state through no influence of anterior circumstances. To escape from the other difficulties, a favourite contrivance has been the fiction of a contract, whereby at some unknown period all the members of society engaged to obey the laws, and consented to be punished for any disobedience to them; thereby giving to their legislators the right, which it is assumed they would not otherwise have had, of punishing them, either for their own good or for that of society. This happy thought was considered to get rid of the whole difficulty, and to legitimate the infliction of punishment, in virtue of another received maxim of justice, *volenti non fit injuria*; that is not unjust which is done with the consent of the person who is supposed to be hurt by it. I need hardly remark, that even if the consent were not a mere fiction, this maxim is not superior in authority to the others which it is brought in to supersede. It is, on the contrary, an instructive specimen of the loose and irregular manner in which supposed principles of justice grow up. This particular one evidently came into use as a help to the coarse exigencies of courts of law, which are sometimes obliged to be content with very uncertain presumptions, on account of the greater evils which would often arise from any attempt on their part to cut finer. But even courts of law are not able to adhere consistently to the maxim, for they allow voluntary engagements to be set aside on the ground of fraud, and sometimes on that of mere mistake or misinformation.

Again, when the legitimacy of inflicting punishment is admitted, how many conflicting conceptions of justice come to light in discussing the proper apportionment of punishment to offences. No rule on this subject recommends itself so strongly to the primitive and spontaneous sentiment of justice as the *lex talionis*, an eye for an eye and a tooth for a tooth. Though this principle of the Jewish and of the Muhammadan law has been generally abandoned in Europe as a practical maxim, there is, I suspect, in most minds, a secret hankering after it; and when retribution accidentally falls on an offender in that precise shape, the general feeling of satisfaction evinced, bears witness how natural is the sentiment to which this repayment in kind is acceptable. With many the test of justice in penal infliction is that the punishment should be proportioned to the offence; meaning that it should be exactly measured by the moral guilt of the culprit (whatever be their standard for measuring moral guilt): the consideration, what amount of punishment is necessary to deter from the offence, having nothing to do with the question of justice, in their estimation: while there are others to whom that consideration is all in all; who maintain that it is not just, at least for man, to inflict on a fellow creature, whatever may be his offences, any amount of suffering beyond the least that will suffice to prevent him from repeating, and others from imitating, his misconduct.

To take another example from a subject already once referred to. In a co-operative industrial association, is it just or not that talent or skill should give a title to superior remuneration? On the negative side of the question it is argued that whoever does the best he can, deserves equally well, and ought not in justice to be put in a position of inferiority for no fault of his own; that superior abilities have already advantages more than enough, in the admiration they excite, the personal influence they command, and the internal sources of satisfaction attending them, without adding to these a superior share of the world's goods; and that society is bound in justice rather to make compensation to the less favoured, for this unmerited inequality of advantages, than to aggravate it. On the contrary side it is contended that society receives more from the more efficient labourer; that his services being more useful, society owes him a larger return for them; that a greater share of the joint result is actually his work, and not to allow his claim to it is a kind of robbery; that if he is only to receive as much as others, he can only be justly required to produce as much, and to give a smaller amount of time and exertion, proportioned to his superior efficiency. Who shall decide between these appeals to conflicting principles of justice? Justice has in this case two sides to it, which it is impossible to bring into harmony, and the two disputants have chosen opposite sides; the one looks to what it is just that the individual should receive, the other to what it is just that the community should give. Each, from his own point of view, is unanswerable; and any choice between them, on grounds of justice, must be perfectly arbitrary. Social utility alone can decide the preference.

How many, again, and how irreconcilable, are the standards of justice to which reference is made in discussing the repartition of taxation. One opinion is, that payment to the State should be in numerical proportion to pecuniary means. Others think that justice dictates what they term graduated taxation; taking a higher percentage from those who have more to spare. In point of natural justice a strong case might be made for disregarding means altogether, and taking the same absolute sum (whenever it could be got) from every one: as the subscribers to a mess, or to a club, all pay the same sum for the same privileges, whether they can all equally afford it or not. Since the protection (it might be said) of law and government is afforded to, and is equally required by, all, there is no justice in making all buy it at the same price. It is reckoned justice, not injustice, that a dealer should charge to all customers the same price for the same article, not a price varying according to their means of payment. This doctrine, as applied to taxation, finds no advocates, because it conflicts strongly with men's feelings of humanity and perceptions of social expediency; but the principle of justice which it invokes is as true and as binding as those which can be appealed to against it. Accordingly, it exerts a tacit influence on the line of defence employed for other modes of assessing taxation. People feel obliged to argue that the State does more for the rich than for the poor, as a justification for its taking more from them: though this is in reality not true, for the rich would be far better able to protect themselves, in the absence of law or government, than the poor, and indeed would probably be successful in converting the poor into their slaves. Others, again, so far defer to the same conception of justice, as to maintain that all should pay an equal capitation tax for the protection of their persons (these being of equal value to all), and an unequal tax for the protection of their property, which is unequal. To this others reply, that the all of one man is as valuable to him as the all of another. From these confusions there is no other mode of extrication than the utilitarian.

Is, then, the difference between the Just and the Expedient a merely imaginary distinction? Have mankind been under a delusion in thinking that justice is a more sacred thing than policy, and that the latter ought only to be listened to after the former has been satisfied? By no means. The exposition we have given of the nature and origin of the sentiment recognizes a real distinction; and no one of those who profess the most sublime contempt for the consequences of actions as an element in their morality, attaches more importance to the distinction than I do. While I dispute the pretensions of any theory which sets up an imaginary standard of justice not grounded on utility, I account the justice which is grounded on utility to be the chief part, and incomparably the most sacred and binding part, of all morality. Justice is a name for certain classes of moral rules, which concern the essentials of human well-being more nearly, and are therefore of more absolute obligation, than any other rules for the guidance of life; and the notion which we have found to be of the essence of the idea of justice, that of a right residing in an individual, implies and testifies to this more binding obligation.

The moral rules which forbid mankind to hurt one another (in which we must never forget to include wrongful interference with each other's freedom) are more vital to human well-being than any maxims, however important, which only point out the best mode of managing some department of human affairs. They have also the peculiarity, that they are the main element in determining the whole of the social feelings of mankind. It is their observance which alone preserves peace among human beings: if obedience to them were not the rule, and disobedience the exception, every one would see in every one else a probable enemy, against whom he must be perpetually guarding himself. What is hardly less important, these are the precepts which mankind have the strongest and the most direct inducements for impressing upon one another. By merely giving to each other prudential instruction or exhortation, they may gain, or think they gain, nothing: in inculcating in each other the duty of positive beneficence they have an unmistakable interest, but far less in degree: a person may possibly not need the benefits of others; but he always needs that they should not do him hurt. Thus the moralities which protect every individual from being harmed by others, either directly or by being hindered in his freedom of pursuing his own good, are at once those which he himself has most at heart, and those which he has the strongest interest in publishing and enforcing by word and deed. It is by a person's observance of these that his fitness to exist as one of the fellowship of human beings is tested and decided; for on that depends his being a nuisance or not to those with whom he is in contact. Now it is these moralities primarily which compose the obligations of justice. The most marked cases of injustice, and those which give the tone to the feeling of repugnance which characterizes the sentiment, are acts of wrongful aggression, or wrongful exercise of power over someone; the next are those which consist in wrongfully withholding from him something which is his due; in both cases, inflicting on him a positive hurt, either in the form of direct suffering or of the privation of some good which he had reasonable ground, either of a physical or of a social kind, for counting upon.

The same powerful motives which command the observance of these primary moralities, enjoin the punishment of those who violate them; and as the impulses of self-defence, of defence of others, and of vengeance, are all called forth against such persons, retribution, or evil for evil, becomes closely connected with the sentiment of justice, and is universally included in the idea. Good for good is also one of the dictates of justice; and this, though its social utility is evident, and though it carries with it a natural human feeling, has not at first sight that obvious connection with hurt or injury which, existing in the most elementary cases of just and unjust, is the source of the characteristic intensity of the sentiment. But the connection, though less obvious, is not less real. He who accepts benefits, and denies a return of them when needed, inflicts a real hurt, by disappointing one of the most natural and reasonable of expectations, and one which he must at least tacitly have encouraged, otherwise the benefits would seldom have been conferred. The important rank, among human evils and wrongs, of the disappointment of expectation, is shown in the fact that it constitutes the principal criminality of two such highly immoral acts as a breach of friendship and a breach of promise. Few hurts which human beings can sustain are greater, and none wound more, than when that on which they habitually and with full assurance relied fails them in the hour of need; and few wrongs are greater than this mere withholding of good; none excite more resentment, either in the person suffering, or in a sympathizing spectator. The principle, therefore, of giving to each what they deserve, that is, good for good as well as evil for evil, is not only included within the idea of Justice as we have defined it, but is a proper object of that intensity of sentiment, which places the Just, in human estimation, above the simply Expedient.

Most of the maxims of justice current in the world, and commonly appealed to in its transactions, are simply instrumental to carrying into effect the principles of justice which we have now spoken of. That a person is only responsible for what he has done voluntarily, or could voluntarily have avoided; that it is unjust to condemn any person unheard; that the punishment ought to be proportioned to the offence, and the like, are maxims intended to prevent the just principle of evil for evil from being perverted to the infliction of evil without that justification. The greater part of these common maxims have come into use from the practice of courts of justice, which have been naturally led to a more complete recognition and elaboration than was likely to suggest itself to others, of the rules necessary to enable them to fulfil their double function, of inflicting punishment when due, and of awarding to each person his right.

That first of judicial virtues, impartiality, is an obligation of justice, partly for the reason last mentioned; as being a necessary condition of the fulfilment of the other obligations of justice. But this is not the only source of the exalted rank, among human obligations, of those maxims of equality and impartiality which, both in popular estimation and in that of the most enlightened, are included among the precepts of justice. In one point of view, they may be considered as corollaries from the principles already laid down. If it is a duty to do to each according to his deserts, returning good for good as well as repressing evil by evil, it necessarily follows that we should treat all equally well (when no higher duty forbids) who have deserved equally well of us, and that society should treat all equally well who have deserved equally well of it, that is, who have deserved equally well absolutely. This is the highest abstract standard of social and distributive justice; towards which all institutions, and the efforts of all virtuous citizens, should be made in the utmost possible degree to converge. But this great moral duty rests upon a still deeper foundation, being a direct emanation from the first principle of morals, and not a mere logical corollary from secondary or derivative doctrines. It is involved in the very meaning of Utility, or the Greatest Happiness Principle. That principle is a mere form of words without rational signification, unless one person's happiness, supposed equal in degree (with the proper allowance made for kind), is counted for exactly as much as another's. Those conditions being supplied, Bentham's dictum, 'everybody to count for one, nobody for more than one', might be written under the principle of utility as an explanatory commentary.[1] The equal claim of everybody to happiness in the estimation of the moralist and the legislator, involves an equal claim to all the means of happiness, except in so far as the inevitable conditions of human life, and the general interest, in which that of every individual is included, set limits to the maxim; and those limits ought to be strictly construed. As every other maxim of justice, so this, is by no means applied or held applicable universally; on the contrary, as I have already

[1] This implication, in the first principle of the utilitarian scheme, of perfect impartiality between persons, is regarded by Mr Herbert Spencer (in his *Social Statics*) as a disproof of the pretensions of utility to be a sufficient guide to right; since (he says) the principle of utility presupposes the anterior principle that everybody has an equal right to happiness. It may be more correctly described as supposing that equal amounts of happiness are equally desirable, whether felt by the same or by different persons. This, however, is not a presupposition; not a premiss needful to support the principle of utility, but the very principle itself; for what is the principle of utility, if it be not that 'happiness' and 'desirable' are synonymous terms? If there is any anterior principle implied, it can be no other than this, that the truths of arithmetic are applicable to the valuation of happiness, as of all other measurable quantities.

Mr Herbert Spencer, in a private communication on the subject of the preceding Note, objects to being considered an opponent of Utilitarianism, and states that he regards happiness as the ultimate end of morality; but deems that end only partially attainable by empirical generalizations from the observed results of conduct, and completely attainable only by deducing, from the laws of life and the conditions of existence, what kinds of action necessarily tend to produce happiness and what kinds to produce unhappiness. With the exception of the word 'necessarily', I have no dissent to express from this doctrine; and (omitting that word) I am not aware that any modern advocate of utilitarianism is of a different opinion. Bentham, certainly, to whom in the *Social Statics* Mr Spencer particularly referred, is, least of all writers, chargeable with unwillingness to deduce the effect of actions on happiness from the laws of human nature and the universal conditions of human life. The common charge against him is of relying too exclusively upon such deductions, and declining altogether to be bound by the generalizations from specific experience which Mr Spencer thinks that utilitarians generally confine themselves to. My own opinion (and, as I collect, Mr Spencer's) is, that in ethics, as in all other branches of scientific study, the consilience of the results of both these processes, each corroborating and verifying the other, is requisite to give to any general proposition the kind and degree of evidence which constitutes scientific proof.

remarked, it bends to every person's ideas of social expediency. But in whatever case it is deemed applicable at all, it is held to be the dictate of justice. All persons are deemed to have a *right* to equality of treatment, except when some recognized social expediency requires the reverse. And hence all social inequalities which have ceased to be considered expedient, assume the character not of simple inexpediency, but of injustice, and appear so tyrannical, that people are apt to wonder how they ever could have been tolerated; forgetful that they themselves perhaps tolerate other inequalities under an equally mistaken notion of expediency, the correction of which would make that which they approve seem quite as monstrous as what they have at last learnt to condemn. The entire history of social improvement has been a series of transitions, by which one custom or institution after another, from being a supposed primary necessity of social existence, has passed into the rank of a universally stigmatized injustice and tyranny. So it has been with the distinctions of slaves and freemen, nobles and serfs, patricians and plebeians; and so it will be, and in part already is, with the aristocracies of colour, race, and sex.

It appears from what has been said, that justice is a name for certain moral requirements, which, regarded collectively, stand higher in the scale of social utility, and are therefore of more paramount obligation, than any others; though particular cases may occur in which some other social duty is so important, as to overrule any one of the general maxims of justice. Thus to save a life, it may not only be allowable, but a duty, to steal, or take by force, the necessary food or medicine, or to kidnap, and compel to officiate the only qualified medical practitioner. In such cases, as we do not call anything justice which is not a virtue, we usually say, not that justice must give way to some other moral principle, but that what is just in ordinary cases is, by reason of that other principle, not just in the particular case. By this useful accommodation of language, the character of indefeasibility attributed to justice is kept up, and we are saved from the necessity of maintaining that there can be laudable injustice.

The considerations which have now been adduced resolve, I conceive, the only real difficulty in the utilitarian theory of morals. It has always been evident that all cases of justice are also cases of expediency: the difference is in the peculiar sentiment which attaches to the former, as contradistinguished from the latter. If this characteristic sentiment has been sufficiently accounted for; if there is no necessity to assume for it any peculiarity of origin; if it is simply the natural feeling of resentment, moralized by being made coextensive with the demands of social good; and if this feeling not only does but ought to exist in all the classes of cases to which the idea of justice corresponds: that idea no longer presents itself as a stumbling-block to the utilitarian ethics. Justice remains the appropriate name for certain social utilities which are vastly more important, and therefore more absolute and imperative, than any others are as a class (though not more so than others may be in particular cases); and which, therefore, ought to be, as well as naturally are, guarded by a sentiment not only different in degree, but also in kind; distinguished from the milder feeling which attaches to the mere idea of promoting human pleasure or convenience, at once by the more definite nature of its commands, and by the sterner character of its sanctions.

6

DISTRIBUTIVE JUSTICE[1]

JOHN RAWLS

I

We may think of a human society as a more or less self-sufficient association regulated by a common conception of justice and aimed at advancing the good of its members. As a co-operative venture for mutual advantage, it is characterized by a conflict as well as an identity of interests. There is an identity of interests since social co-operation makes possible a better life for all than any would have if everyone were to try to live by his own efforts; yet at the same time men are not indifferent as to how the greater benefits produced by their joint labours are distributed, for in order to further their own aims each prefers a larger to a lesser share. A conception of justice is a set of principles for choosing between the social arrangements which determine this division and for underwriting a consensus as to the proper distributive shares.

Now at first sight the most rational conception of justice would seem to be utilitarian. For consider: each man in realizing his own good can certainly balance his own losses against his own gains. We can impose a sacrifice on ourselves now for the sake of a greater advantage later. A man quite properly acts, as long as others are not affected, to achieve his own greatest good, to advance his ends as far as possible. Now, why should not a society act on precisely the same principle? Why is not that which is rational in the case of one man right in the case of a group of men? Surely the simplest and most direct conception of the right, and so of justice, is that of maximizing the good. This assumes a prior understanding of what is good, but we can think of the good as already given by the interests of rational

John Rawls, 'Distributive Justice', from Robert M. Stewart (ed.), *Readings in Social and Political Philosophy* (Oxford University Press: New York 1986). Originally published in P. Laslett and W. G. Runciman (eds.), *Philosophy, Politics and Society* (Basil Blackwell: Oxford, 1967). Reprinted by permission of author and publishers.

[1] In this essay I try to work out some of the implications of the two principles of justice discussed in 'Justice as Fairness' which first appeared in the *Philosophical Review* in 1958 and which is reprinted in *Philosophy, Politics and Society*, Series 2, pp. 132–57.

individuals. Thus just as the principle of individual choice is to achieve one's greatest good, to advance so far as possible one's own system of rational desires, so the principle of social choice is to realize the greatest good (similarly defined) summed over all the members of society. We arrive at the principle of utility in a natural way: by this principle a society is rightly ordered, and hence just, when its institutions are arranged so as to realize the greatest sum of satisfactions.

The striking feature of the principle of utility is that it does not matter, except indirectly, how this sum of satisfactions is distributed among individuals, any more than it matters, except indirectly, how one man distributes his satisfactions over time. Since certain ways of distributing things affect the total sum of satisfactions, this fact must be taken into account in arranging social institutions; but according to this principle the explanation of common-sense precepts of justice and their seemingly stringent character is that they are those rules which experience shows must be strictly respected and departed from only under exceptional circumstances if the sum of advantages is to be maximized. The precepts of justice are derivative from the one end of attaining the greatest net balance of satisfactions. There is no reason in principle why the greater gains of some should not compensate for the lesser losses of others; or why the violation of the liberty of a few might not be made right by a greater good shared by many. It simply happens, at least under most conditions, that the greatest sum of advantages is not generally achieved in this way. From the standpoint of utility the strictness of common-sense notions of justice has a certain usefulness, but as a philosophical doctrine it is irrational.

If, then, we believe that as a matter of principle each member of society has an inviolability founded on justice which even the welfare of everyone else cannot override, and that a loss of freedom for some is not made right by a greater sum of satisfactions enjoyed by many, we shall have to look for another account of the principles of justice. The principle of utility is incapable of explaining the fact that in a just society the liberties of equal citizenship are taken for granted, and the rights secured by justice are not subject to political bargaining nor to the calculus of social interests. Now, the most natural alternative to the principle of utility is its traditional rival, the theory of the social contract. The aim of the contract doctrine is precisely to account for the strictness of justice by supposing that its principles arise from an agreement among free and independent persons in an original position of equality and hence reflect the integrity and equal sovereignty of the rational persons who are the contractees. Instead of supposing that a conception of right, and so a conception of justice, is simply an extension of the principle of choice for one man to society as a whole, the contract doctrine assumes that the rational individuals who belong to society must choose together, in one joint act, what is to count among them as just and unjust. They are to decide among themselves once and for all what is to be their conception of justice. This decision is thought of as being made in a suitably defined initial situation one of the significant features of which is that no one knows his position in society, nor even his place in the distribution of natural talents and abilities. The principles of justice to which all are forever bound are chosen in the absence of this sort of specific information. A veil of ignorance prevents anyone from being advantaged or disadvantaged by the contingencies of social class and fortune; and hence the bargaining problems which arise in everyday life from the possession of this knowledge do not affect the choice of principles. On the contract doctrine, then, the theory of justice, and indeed ethics itself, is part of the general theory of rational choice, a fact perfectly clear in its Kantian formulation.

Once justice is thought of as arising from an original agreement of this kind, it is evident that the principle of utility is problematical. For why should rational individuals who have a system of ends they wish to advance agree to a violation of their liberty for the sake of a greater balance of satisfactions enjoyed by others? It seems more plausible to suppose that, when situated in an original position of equal right, they would insist upon institutions which returned compensating advantages for any sacrifices required. A rational man would not accept an institution merely because it maximized the sum of advantages irrespective of its effect on his own interests. It appears, then, that the principle of utility would be rejected as a principle of justice, although we shall not try to argue this important question here. Rather, our aim is to give a brief sketch of the conception of distributive shares implicit in the principles of justice which, it seems, would be chosen in the original position. The philosophical appeal of utilitarianism is that it seems to offer a single principle on the basis of which a consistent and complete conception of right can be developed. The problem is to work out a contractarian alternative in such a way that it has comparable if not all the same virtues.

2

In our discussion we shall make no attempt to derive the two principles of justice which we shall examine; that is, we shall not try to show that they would be chosen in the original position.[2] It must suffice that it is plausible that they would be, at least in preference to the standard forms of traditional theories. Instead we shall be mainly concerned with three questions: first, how to interpret these principles so that they define a consistent and complete conception of justice; second, whether it is possible to arrange the institutions of a constitutional democracy so that these principles are satisfied, at least approximately; and third, whether the conception of distributive shares which they define is compatible with common-sense notions of justice. The significance of these principles is that they allow for the strictness of the claims of justice; and if they can be understood so as to yield a consistent and complete conception, the contractarian alternative would seem all the more attractive.

The two principles of justice which we shall discuss may be formulated as follows: first, each person engaged in an institution or affected by it has an equal right to the most extensive liberty compatible with a like liberty for all; and second, inequalities as defined by the institutional structure or fostered by it are arbitrary unless it is reasonable to expect that they will work out to everyone's advantage and provided that the positions and offices to which they attach or from which they may be gained are open to all. These principles regulate the distributive aspects of institutions by controlling the assignment of rights and duties throughout the whole social structure, beginning with the adoption of a political constitution in accordance with which they are then to be applied to legislation. It is upon a correct choice of a basic structure of society, its fundamental system of rights and duties, that the justice of distributive shares depends.

The two principles of justice apply in the first instance to this basic structure, that is, to the main institutions of the social system and their arrangement, how they are combined together. Thus this structure includes the political constitution and the principal economic and social institutions which together define a person's

---

[2] This question is discussed very briefly in 'Justice as Fairness', 138–41. The intuitive idea is as follows. Given the circumstances of the original position, it is rational for a man to choose as if he were designing a society in which his enemy is to assign him his place. Thus, in particular, given the complete lack of knowledge (which makes the choice one under uncertainty), the fact that the decision involves one's life-prospects as a whole and is constrained by obligations to third parties (e.g. one's descendants) and duties to certain values (e.g. to religious truth), it is rational to be conservative and so to choose in accordance with an analogue of the maxim in principle. Viewing the situation in this way, the interpretation given to the principles of justice in Section 4 is perhaps natural enough. Moreover, it seems clear how the principle of utility can be interpreted: it is the analogue of the Laplacean principle for choice uncertainty. (For a discussion of these choice criteria, see R. D. Luce and H. Raiffa, *Games and Decisions* (1957), 275–98.)

liberties and rights and affect his life-prospects, what he may expect to be and how well he may expect to be and how well he may expect to fare. The intuitive idea here is that those born into the social system at different positions, say in different social classes, have varying life-prospects determined, in part, by the system of political liberties and personal rights, and by the economic and social opportunities which are made available to these positions. In this way the basic structure of society favours certain men over others, and these are the basic inequalities, the ones which affect their whole life-prospects. It is inequalities of this kind, presumably inevitable in any society, with which the two principles of justice are primarily designed.

Now the second principle holds that an inequality is allowed only if there is reason to believe that the institution with the inequality, or permitting it, will work out for the advantage of every person engaged in it. In the case of the basic structure this means that all inequalities which affect life prospects, say the inequalities of income and wealth which exist between social classes, must be to the advantage of everyone. Since the principle applies to institutions, we interpret this to mean that inequalities must be to the advantage of the representative man for each relevant social position; they should improve each such man's expectation. Here we assume that it is possible to attach to each position an expectation, and that this expectation is a function of the whole institutional structure: it can be raised and lowered by reassigning rights and duties throughout the system. Thus the expectation of any position depends upon the expectations of the others, and these in turn depend upon the pattern of rights and duties established by the basic structure. But it is not clear what is meant by saying that inequalities must be to the advantage of every representative man, and hence our first question.

3

One possibility is to say that everyone is made better off in comparison with some historically relevant benchmark. An interpretation of this kind is suggested by Hume.[3] He sometimes says that the institutions of justice, that is, the rules regulating property and contracts, and so on, are to everyone's advantage, since each man can count himself the gainer on balance when he considers his permanent interests. Even though the application of the rules is sometimes to his disadvantage, and he loses in the particular case,

[3] For this observation I am indebted to Brian Barry.

each man gains in the long run by the steady administration of the whole system of justice. But all Hume seems to mean by this is that everyone is better off in comparison with the situation of men in the state of nature, understood either as some primitive condition or as the circumstances which would obtain at any time if the existing institutions of justice were to break down. While this sense of everyone's being made better off is perhaps clear enough, Hume's interpretation is surely unsatisfactory. For even if all men including slaves are made better off by a system of slavery than they would be in the state of nature, it is not true that slavery makes everyone (even a slave) better off, at least not in a sense which makes the arrangement just. The benefits and burdens of social co-operation are unjustly distributed even if everyone does gain in comparison with the state of nature; this historical or hypothetical benchmark is simply irrelevant to the question of justice. In fact, any past state of society other than a recent one seems irrelevant offhand, and this suggests that we should look for an interpretation independent of historical comparisons altogether. Our problem is to identify the correct hypothetical comparisons defined by currently feasible changes.

Now the well-known criterion of Pareto[4] offers a possibility along these lines once it is formulated so as to apply to institutions. Indeed, this is the most natural way of taking the second principle (or rather the first part of it, leaving aside the requirement about open positions). This criterion says that group welfare is at an optimum when it is impossible to make any one man better off without at the same time making at least one other man worse off. Applying this criterion to allocating a given bundle of goods among given individuals, a particular allocation yields an optimum if there is no redistribution which would improve one individual's position without worsening that of another. Thus a distribution is optimal when there is no further exchange which is to the advantage of both parties, or to the advantage of one and not to the disadvantage of the other. But there are many such distributions, since there are many ways of allocating commodities so that no further mutually beneficial exchange is possible. Hence the Pareto criterion as important as it is, admittedly does not identify the best distribution, but rather a class of optimal, or efficient, distributions. Moreover, we cannot say that a given optimal distribution is better than any non-optimal one; it is only superior to those which it dominates. The criterion is at best an incomplete principle for ordering distributions.

---

[4] Introduced by him in his *Manuel d'économie politique* (1909) and long since a basic principle of welfare economics.

Pareto's idea can be applied to institutions. We assume, as remarked above, that it is possible to associate with each social position an expectation which depends upon the assignment of rights and duties in the basic structure. Given this assumption, we get a principle which says that the pattern of expectations (inequalities in life-prospects) is optimal if and only if it is impossible to change the rules, to redefine the scheme of rights and duties, so as to raise the expectations of any representative man without at the same time lowering the expectations of some other representative man. Hence the basic structure satisfies this principle when it is impossible to change the assignment of fundamental rights and duties and to alter the availability of economic and social opportunities so as to make some representative man better off without making another worse off. Thus, in comparing different arrangements of the social system, we can say that one is better than another if in one arrangement all expectations are at least as high, and some higher, than in the other. The principle gives grounds for reform, for if there is an arrangement which is optimal in comparison with the existing state of things, then, other things equal, it is a better situation all around and should be adopted.

The satisfaction of this principle, then, defines a second sense in which the basic structure makes everyone better off; namely, that from the standpoint of its representative men in the relevant positions, there exists no change which would improve anyone's condition without worsening that of another. Now we shall assume that this principle would be chosen in the original position, for surely it is a desirable feature of a social system that it is optimal in this sense. In fact, we shall suppose that this principle defines the concept of efficiency for institutions, as can be seen from the fact that if the social system does not satisfy it, this implies that there is some change which can be made which will lead people to act more effectively so that the expectations of some at least can be raised. Perhaps an economic reform will lead to an increase in production with given resources and techniques, and with greater output someone's expectations are raised.

It is not difficult to see, however, that while this principle provides another sense for an institution's making everyone better off, it is an inadequate conception of justice. For one thing, there is the same incompleteness as before. There are presumably many arrangements of an institution and of the basic structure which are optimal in this sense. There may also be many arrangements which are optimal with respect to existing conditions, and so many reforms which would be improvements by this principle. If so, how is one to choose between them? It is impossible to say that the many optimal arrangements are equally just, and the choice between them a matter of indifference, since efficient institutions allow extremely wide variations in the pattern of distributive shares.

Thus it may be that under certain conditions serfdom cannot be significantly reformed without lowering the expectations of some representative man, say that of landowners, in which case serfdom is optimal. But equally it may happen under the same conditions that a system of free labour could not be changed without lowering the expectations of some representative man, say that of free labourers, so that this arrangement likewise is optimal. More generally, whenever a society is relevantly divided into a number of classes, it is possible, let's suppose, to maximize with respect to any one of its representative men at a time. These maxima give at least this many optimal positions, for none of them can be departed from to raise the expectations of any man without lowering those of another, namely, the man with respect to whom the maximum is defined. Hence each of these extremes is optimal. All this corresponds to the obvious fact that, in distributing particular goods to given individuals, those distributions are also optimal which give the whole stock to any one person; for once a single person has everything, there is no change which will not make him worse off.

We see, then, that social systems which we should judge very differently from the standpoint of justice may be optimal by this criterion. This conclusion is not surprising. There is no reason to think that, even when applied to social systems, justice and efficiency come to the same thing. These reflections only show what we knew all along, which is that we must find another way of interpreting the second principle, or rather the first part of it. For while the two principles taken together incorporate strong require-ments of equal liberty and equality of opportunity, we cannot be sure that even these constraints are sufficient to make the social structure acceptable from the standpoint of justice. As they stand the two principles would appear to place the burden of ensuring justice entirely upon these prior constraints and to leave indeter-minate the preferred distributive shares.

4

There is, however, a third interpretation which is immediately suggested by the previous remarks, and this is to choose some social position by reference to which the pattern of expectations as a whole is to be judged, and then to maximize with respect to the expectations of this representative man consistent with the demands of equal liberty and equality of opportunity. Now, the one obvious candidate is the representative man of those who are least favoured by the system of institutional inequalities. Thus we arrive at the following idea: the basic structure of the social system affects the life-prospects of typical individuals according to their initial places in society, say the various income classes into which they are born, or depending upon certain natural attributes, as when institutions make discriminations between men and women or allow certain advantages to be gained by those with greater natural abilities. The fundamental problem of distributive justice concerns the differences in life-prospect which come about in this way. We interpret the second principle to hold that these differences are just if and only if the greater expectations of the more advantaged, when playing a part in the working of the whole social system, improve the expectations of the least advantaged. The basic structure is just throughout when the advantages of the more fortunate promote the well-being of the least fortunate, that is, when a decrease in their advantages would make the least fortunate even worse off than they are. The basic structure is perfectly just when the prospects of the least fortunate are as great as they can be.

In interpreting the second principle (or rather the first part of it which we may, for obvious reasons, refer to as the difference principle), we assume that the first principle requires a basic equal liberty for all, and that the resulting political system, when circumstances permit, is that of a constitutional democracy in some form. There must be liberty of the person and political equality as well as liberty of conscience and freedom of thought. There is one class of equal citizens which defines a common status for all. We also assume that there is equality of opportunity and a fair competition for the available positions on the basis of reasonable qualifications. Now, given this background, the differences to be justified are the various economic and social inequalities in the basic structure which must inevitably arise in such a scheme. These are the inequalities in the distribution of income and wealth and the distinctions in social prestige and status which attach to the various positions and classes. The difference principle says that these inequalities are just if and only if they are part of a larger system in which they work out to the advantage of the most unfortunate representative man. The just distributive shares determined by the basic structure are those specified by this constrained maximum principle.

Thus, consider the chief problem of distributive justice, that concerning the distribution of wealth as it affects the life-prospects of those starting out in the various income groups. These income classes define the relevant representative men from which the social system is to be judged. Now, a son of a member of the entrepreneurial class (in a capitalist society) has a better prospect than that of the son of an unskilled labourer. This will be true, it seems, even when the social injustices which presently exist are removed and the two men are of equal talent and ability; the inequality cannot be done away with as long as something like the family is maintained. What, then, can justify this inequality in life-prospects? According to the second principle it is justified only if it is to the advantage of the representative man who is worst off, in this case the representative unskilled labourer. The inequality is permissible because lowering it would, let's suppose, make the working man even worse off than he is. Presumably, given the principle of open offices (the second part of the second principle), the greater expectations allowed to entrepreneurs has the effect in the longer run of raising the life-prospects of the labouring class. The inequality in expectation provides an incentive so that the economy is more efficient, industrial advance proceeds at a quicker pace, and so on, the end result of which is that greater material and other benefits are distributed throughout the system. Of course, all of this is familiar, and whether true or not in particular cases, it is the sort of thing which must be argued if the inequality in income and wealth is to be acceptable by the difference principle.

We should now verify that this interpretation of the second principle gives a natural sense in which everyone may be said to be made better off. Let us suppose that inequalities are chain-connected: that is, if an inequality raises the expectations of the lowest position, it raises the expectations of all positions in between. For example, if the greater expectations of the representative entrepreneur raises that of the unskilled labourer, it also raises that of the semi-skilled. Let us further assume that inequalities are close-knit: that is, it is impossible to raise (or lower) the expectation of any representative man without raising (or lowering) the expectations of every other representative man, and in particular, without affecting one way or the other that of the least fortunate. There is no loose-jointedness, so to speak, in the way in which expectations depend upon one another. Now, with these assumptions, everyone does benefit from an inequality which satisfies the difference principle, and the second principle as we have formulated it reads correctly. For the representative man who is better off in any pairwise comparison gains by being allowed to have his advantage, and the man who is worse off benefits from the contribution which all inequalities make to each position below. Of course, chain-connection and close-knitness may not obtain; but in this case those who are better off should not have a veto over the advantages available for the least advantaged. The stricter interpretation of the difference principle should be followed, and all inequalities should be arranged for the advantage of those in middle positions. Should these conditions fail, then, the second principle would have to be stated in another way.

It may be observed that the difference principle represents, in effect, an original agreement to share in the benefits of the distribution of natural talents and abilities, whatever this distribution turns out to be, in order to alleviate as far as possible the arbitrary handicaps resulting from our initial starting places in society. Those who have been favoured by nature, whoever they are, may gain from their good fortune only on terms that improve the well-being of those who have lost out. The naturally advantaged are not to gain simply because they are more gifted, but only to cover the costs of training and cultivating their endowments and for putting them to use in a way which improves the position of the less fortunate. We are led to the difference principle if we wish to arrange the basic social structure so that no one gains (or loses) from his luck in the natural lottery of talent and ability, or from his initial place in society, without giving (or receiving) compensating advantages in return. (The parties in the original position are not said to be attracted by this idea and so agree to it; rather, given the symmetries of their situation, and particularly their lack of knowledge, and so on, they will find it to their interest to agree to a principle which can be understood in this way.) And we should note also that when the difference principle is perfectly satisfied, the basic structure is optimal by the efficiency principle. There is no way to make anyone better off without making someone else worse off, namely, the least fortunate representative man. Thus the two principles of justice define distributive shares in a way compatible with efficiency, at least as long as we move on this highly abstract level. If we want to say (as we do, although it cannot be argued here) that the demands of justice have an absolute weight with respect to efficiency, this claim may seem less paradoxical when it is kept in mind that perfectly just institutions are also efficient.

5

Our second question is whether it is possible to arrange the institutions of a constitutional democracy so that the two principles of justice are satisfied, at least approximately. We shall try to show that this can be done provided the government regulate a free economy in a certain way. More fully, if law and government act effectively to keep markets competitive, resources fully employed, property and wealth widely distributed over time, and to maintain the appropriate social minimum, then if there is equality of opportunity underwritten by education for all, the resulting distribution will be just. Of course, all of these arrangements and policies are familiar. The only novelty in the following remarks, if there is any novelty at all, is that this framework of institutions can be made to satisfy the difference principle. To argue this, we must sketch the relations of these institutions and how they work together.

First of all, we assume that the basic social structure is controlled by a just constitution which secures the various liberties of equal citizenship. Thus the legal order is administered in accordance with the principle of legality, and liberty of conscience and freedom of thought are taken for granted. The political process is conducted, so far as possible, as a just procedure for choosing between governments and for enacting just legislation. From the standpoint of distributive justice, it is also essential that there be equality of opportunity in several senses. Thus, we suppose that, in addition to maintaining the usual social overhead capital, government provides for equal educational opportunities for all either by subsidizing private schools or by operating a public school system. It also enforces and underwrites equality of opportunity in commercial ventures and in the free choice of occupation. This result is achieved by policing business behaviour and by preventing the establishment of barriers and restriction to the desirable positions and markets. Lastly, there is a guarantee of a social minimum which the government meets by family allowances and special payments in times of unemployment, or by a negative income tax.

In maintaining this system of institutions the government may be thought of as divided into four branches. Each branch is represented by various agencies (or activities thereof) charged with preserving certain social and economic conditions. These branches do not necessarily overlap with the usual organization of government, but should be understood as purely conceptual. Thus the allocation branch is to keep the economy feasibly competitive, that is, to prevent the formation of unreasonable market power. Markets are competitive in this sense when they cannot be made more so consistent with the requirements of efficiency and the acceptance of the fact of consumer preferences and geography. The allocation branch is also charged with identifying and correcting, say by suitable taxes and subsidies wherever possible, the more obvious departures from efficiency caused by the failure of prices to measure accurately social benefits and costs. The stabilization branch strives to maintain reasonably full employment so that there is no waste through failure to use resources and the free choice of occupation and the deployment of finance is supported by strong effective demand. These two branches together are to preserve the efficiency of the market economy generally.

The social minimum is established through the operations of the transfer branch. Later on we shall consider at what level this minimum should be set, since this is a crucial matter; but for the moment, a few general remarks will suffice. The main idea is that the workings of the transfer branch take into account the precept of need and assign it an appropriate weight with respect to the other common-sense precepts of justice. A market economy ignores the claims of need altogether. Hence there is a division of labour between the parts of the social system as different institutions answer to different common-sense precepts. Competitive markets (properly supplemented by government operations) handle the problem of the efficient allocation of labour and resources and set a weight to the conventional precepts associated with wages and earnings (the precepts of each according to his work and experience, or responsibility and the hazards of the job, and so on), whereas the transfer branch guarantees a certain level of well-being and meets the claims of need. Thus it is obvious that the justice of distributive shares depends upon the whole social system and how it distributes total income, wages plus transfers. There is with reason strong objection to the competitive determination of total income, since this would leave out of account the claims of need and of a decent standard of life. From the standpoint of the original position it is clearly rational to insure oneself against these contingencies. But now, if the appropriate minimum is provided by transfers, it may be perfectly fair that the other part of total income is competitively determined. Moreover, this way of dealing with the claims of need is doubtless more efficient, at least from a theoretical point of view, than trying to regulate prices by minimum wage standards and so on. It is preferable to handle these claims by a separate branch which supports a social minimum. Henceforth, in considering whether the second principle of justice is satisfied, the answer turns on whether the total income of the least advantaged, that is, wages plus transfers, is such as to maximize their long-term expectations consistent with the demands of liberty.

Finally, the distribution branch is to preserve an approximately just distribution of income and wealth over time by affecting the background conditions of the market from period to period. Two aspects of this branch may be distinguished. First of all, it operates a system of inheritance and gift taxes. The aim of these levies is not to raise revenue, but gradually and continually to correct the distribution of wealth and to prevent the concentrations of power to the detriment of liberty and equality of opportunity. It is perfectly true, as some have said,[5] that unequal inheritance of wealth is no more inherently unjust than unequal inheritance of intelligence; as far as possible the inequalities founded on either should satisfy the difference principle. Thus, the inheritance of greater wealth is just as long as it is to the advantage of the worst off and consistent with liberty, including equality of opportunity. Now by the latter we do not mean, of course, the equality of expectations between classes, since differences in life-prospects arising from the basic structure are inevitable, and it is precisely the aim of the second principle to say when these differences are just. Instead, equality of opportunity is a certain set of institutions which assures equally good education and chances of culture for all and which keeps open the competition for positions on the basis of qualities reasonably related to performance, and so on. It is these institutions which are put in jeopardy when inequalities and concentrations of wealth reach a certain limit; and the taxes imposed by the distribution branch are to prevent this limit from being exceeded. Naturally enough where this limit lies is a matter for political judgement guided by theory, practical experience, and plain hunch; on this question the theory of justice has nothing to say.

The second part of the distribution branch is a scheme of taxation for raising revenue to cover the costs of public goods, to make transfer payments, and the like. This scheme belongs to the distribution branch since the burden of taxation must be justly shared. Although we cannot examine the legal and economic complications involved, there are several points in favour of proportional expenditure taxes as part of an ideally just arrangement. For one thing, they are preferable to income taxes at the level of common-sense precepts of justice, since they impose a levy according to how much he contributes (assuming that income is fairly earned in return for productive efforts). On the other hand, proportional taxes treat everyone in a clearly defined uniform way (again assuming that income is fairly earned) and hence it is preferable to use progressive rates only when they are necessary to preserve the justice of the system as a whole, that is, to prevent large fortunes hazardous to liberty and equality of opportunity, and the like. If proportional expenditure taxes should also prove more efficient, say because they interfere less with incentives, or whatever, this would make the case for them decisive provided a feasible

[5] See, for example, F. von Hayek, *The Constitution of Liberty* (1960), 90.

scheme could be worked out.[6] Yet these are questions of political judgement which are not our concern; and, in any case, a proportional expenditure tax is part of an idealized scheme which we are describing. It does not follow that even steeply progressive income taxes, given the injustice of existing systems, do not improve justice and efficiency all things considered. In practice we must usually choose between unjust arrangements and then it is a matter of finding the lesser injustice.

Whatever form the distribution branch assumes, the argument for it is to be based on justice: we must hold that once it is accepted the social system as a whole—the competitive economy surrounded by a just constitutional and legal framework—can be made to satisfy the principles of justice with the smallest loss in efficiency. The long-term expectations of the least advantaged are raised to the highest level consistent with the demands of equal liberty. In discussing the choice of a distribution scheme we have made no reference to the traditional criteria of taxation according to ability to pay or benefits received; nor have we mentioned any of the variants of the sacrifice principle. These standards are subordinate to the two principles of justice; once the problem is seen as that of designing a whole social system, they assume the status of secondary precepts with no more independent force than the precepts of common sense in regard to wages. To suppose otherwise is not to take a sufficiently comprehensive point of view. In setting up a just distribution branch these precepts may or may not have a place depending upon the demands of the two principles of justice when applied to the entire system.

6

Our problem now is whether the whole system of institutions which we have described, the competitive economy surrounded by the four branches of government, can be made to satisfy the two principles of justice. It seems intuitively plausible that this can be done, but we must try to make sure. We assume that the social system as a whole meets the demands of liberty; it secures the rights required by the first principle and the principle of open offices. Thus the question is whether, consistent with these liberties, there is any way of operating the four branches of government so as to bring the inequalities of the basic structure in line with the difference principle.

[6] See N. Kaldor, *An Expenditure Tax* (1955).

Now, quite clearly the thing to do is to set the social minimum at the appropriate level. So far we have said nothing about how high this minimum should be. Common sense might be content to say that the right level depends on the average wealth of the country, and that, other things equal, the minimum should be higher if this average is higher; or it might hold that the proper level depends on customary expectations. Both of these ideas are unsatisfactory. The first is not precise enough since it does not state how the minimum should depend on wealth and it overlooks other relevant considerations such as distribution; and the second provides no criterion for when customary expectations are themselves reasonable. Once the difference principle is accepted, however, it follows that the minimum should be set at the level which, taking wages into account, maximizes the expectations of the lowest income class. By adjusting the amount of transfers, and the benefits from public goods which improve their circumstances, it is possible to increase or decrease the total income of the least advantaged (wages plus transfers plus benefits from public goods). Controlling the sum of transfers, thereby raising or lowering the social minimum, gives sufficient leeway in the whole scheme to satisfy the difference principle.

Now, offhand it might appear that this arrangement requires a very high minimum. It is easy to imagine the greater wealth of those better off being scaled down until arrangement of institutions working over time results in a definite pattern of distributive shares, and each man receives a total income (wages plus transfers) to which he is entitled under the rules upon which his legitimate expectations are founded. Now an essential feature of this whole scheme is that it contains an element of pure procedural justice. That is, no attempt is made to specify the just distribution of particular goods and services to particular persons, as if there were only one way in which, independently of the choices of economic agents, these things should be shared. Rather, the idea is to design a scheme such that the resulting distribution, whatever it is, which is brought about by the efforts of those engaged in co-operation and elicited by their legitimate expectations, is just.

The option of pure procedural justice may be explained by a comparison with perfect and imperfect procedural justice. Consider the simplest problem of fair division. A number of men are to divide a cake: assuming that a fair division is an equal one, which procedure will give this outcome? The obvious solution is to have the man who divides the cake take the last piece. He will divide it equally, since in this way he assures for himself as large a share as he can. Now in this case there is an independent criterion for which is the fair division. The problem is to devise a procedure, a set of rules for dividing the cake, which will yield this outcome. The problem of fair division exemplifies the features of perfect procedural justice. There is an independent criterion for which outcome is just—and we can design a procedure guaranteed to lead to it.

The case of imperfect procedural justice is found in a criminal trial. The desired outcome is that the defendant should be declared guilty if and only if he has committed the offence as charged. The trial procedure is framed to search for and to establish this result, but we cannot design rules guaranteed to reach it. The theory of trial procedures examines which rules of evidence, and the like, are best calculated to advance this purpose. Different procedures may reasonably be expected in different circumstances to yield the right result, not always, but at least most of the time. Hence a trial is a case of imperfect procedural justice. Even though the law may be carefully followed, and the trial fairly and properly conducted, it may reach the wrong outcome. An innocent man may be found guilty, a guilty man may be set free. In such cases we speak of a miscarriage of justice: the injustice springs from no human fault but from a combination of circumstances which defeats the purpose of the rules.

The notion of pure procedural justice is illustrated by gambling. If a number of persons engage in a series of fair bets, the distribution of cash after the last bet is fair, or at least not unfair, whatever this distribution is. (We are assuming, of course, that fair bets are those which define a zero expectation, that the bets are made voluntarily, that no one cheats, and so on.) Any distribution summing to the initial stock of cash held by everyone could result from a series of fair bets; hence all of these distributions are, in this sense, equally fair. The distribution which results is fair simply because it is the outcome. Now when there is pure procedural justice, the procedure for determining the just result must actually be carried out; for in this case there is no independent criterion by reference to which an outcome can be known to be just. Obviously we cannot say that a particular state of affairs is just because it could have been reached by following a just procedure. This would permit far too much and lead to absurdly unjust consequences. In the case of gambling, for example, it would entail that any distribution whatever could be imposed. What makes the final outcome of the betting fair, or not unfair, is that it is the one which has arisen after a series of fair gambles.

In order, therefore, to establish just distributive shares a just total system of institutions must be set up and impartially administered. Given a just constitution and the smooth working of the four branches of government, and so on, there exists a procedure such that the actual distribution of wealth, whatever it turns out to be, is just. It will have come about as a consequence of just system of institutions satisfying the principles to which everyone would agree and against which no one can complain. The situation is one of pure procedural justice, since there is no independent criterion by which the outcome can be judged. Nor can we say that a particular distribution of wealth is just because it is one which could have resulted from just institutions although it has not, as this would be to allow too much. Clearly there are many distributions which may be reached by just institutions, and this is true whether we count distributions of particular goods and services among particular individuals. There are indefinitely many outcomes and what makes one of these just is that it has been achieved by actually carrying out a just scheme of co-operation as it is publicly understood. It is the result which has arisen when everyone receives that to which he is entitled given his and others' actions guided by their legitimate expectations and their obligations to one another. We can no more arrive at a just distribution of wealth except by working together within the framework of a just system of institutions than we can win or lose fairly without actually betting.

This account of distributive shares is simply an elaboration of the familiar idea that economic rewards will be just once a perfectly competitive price system is organized as a fair game. But in order to do this we have to begin with the choice of a social system as a whole, for the basic structure of the entire arrangement must be just. The economy must be surrounded with the appropriate framework of institutions, since even a perfectly efficient price system has no tendency to determine just distributive shares when left to itself. Not only must economic activity be regulated by a just constitution and controlled by the four branches of government, but a just saving-function must be adopted to estimate the provision to be made for future generations. Thus, we cannot, in general, consider only piecewise reforms, for unless all of these fundamental questions are properly handled, there is no assurance that the resulting distributive shares will be just; while if the correct initial choices of institutions are made, the matter of distributive justice may be left to take care of itself. Within the framework of a just system men may be permitted to form associations and groupings as they please so long as they respect the like liberty of others. With social ingenuity it should be possible to invent many different kinds of economic and social activities appealing to a wide variety of tastes and talents; and as long as the justice of the basic structure of the whole is not affected, men may be allowed, in accordance with the principle of free association, to enter into and to take part in whatever activities they wish. The resulting distribution will be just whatever it happens to be. The system of institutions which we have described is, let's suppose, the basic structure of a well-ordered society. This system exhibits the content of the two principles of justice by showing how they may be perfectly satisfied; and it defines a social ideal by reference to which political judgement among second-bests, and the long range direction of reform, may be guided.

8

We may conclude by considering the third question: whether this conception of distributive shares is compatible with common-sense notions of justice. In elaborating the contract doctrine we have been led to what seems to be a rather special, even eccentric, conception the peculiarities of which centre in the difference principle. Clear statements of it seem to be rare, and it differs rather widely from traditional utilitarian and intuitionist notions.[7] But this question is not an easy one to answer, for philosophical conceptions of justice, including the one we have just put forward, and our common-sense convictions, are not very precise. Moreover, a comparison is made difficult by our tendency in practice to adopt combinations of principles and precepts the consequences of which depend essentially upon how they are weighted; but the weighting may be undefined and allowed to vary with circumstances, and thus relies on the intuitive judgements which we are trying to systematize.

Consider the following conception of right: social justice depends positively on two things, on the equality of distribution (understood as equality in levels of well-being) and total welfare (understood as the sum of utilities taken over all individuals). On this view one social system is better than another without ambiguity if it is better on both counts, that is, if the expectations it defines are both less unequal and sum to a larger total. Another conception of right can be obtained by substituting the principle of a social minimum for the principle of equality; and thus an arrangement of institutions is preferable to another without ambiguity if the expectations sum to a

---

[7] The nearest statement known to me is by Santayana. See the last part of chap. 4 in *Reason and Society* (1906) on the aristocratic ideal. He says, for example, ' . . . an aristocratic regimen can only be justified by radiating benefit and by proving that were less given to those above, less would be attained by those beneath them.' But see also Christian Bay, *The Structure of Freedom* (1958), who adopts the principle of maximizing freedom, giving special attention to the freedom of the marginal, least privileged man. Cf. pp. 59, 374 f.

larger total and it provides for a higher minimum. The idea here is to maximize the sum of expectations subject to the constraint that no one be allowed to fall below some recognized standard of life. In these conceptions the principles of equality and of a social minimum represent the demands of justice, and the principle of total welfare that of efficiency. The principle of utility assumes the role of the principle of efficiency the force of which is limited by a principle of justice.

Now in practice combinations of principles of this kind are not without value. There is no question but that they identify plausible standards by reference to which policies may be appraised, and given the appropriate background of institutions, they may give correct conclusions. Consider the first conception: a person guided by it may frequently decide rightly. For example, he would be in favour of equality of opportunity, for it seems evident that having more equal chances for all both improves efficiency and decreases inequality. The real question arises, however, when an institution is approved by one principle but not by the other. In this case everything depends on how the principles are weighted, but how is this to be done? The combination of principles yields no answer to this question, and the judgement must be left to intuition. For every arrangement combining a particular total welfare with a particular degree of inequality one simply has to decide, without the guidance from principle, how much of an increase (or decrease) in total welfare, say, compensates for a given decrease (or increase) in equality.

Anyone using the two principles of justice, however, would also appear to be striking a balance between equality and total welfare. How do we know, then, that a person who claims to adopt a combination of principles does not, in fact, rely on the two principles of justice in weighing them, not consciously certainly, but in the sense that the weights he gives to equality and total welfare are those which he would give to them if he applied the two principles of justice? We need not say, of course, that those who in practice refer to a combination of principles, or whatever, rely on the contract doctrine, but only that until their conception of right is completely specified the question is still open. The leeway provided by the determination of weights leaves the matter unsettled.

Moreover, the same sort of situation arises with other practical standards. It is widely agreed, for example, that the distribution of income should depend upon the claims of entitlement, such as training and experience, responsibility and contribution, and so on, weighed against the claims of need and security. But how are these common-sense precepts to be balanced? Again, it is generally accepted that the ends of economic policy are competitive efficiency, full employment, and appropriate rate of growth, a decent social minimum, and a more equal distribution of income. In a modern democratic state these aims are to be advanced in ways consistent with equal liberty and equality of opportunity. There is no argument with these objectives; they would be recognized by anyone who accepted the two principles of justice. But different political views balance these ends differently, and how are we to choose between them? The fact is that we agree too little when we acknowledge precepts and ends of this kind; it must be recognized that a fairly detailed weighting is implicit in any complete conception of justice. Often we content ourselves with enumerating common-sense precepts and objectives of policy, adding that on particular questions we must strike a balance between them having studied the relevant facts. While this is sound practical advice, it does not express a conception of justice. Whereas on the contract doctrine all combinations of principle, precepts, and objectives of policy are given a weight in maximizing the expectations of the lowest income class consistent with making the required saving and maintaining the system of equal liberty and equality of opportunity.

Thus despite the fact that the contract doctrine seems at first to be a somewhat special conception, particularly in its treatment of inequalities, it may still express the principles of justice which stand in the background and control the weights expressed in our everyday judgements. Whether this is indeed the case can be decided only by developing the consequences of the two principles in more detail and noting if any discrepancies turn up. Possibly there will be no conflicts; certainly we hope there are none with the fixed points of our considered judgements. The main question perhaps is whether one is prepared to accept the further definition of one's conception of right which the two principles represent. For, as we have seen, common sense presumably leaves the matter of weights undecided. The two principles may not so much oppose ordinary ideas as provide a relatively precise principle where common sense has little to say.

Finally, it is a political convention in a democratic society to appeal to the common good. No political party would admit to pressing for legislation to the disadvantage of any recognized social interest. But how, from a philosophical point of view, is this convention to be understood? Surely it is something more than the principle of efficiency (in its Paretian form) and we cannot assume that government always affects everyone's interests equally. Yet since we cannot maximize with respect to more than one point of view, it is natural, given the ethos of a democratic society, to single out that of the least advantaged and maximize their long-term prospects consistent with the liberties of equal citizenship. Moreover, it does seem that the policies which we most confidently think to be just do at least contribute positively to the well-being of this class, and hence that these policies are just throughout. Thus the difference principle is a reasonable extension of the political convention of a democracy once we face up to the necessity of choosing a complete conception of justice.

7

DISTRIBUTIVE JUSTICE

ROBERT NOZICK

The term 'distributive justice' is not a neutral one. Hearing the term 'distribution', most people presume that some thing or mechanism uses some principle or criterion to give out a supply of things. Into this process of distributing shares some error may have crept. So it is an open question, at least, whether *re*distribution should take place; whether we should do again what has already been done once, though poorly. However, we are not in the position of children who have been given portions of pie by someone who now makes last-minute adjustments to rectify careless cutting. There is no *central* distribution, no person or group entitled to control all the resources, (jointly) deciding how they are to be doled out. What each person gets, he gets from others who give to him in exchange for something, or as a gift. In a free society, diverse persons control different resources, and new holdings arise out of the voluntary exchanges and actions of persons. There is no more a distributing or distribution of shares than there is a distributing of mates in a society in which persons choose whom they shall marry. The total result is the product of many individual decisions which the different individuals involved are entitled to make. Some uses of the term 'distribution', it is true, do not imply a previous distributing appropriately judged by some criterion (e.g. 'probability distribution'); nevertheless, despite the title of this essay, it would be best to use a terminology that clearly is neutral. We shall speak of people's holdings; a principle of justice in holdings describes (part of) what justice tells us (requires) about holdings. I shall state first what I take to be the correct view about justice in holdings, and then turn to the discussion of alternative views.[1]

Robert Nozick, 'Distributive Justice', part I, ss. 1–6, from *Anarchy, State and Utopia* (1974). Copyright © 1974 by Basic Books, Inc. Publishers, and Basil Blackwell. Reprinted by permission of Basic Books Inc., a division of HarperCollins Publishers, and Basil Blackwell. (Abridged following Robert M. Stewart, *Readings in Social and Political Philosophy* (Oxford University Press: New York, 1986).

[1] The reader who has read *Anarchy, State and Utopia* and seen that the second part of this chapter discusses Rawls's theory, mistakenly may think that every remark or argument in the first part against alternative theories of justice is meant to apply to or anticipate a criticism of his theory. This is not so; there are other theories also worth criticizing.

THE ENTITLEMENT THEORY

The subject of justice in holdings consists of three major topics. The first is the *original acquisition of holdings*, the appropriation of unheld things. This includes the issues of how unheld things may come to be held, the process(es) by which unheld things may come to be held, the things that may come to be held by these processes, the extent of what comes to be held by a particular process, and so on. We shall refer to the complicated truth about this topic, which we shall not formulate here, as the principle of justice in acquisition. The second topic concerns the *transfer of holdings* from one person to another. By what processes may a person transfer holdings to another? How may a person acquire a holding from another who holds it? Under this topic come general descriptions of voluntary exchange, and gift, and (on the other hand) fraud, as well as reference to particular conventional details fixed upon a given society. The complicated truth about this subject (with placeholders for conventional details) we shall call the principle of justice in transfer. (And we shall suppose it also includes principles governing how a person may divest himself of a holding, passing it into an unheld state.)

If the world were wholly just, the following inductive definition would exhaustively cover the subject of justice in holdings.

(1) A person who acquires a holding in accordance with the principle of justice in acquisition is entitled to that holding.

(2) A person who acquires a holding in accordance with the principle of justice in transfer, from someone else entitled to the holding, is entitled to the holding.

(3) No one is entitled to a holding except by (repeated) applications of (1) and (2).

The complete principle of distributive justice would say simply that a distribution is just if everyone is entitled to the holdings they possess under the distribution.

A distribution is just if it arises from another (just) distribution by legitimate means. The legitimate means of moving from one distribution to another are specified by the principle of justice in transfer. The legitimate first 'moves' are specified by the principle of justice in acquisition.[2] Whatever arises from a just situation by just

---

[2] Applications of the principle of justice in acquisition may also occur as part of the move from one distribution to another. You may find an unheld thing now, and appropriate it. Acquisitions also are to be understood as included when, to simplify, I speak only of transitions by transfers.

steps is itself just. The means of change specified by the principle of justice in transfer, preserve justice. As correct rules of inference are truth preserving, and any conclusion deduced via repeated application of such rules from only true premisses is itself true, so the means of transition from one situation to another specified by the principle of justice in transfer are justice preserving, and any situation actually arising from repeated transitions in accordance with the principle from a just situation is itself just. The parallel between justice-preserving transformations and truth-preserving transformations illuminates where it fails as well as where it holds. That a conclusion could have been deduced by truth-preserving means from premisses that are true suffices to show its truth. That from a just situation a situation *could* have arisen via justice-preserving means does *not* suffice to show its justice. The fact that a thief's victims voluntarily *could* have presented him with gifts, does not entitle the thief to his ill-gotten gains. Justice in holdings is historical; it depends upon what actually has happened. We shall return to this point later.

Not all actual situations are generated in accordance with the two principles of justice in holdings: the principle of justice in acquisition and the principle of justice in transfer. Some people steal from others, or defraud them, or enslave them seizing their product and preventing them from living as they choose, or forcibly exclude others from competing in exchanges. None of these are permissible modes of transition from one situation to another. And some persons acquire holdings by means not sanctioned by the principle of justice in acquisition. The existence of past injustice (previous violations of the first two principles of justice in holdings) raises the third major topic under justice in holdings: the rectification of injustice in holdings. If past injustice has shaped present holdings in various ways, some identifiable and some not, what now, if anything, ought to be done to rectify these injustices? What obligations are the performers of injustice under to their victims? What obligations do the beneficiaries of injustice have to those whose position is worse than it would have been had the injustice not been done? Or, than it would have been had compensation been paid promptly? How, if at all, do things change if the beneficiaries and those made worse off are not the direct parties in the act of injustice, but, for example, their descendants? Is an injustice done to someone whose holding was itself based upon an unrectified injustice? How far back must one go in wiping clean the historical slate of injustices? What may victims of injustice permissibly do in order to rectify the injustices being done to them, including the many injustices done by persons acting through their government? I do not know of a thorough or theoretically sophisticated treatment of such issues. Idealizing greatly, let us suppose theoretical investigation will produce a principle of rectification. This principle uses historical information about previous situations and injustices done in them (as defined by the first two principles of justice, and rights against interference), and information about the actual course of events that flowed from these injustices, up until the present, and it yields a description (or descriptions) of holdings in the society. The principle of rectification presumably will make use of (its best estimate of) subjunctive information about what would have occurred (or a probability distribution over what might have occurred, using the expected value) if the injustice had not taken place. If the actual description of holdings turns out not to be one of the descriptions yielded by the principle, then one of the descriptions yielded must be realized.[3]

The general outlines of the theory of justice in holdings are that the holdings of a person are just if he is entitled to them by the principles of justice in acquisition and transfer, or by the principle of rectification of injustice (as specified by the first two principles). If each person's holdings are just then the total set (distribution) of holdings is just. To turn these general outlines into a specific theory we would have to specify the details of each of the three principles of justice in holdings: the principle of acquisition of holdings, the principle of transfer of holdings, and the principle of rectification of violations of the first two principles. I shall not attempt that task here. (Locke's principle of justice in acquisition is discussed below.)

Historical Principles and End-Result Principles

The general outlines of the entitlement theory illuminate the nature and defects of other conceptions of distributive justice. The entitlement theory of justice in distribution is *historical*; whether a distribution is just depends upon how it came about. In contrast, *current time-slice principles* of justice hold that the justice of a distribution is determined by how things are distributed (who has what) as judged by some *structural* principle(s) of just distribution. A utilitarian who judges between any two distributions by seeing which has the greater sum of utility and, if these tie, who applies

---

[3] If the principle of rectification of violations of the first two principles yields more than one description of holdings, then some choice must be made as to which of these is to be realized. Perhaps the sort of considerations about distributive justice and equality I argue against play a legitimate role in *this* subsidiary choice. Similarly, there may be room for such considerations in deciding which otherwise arbitrary features a statute will embody, when such features are unavoidable because other considerations do not specify a precise line, yet one must be drawn.

some fixed equality criterion to choose the more equal distribution, would hold a current time-slice principle of justice. As would someone who had a fixed schedule of trade-offs between the sum of happiness and equality. All that needs to be looked at, in judging the justice of a distribution, according to a current time-slice principle, is who ends up with what; in comparing any two distributions one need look only at the matrix presenting the distributions. No further information need be fed into a principle of justice. It is a consequence of such principles of justice that any two structurally identical distributions are equally just. (Two distributions are structurally identical if they present the same profile, but (perhaps) have different persons occupying the particular slots. My having ten and your having five, and my having five and your having ten are structurally identical distributions.) Welfare economics is the theory of current time-slice principles of justice. The subject is conceived as operating on matrices representing only current information about distribution. This, as well as some of the usual conditions (e.g. the choice of distribution is invariant under relabelling of columns), guarantees that welfare economics will be a current time-slice theory, with all of its inadequacies.

Most persons do not accept current time-slice principles as constituting the whole story about distributive shares. They think it relevant in assessing the justice of a situation to consider not only the distribution it embodies, but also how that distribution came about. If some persons are in prison for murder or war crimes, we do not say that to assess the justice of the distribution in the society we must look only at what this person has, and that person has, and that person has . . . , at the current time. We think it relevant to ask whether someone did something so that he *deserved* to be punished, deserved to have a lower share. Most will agree to the relevance of further information with regard to punishments and penalties. Consider also desired things. One traditional socialist view is that workers are entitled to the product and full fruits of their labour; they have earned it; a distribution is unjust if it does not give the workers what they are entitled to. Such entitlements are based upon some past history. No socialist holding this view would find it comforting to be told that because the actual distribution A happens to coincide structurally with the one he desires D, A therefore is no less just than D; it differs only in that the 'parasitic' owners of capital receive under A what the workers are entitled to under D, and the workers receive under A what the owners are entitled to (under D), namely very little. Rightly in my view, this socialist holds onto the notions of earning, producing, entitlement, desert, etc. and he rejects (current time-slice) principles that look only to the structure of the resulting set of holdings. (The set of holdings resulting from what? Isn't it implausible that how holdings are produced and come to exist has no effect at all on who should hold what?) His mistake lies in his view of what entitlements arise out of what sorts of productive processes.

We construe the position we discuss too narrowly by speaking of *current* time-slice principles. Nothing is changed if structural principles operate upon a time sequence of current time-slice profiles and, for example, give someone more now to counterbalance the less he has had earlier. A utilitarian or an egalitarian or any mixture of the two over time will inherit the difficulties of his more myopic comrades. He is not helped by the fact that *some* of the information others consider relevant in assessing a distribution is reflected, unrecoverably, in past matrices. Henceforth, we shall refer to such unhistorical principles of distributive justice, including the current time-slice principles, as *end-result principles* or *end-state principles*.

In contrast to end-result principles of justice, *historical principles* of justice hold that past circumstances or actions of people can create differential entitlements or differential deserts to things. An injustice can be worked by moving from one distribution to another structurally identical one, for the second, in profile the same, may violate people's entitlements or deserts; it may not fit the actual history.

Patterning

The entitlement principles of justice in holdings that we have sketched are historical principles of justice. To better understand their precise character, we shall distinguish them from another subclass of the historical principles. Consider, as an example, the principle of distribution according to moral merit. This principle requires total distributive shares to vary directly with moral merit; no person should have a greater share than anyone whose moral merit is greater. (If moral merit could be not merely ordered but measured on an interval or ratio scale, stronger principles could be formulated.) Or consider the principle that results by substituting 'usefulness to society' for 'moral merit' in the previous principle. Or instead of 'distribute according to moral merit', or 'distribute according to usefulness to society', we might consider 'distribute according to the weighted sum of moral merit, usefulness to society, and need', with the weights of the different dimensions equal. Let us call a principle of distribution *patterned* if it specifies that a distribution is to vary along with some natural dimension, weighted sum of natural dimensions, or lexicographic ordering of natural dimensions. And let us say a distribution is patterned if it accords with some patterned principle. (I speak of natural dimensions, admittedly without a general criterion for them, because for any set of holdings some artificial dimensions can be gimmicked up to vary along with the distribution of the set.) The principle of distribution in accordance with moral merit is a patterned historical principle, which specifies a patterned distribution. 'Distribute according to IQ' is a patterned principle that looks to information not contained in distributional matrices. It is not historical, however, in that it does not look to any past actions creating differential entitlements to evaluate a distribution; it requires only distributional matrices whose columns are labelled by IQ scores. The distribution in a society, however, may be composed of such simple patterned distributions, without itself being simply patterned. Different sectors may operate different patterns, or some combination of patterns may operate in different proportions across a society. A distribution composed in this manner, from a small number of patterned distributions, we also shall term patterned. And we extend the use of 'pattern' to include the overall designs put forth by combinations of end-state principles.

Almost every suggested principle of distributive justice is patterned: to each according to his moral merit, or needs, or marginal product, or how hard he tries, or the weighted sum of the foregoing, and so on. The principle of entitlement we have sketched is *not* patterned.[4] There is no one natural dimension or weighted sum or combination of (a small number of) natural dimensions that yields the distributions generated in accordance with the principle of entitlement. The set of holdings that results when some persons receive their marginal products, others win at gambling, others receive a share of their mate's income, others receive gifts from foundations, others receive interest on loans, others receive gifts from admirers, others receive returns on investment, others make for

[4] One might try to squeeze a patterned conception of distributive justice into the framework of the entitlement conception, by formulating a gimmicky obligatory 'principle of transfer' that would lead to the pattern. For example, the principle that if one has more than the mean income, one must transfer everything one holds above the mean to persons below the mean so as to bring them up to (but not over) the mean. We can formulate a criterion for a 'principle of transfer' to rule out such obligatory transfers, or we can say that no correct principle of transfer, no principle of transfer in a free society will be like this. The former is probably the better course, though the latter also is true.

Alternatively, one might think to make the entitlement conception instantiate a pattern, by using matrix entries that express the relative strength of a person's entitlements as measured by some real-valued function. But even if the limitation to natural dimensions failed to exclude this function, the resulting edifice would *not* capture our system of entitlements to *particular* things.

themselves much of what they have, others find things, and so on, will not be patterned. Heavy strands of patterns will run through it; significant portions of the variance in holdings will be accounted for by pattern variables. If most people most of the time choose to transfer some of their entitlements to others only in exchange for something from them, then a large part of what many people hold will vary with what they held that others wanted. More details are provided by the theory of marginal productivity. But gifts to relatives, charitable donations, bequests to children, and the like, are not best conceived, in the first instance, in this manner. Ignoring the strands of pattern, let us suppose for the moment that a distribution actually gotten by the operation of the principle of entitlement is random with respect to any pattern. Though the resulting set of holdings will be unpatterned, it will not be incomprehensible, for it can be seen as arising from the operation of a small number of principles. These principles specify how an initial distribution may arise (the principle of acquisition of holdings) and how distributions may be transformed into others (the principle of transfer of holdings). The process whereby the set of holdings is generated will be intelligible, though the set of holdings itself that results from this process will be unpatterned. . . .

How Liberty Upsets Patterns

It is not clear how those holding alternative conceptions of distributive justice can reject the entitlement conception of justice in holdings. For suppose a distribution favoured by one of these non-entitlement conceptions is realized. Let us suppose it is your favourite one and call this distribution D_1; perhaps everyone has an equal share, perhaps shares vary in accordance with some dimension you treasure. Now suppose that Wilt Chamberlain is greatly in demand by basketball teams, being a great gate-attraction. (Also suppose contracts run only for a year, with players being free agents.) He signs the following sort of contract with a team: in each home game, twenty-five cents from the price of each ticket of admission goes to him. (We ignore the question of whether he is 'gouging' the owners, letting them look out for themselves.) The season starts, and people cheerfully attend his team's games; they buy their tickets, each time dropping a separate twenty-five cents of their admission price into a special box with Chamberlain's name on it. They are excited about seeing him play; it is worth the total admission price to them. Let us suppose that in one season one million persons attend his home games, and Wilt Chamberlain winds up with \$250,000, a much larger sum than the average income and larger even than anyone else has. Is he entitled to this income? Is this new distribution D_2 unjust? If so, why? There is *no* question about whether each of the people was entitled to the control over the resources they held, in D_1, because that was the distribution (your favourite) that (for the purposes of argument) we assumed was acceptable. Each of these persons *chose* to give twenty-five cents of their money to Chamberlain. They could have spent it on going to the movies, or on candy bars, or on copies of *Dissent* magazine, or of *Monthly Review*. But they all, at least one million of them, converged on giving it to Wilt Chamberlain in exchange for watching him play basketball. If D_1 was a just distribution, and people voluntarily moved from it to D_2, transferring parts of their shares they were given under D_1 (what was it for if not to do something with?), isn't D_2 also just? If the people were entitled to dispose of the resources to which they were entitled (under D_1), didn't this include their being entitled to give it to, or exchange it with, Wilt Chamberlain? Can anyone else complain on grounds of justice? Each other person already has his legitimate share under D_1. Under D_1 there is nothing that anyone has that anyone else has a claim of justice against. After someone transfers something to Wilt Chamberlain, third parties *still* have their legitimate shares; *their* shares are not changed. By what process could such a transfer among two persons give rise to a legitimate claim of distributive justice on a portion of what was transferred, by a third party who had no claim of justice on any holding of the others *before* the transfer?[5] To cut off objections irrelevant here, we might imagine the exchanges occurring in a socialist society, after hours. After playing whatever basketball he does in his daily work, or doing whatever other daily work he does,

---

[5] Might not a transfer have instrumental effects on a third party, changing his feasible options? (But what if the two parties to the transfer independently had used their holdings in this fashion?) I discuss this question elsewhere, but note here that this question concedes the point for distributions of ultimate intrinsic non-instrumental goods (pure utility experiences, so to speak) that are transferable. It also might be objected that the transfer might make a third party more envious because it worsens his position relative to someone else. I find it incomprehensible how it can be thought that this involves a claim of justice. On envy, see *Anarchy, State, and Utopia*, ch. 8.

Here and elsewhere in this essay, a theory which incorporates elements of pure procedural justice might find what I say acceptable, *if* kept in its proper place; that is, if background institutions exist to ensure the satisfaction of certain conditions on distributive shares. But if these institutions are not themselves the sum or invisible-hand result of people's voluntary (non-aggressive) actions, the constraints they impose require justification. At no point does *our* argument assume any background institutions more extensive than those of the minimal night-watchman state, limited to protecting persons against murder, assault, theft, fraud, etc.

Wilt Chamberlain decides to put in *overtime* to earn additional money. (First his work quota is set; he works time over that.) Or imagine it is a skilled juggler people like to see, who puts on shows after hours.

Why might some people work overtime in a society in which it is assumed their needs are satisfied? Perhaps because they care about things other than needs. I like to write in books that I read, and to have easy access to books for browsing at odd hours. It would be very pleasant and convenient to have the resources of Widener Library in my back yard. No society, I assume, will provide such resources close to each person who would like them as part of his regular allotment (under D_1). Thus, persons either must do without some extra things that they want, or be allowed to do something extra to get (some of) these things. On what basis could the inequalities that would eventuate be forbidden? Notice also that small factories would spring up in a socialist society, unless forbidden. I melt down some of my personal possession (under D_1) and build a machine out of the material. I offer you, and others, a philosophy lecture once a week in exchange for your cranking the handle on my machine, whose products I exchange for yet other things, and so on. (The raw materials used by the machine are given to me by others who possess them under D_1, in exchange for hearing lectures.) Each person might participate to gain things over and above their allotment under D_1. Some persons even might want to leave their job in socialist industry, and work full time in this private sector. I say something more about these issues elsewhere. Here I wish merely to note how private property, even in means of production, would occur in a socialist society that did not forbid people to use as they wished some of the resources they are given under the socialist distribution D_1. The socialist society would have to forbid capitalist acts between consenting adults.[6]

---

[6] See the selection from John Henry MacKay's novel, *The Anarchists*, reprinted in Leonard Krimmerman and Lewis Perry (eds.), *Patterns of Anarchy* (New York, 1966), 16–33, in which an individualist anarchist presses upon a communist anarchist the question: 'Would you, in the system of society which you call "free Communism" prevent individuals from exchanging their labor among themselves by means of their own medium of exchange? And further: Would you prevent them from occupying land for the purpose of personal use?' The novel continues: [the] question was not to be escaped. If he answered "Yes!" he admitted that society had the right of control over the individual and threw overboard the autonomy of the individual which he had always zealously defended; if on the other hand, he answered "No!" he admitted the right of private property which he had just denied so emphatically. . . . Then he answered "In Anarchy any number of men must have the right of forming a voluntary association, and so realizing their ideas in practice. Nor can I understand how any one could justly be driven from the land and house which he uses and occupies . . . every serious man must declare himself: for Socialism, and thereby for force and against liberty, or for Anarchism, and thereby for liberty and against force." ' In

The general point illustrated by the Wilt Chamberlain example and the example of the entrepreneur in a socialist society is that no end-state principle or distributional pattern principle of justice can be continuously realized without continuous interference into people's lives. Any favoured pattern would be transformed into one unfavoured by the principle, by people choosing to act in various ways; e.g. by people exchanging goods and services with other people, or giving things to other people, things the transferrers are entitled to under the favoured distributional pattern. To maintain a pattern one must either continuously interfere to stop people from transferring resources as they wish to, or continually (or periodically) interfere to take from some persons resources that others for some reason chose to transfer to them. (But if some time limit is to be set on how long people may keep resources others voluntarily transfer to them, why let them keep these resources for *any* period of time? Why not have immediate confiscation?) It might be objected that all persons voluntarily will choose to refrain from actions which would upset the pattern. This presupposes unrealistically (*a*) that all will most want to maintain the pattern (are those who don't, to be 're-educated' or forced to undergo 'self-criticism'?); (*b*) that each can gather enough information about his own actions and the ongoing activities will upset the pattern; and (*c*) that diverse and far-flung persons can co-ordinate their actions to dovetail into the pattern. Compare the manner in which the market is neutral among persons' desires, as it reflects and transmits widely scattered information via prices, and co-ordinates persons' activities.

It puts things perhaps a bit too strongly to say that every patterned (or end-state) principle is liable to be thwarted by the voluntary actions of the individual parties transferring some of their shares they receive under the principle. For perhaps some *very* weak patterns are not so thwarted.[7] Any distributional pattern with any

contrast, we find Noam Chomsky writing, 'Any consistent anarchist must oppose private ownership of the means of production,' and 'the consistent anarchist then . . . will be a socialist . . . of a particular sort.' (Introduction to Daniel Guerin, *Anarchism: From Theory to Practice* (New York, 1970), pp. xiii, xv.)

[7] Is the patterned principle stable that requires merely that a distribution be Pareto-optimal? One person might give another a gift or bequest that the second could exchange with a third to their mutual benefit. Before the second makes this exchange, there is not Pareto-optimality. Is a stable pattern presented by a principle choosing that among the Pareto-optimal positions that satisfies some further condition *C*? It may seem there cannot be a counter-example, for won't any voluntary exchange made away from a situation show that the first situation wasn't Pareto-optimal? (Ignore the implausibility of this last claim for the case of bequests.) But principles are to be satisfied over time, during which new possibilities arise. A distribution that at one time satisfies the criterion of Pareto-optimality might not do so when some new possibilities arise (Wilt Chamberlain grows up and starts playing basketball); and though people's activities will tend to move then to a new Pareto-

egalitarian component is overturnable by the voluntary actions of individual persons over time; as is every patterned condition with sufficient content so as actually to have been proposed as presenting the central core of distributive justice. Still, given the possibility that some weak conditions or patterns may not be unstable in this way, it would be better to formulate an explicit description of the kind of (interesting and contentful) patterns under discussion, and to prove a theorem about their instability. Since the weaker the patterning, the more likely it is that the entitlement system itself satisfies it, a plausible conjecture is that any patterning either is unstable or is satisfied by the entitlement system. . . .

Redistribution and Property Rights

Apparently patterned principles allow people to choose to expend upon themselves, but not upon others, those resources they are entitled to (or rather, receive) under some favoured distributional pattern D_1. For if each of several persons chooses to expend some of his D_1 resources upon one other person, then that other person will receive more than his D_1 share, disturbing the favoured distributional pattern. Maintaining a distributional pattern is individualism with a vengeance! Patterned distributional principles do not give people what entitlement principles do, only better distributed. For they do not give the right to choose what to do with what one has; they do not give the right to choose to pursue an end involving (intrinsically, or as a means) the enhancement of another's position. To such views, families are disturbing; for within a family occur transfers that upset the favoured distributional pattern. Either families themselves become units to which distribution takes place, the column occupiers (on what rationale?), or loving behaviour is forbidden. We should note in passing the ambivalent position of radicals towards the family. Its loving relationships are seen as a model to be emulated and extended across the whole society, while it is denounced as a suffocating institution to be broken, and condemned as a focus of parochial concerns that interfere with achieving radical goals. Need we say that it is not appropriate to enforce across the wider society the relationships of love and care appropriate within family, relationships which are voluntarily undertaken?[8] Incidentally, love is an interesting instance of another

optimal position, *this* new one need not satisfy the contentful condition C. Continual interference will be needed to ensure the continual satisfaction of C. (The theoretical possibility should be investigated of a pattern's being maintained by some invisible-hand process that brings it back to an equilibrium that fits the pattern when deviations occur.)

[8] One indication of the stringency of Rawls's difference principle, which we attend to in the second part of this essay, is its inappropriateness as a governing

relationship that is historical, in that (like justice) it depends upon what actually occurred. An adult may come to love another because of the other's characteristics; but it is the other person, and not the characteristics, that is loved. The love is not transferable to someone else with the same characteristics, even to one who 'scores' higher for these characteristics. And the love endures through changes of the characteristics that gave rise to it. One loves the particular person one actually encountered. Why love is historical, attaching to persons in this way and not to characteristics, is an interesting and puzzling question.

Proponents of patterned principles of distributive justice focus upon criteria for determining who is to receive holdings; they consider the reasons for which someone should have something, and also the total picture of holdings. Whether or not it is better to give than to receive, proponents of patterned principles ignore giving altogether. In considering the distribution of goods, income, etc., their theories are theories of recipient-justice; they completely ignore any right a person might have to give something to someone. Even in exchanges where each party is simultaneously giver and recipient, patterned principles of justice focus only upon the recipient role and its supposed rights. Thus discussions tend to focus on whether people (should) have a right to inherit, rather than on whether people (should) have a right to bequeath or on whether persons who have a right to hold also have a right to choose that others hold in their place. I lack a good explanation of why the usual theories of distributive justice are so recipient-oriented; ignoring givers and transferrers and their rights is of a piece with ignoring producers and their entitlements. But why is it *all* ignored?

Patterned principles of distributive justice necessitate *re*distributive activities. The likelihood is small that any actual freely arrived at set of holdings fits a given pattern; and the likelihood is nil that it will continue to fit the pattern as people exchange and give. From the point of view of an entitlement theory, redistribution is a serious matter indeed, involving, as it does, the violation of people's rights. (An exception is those takings that fall under the principle of the rectification of injustices.) From other points of view, also, it is serious.

principle even within a family of individuals who love one another. Should a family devote its resources to maximizing the position of its least well-off and talented child, holding back the other children or using resources for their education and development only if they will follow a policy throughout their lifetimes of maximizing the position of their least fortunate sibling? Surely not. How then can this even be considered as the appropriate policy for enforcement in the wider society? (I discuss below what I think would be Rawls's reply: that some principles apply at the macro-level which do not apply to microsituations.)

Taxation of earnings from labour is on a par with forced labour.[9] Some persons find this claim obviously true: taking the earnings of *n* hours labour is like taking *n* hours from the person; it is like forcing the person to work *n* hours for another's purpose. Others find the claim absurd. But even these, *if* they object to forced labour, would oppose forcing unemployed hippies to work for the benefit of the needy.[10] And they also would object to forcing each person to work five extra hours each week for the benefit of the needy. But a system that takes five hours' wages in taxes does not seem to them like one that forces someone to work five hours, since it offers the forcee a wider range of choice in activities than does taxation in kind with the particular labour specified. (But we can imagine a gradation of systems of forced labour, from one that specifies a particular activity, to one that gives a choice among two activities, to . . . ; and so on up.) Furthermore, people envisage a system with something like a proportional tax on everything above the amount necessary for basic needs. Some think this does not force someone to work extra hours, since there is no fixed number of extra hours he is forced to work, and since he can avoid the tax entirely by earning only enough to cover his basic needs. This is a very uncharacteristic view of forcing for those who *also* think people are forced to do something *whenever* the alternatives they face are considerably worse. However, *neither* view is correct. The fact that others intentionally intervene, in violation of a side-constraint against aggression, to threaten force to limit the alternatives, in this case to paying taxes or (presumably the worse alternative) bare subsistence, makes the taxation system one of forced labour, and distinguishes it from other cases of limited choices which are not forcings.[11]

The man who chooses to work longer to gain an income more than sufficient for his basic needs prefers some extra goods or services to the leisure and activities he could perform during the possible non-

---

[9] I am unsure as to whether the arguments I present below show that such taxation just *is* forced labour; so that 'is on a par with' means 'is one kind of.' Or alternatively, whether the arguments emphasize the great similarities between such taxation and forced labour, to show it is plausible and illuminating to view such taxation in the light of forced labour. This latter approach would remind one of how John Wisdom conceives of the claims of metaphysicians.

[10] Nothing hangs on the fact that here and elsewhere I speak loosely of *needs*; since I go on, each time, to reject the criterion of justice which includes it. If, however, something did depend upon the notion, one would want to examine it more carefully. For a sceptical view, see Kenneth Minogue, *The Liberal Mind* (New York, 1963), 103–12.

[11] Further details that this statement should include are contained in my essay, 'Coercion,' in S. Morgenbesser, P. Suppes, and M. White (eds.), *Philosophy, Science, and Method* (New York, 1969).

working hours; whereas the man who chooses not to work the extra time prefers the leisure activities to the extra goods or services he could acquire by working more. Given this, if it would be illegitimate for a tax system to seize some of a man's leisure (forced labour) for the purpose of serving the needy, how can it be legitimate for a tax system to seize some of a man's goods for that purpose? Why should we treat the man whose happiness requires certain material goods or services differently from the man whose preferences and desires make such goods unnecessary for his happiness? Why should the man who prefers seeing a movie (and who has to earn money for a ticket) be open to the required call to aid the needy, while the person who prefers looking at a sunset (and hence need earn no extra money) is not? Indeed, isn't it surprising that redistributionists choose to ignore the man whose pleasures are so easily attainable without extra labour, while adding yet another burden to the poor unfortunate who must work for his pleasures? If anything, one would have expected the reverse. Why is the person with the non-material or non-consumption desire allowed to proceed unimpeded to his most favoured feasible alternative, whereas the man whose pleasures or desires involve material things and who must work for extra money (thereby serving whoever considers his activities valuable enough to pay him) is constrained in what he can realize? Perhaps there is no difference in principle. And perhaps some think the answer concerns merely administrative convenience. (These questions and issues will not disturb those who think forced labour to serve the needy or realize some favoured end-state pattern acceptable.) In a fuller discussion we would have (and want) to extend our argument to include interest, entrepreneurial profits, etc. Those who doubt that this extension can be carried through, and who draw the line here at taxation of income from labour, will have to state rather complicated patterned *historical* principles of distributive justice; since end-state principles would not distinguish *sources* of income in any way. It is enough for now to get away from end-state principles and to make clear how various patterned principles are dependent upon particular views about the sources or the illegitimacy or the lesser legitimacy of profits, interest, etc.; which particular views may well be mistaken.

What sort of right over others does a legally institutionalized end-state pattern give one? The central core of the notion of a property right in X, relative to which other parts of the notion are to be explained, is the right to determine what shall be done with X; the right to choose which of the constrained set of options concerning X shall be realized or attempted.[12] The constraints are set by other

---

[12] On the themes in this and the next paragraph, see the writings of Armen Alchian.

principles or laws operating in the society; in our theory by the Lockean rights people possess (under the minimal state). My property rights in my knife allow me to leave it where I will, but not in your chest. I may choose which of the acceptable options involving the knife is to be realized. This notion of property helps us to understand why earlier theorists spoke of people as having property in themselves and their labour. They viewed each person as having a right to decide what would become of himself and what he would do, and as having a right to reap the benefits of what he did.

This right of selecting the alternative to be realized from the constrained set of alternatives may be held by an *individual* or by a *group* with some procedure for reaching a joint decision; or the right may be passed back and forth, so that one year I decide what's to become of X, and the next year you do (with the alternative of destruction, perhaps, being excluded). Or, during the same time period, some types of decisions about X may be made by me, and others by you. And so on. We lack an adequate, fruitful, analytical apparatus for classifying the *types* of constraints on the set of options among which choices are to be made, and the *types* of ways decision powers can be held, divided, and amalgamated. A *theory* of property would, among other things, contain such a classification of constraints and decision modes, and from a small number of principles would follow a host of interesting statements about the *consequences* and effects of certain combinations of constraints and modes of decision.

When end-result principles of distributive justice are built into the legal structure of a society, they (as do most patterned principles) give each citizen an enforceable claim to some portion of the total social product; that is, to some portion of the sum total of the individually and jointly made products. This total product is produced by individuals labouring, using means of production others have saved to bring into existence, by people organizing production or creating means to produce new things or things in a new way. It is on this batch of individual activities that patterned distributional principles give each individual an enforceable claim. Each person has a claim to the activities and the products of other persons, independently of whether the other persons enter into particular relationships that give rise to these claims, and independently of whether they voluntarily take these claims upon themselves, in charity or in exchange for something.

Whether it is done through taxation on wages or on wages over a certain amount, or through seizure of profits, or through there being a big *social pot* so that it's not clear what's coming from where and what's going where, patterned principles of distributive justice involve appropriating the actions of other persons. Seizing the results of someone's labour is equivalent to seizing hours from him and directing him to carry on various activities. If people force you to do certain work, or unrewarded work, for a certain period of time, they decide what you are to do and what purposes your work is to serve apart from your decisions. This process whereby they take this decision from you makes them a *part owner* of you; it gives them a property right in you. Just as having such partial control and power of decision, by right, over an animal or inanimate object would be to have a property right in it.

End-state and most patterned principles of distributive justice institute (partial) ownership by others of people and their actions and labour. These principles involve a shift from the classical liberals' notion of self-ownership to a notion of (partial) property rights in *other* people.

Considerations such as thcsc confront end-state and other patterned conceptions of justice with the question of whether the actions necessary to achieve the selected pattern don't themselves violate moral side-constraints. Any view holding that there are moral side-constraints on actions, that not all moral considerations can be built into end-states that are to be achieved,[13] must face the possibility that some of its goals are not achievable by any morally permissible available means. An entitlement theorist will face such conflicts in a society that deviates from the principles of justice for the generation of holdings, if and only if the only actions available to realize the principles themselves violate some moral constraints. Since deviation from the first two principles of justice (in acquisition and transfer) will involve other persons' direct and aggressive intervention to violate rights, and since moral constraints will not exclude defensive or retributive action in such cases, the entitlement theorist's problem rarely will be pressing. And whatever difficulties he has in applying the principle of rectification to persons who did not themselves violate the first two principles, are difficulties in balancing the conflicting considerations so as correctly to formulate the complex principle of rectification itself; he will not violate moral side-constraints by applying the principle. Proponents of patterned conceptions of justice, however, often will face head-on clashes (and poignant ones if they cherish each party to the clash) between moral side-constraints on how individuals may be treated on the one hand and, on the other, their patterned conception of justice that presents an end-state or other pattern that *must* be realized.

[13] See *Anarchy, State, and Utopia*, ch. 3.

May a person emigrate from a nation that has institutionalized some end-state or patterned distributional principle? For some principles (e.g. Hayek's) emigration presents no theoretical problem. But for others it is a tricky matter. Consider a nation having a compulsory scheme of minimal social provision to aid the neediest (or one organized so as to maximize the position of the worst-off group); no one may opt out of participating in it. (None may say, 'don't compel me to contribute to others and don't provide for me via this compulsory mechanism if I am in need.') Everyone above a certain level is forced to contribute to aid the needy. But if emigration from the country were allowed, anyone could choose to move to another country that did not have compulsory social provision but otherwise was (as much as possible) identical. In such a case, the person's only motive for leaving would be to avoid participating in the compulsory scheme of social provision. And if he does leave, the needy in this initial country will receive no (compelled) help from him. What rationale yields the result that the person be permitted to emigrate, yet forbidden to stay and opt out of the compulsory scheme of social provision? If providing for the needy is of overriding importance, this does militate against allowing internal opting out; but it also speaks against allowing external emigration. (Would it also support, to some extent, the kidnapping of persons living in a place without compulsory social provision, who could be forced to make a contribution to the needy in your community?) Perhaps the crucial component of the position that allows emigration solely to avoid certain arrangements, while not allowing anyone internally to opt out of them, is a concern for fraternal feelings within the country. 'We don't want anyone here who doesn't contribute, who doesn't care enough about the others to contribute.' That concern, in this case, would have to be tied to the view that forced aiding tends to produce fraternal feelings between the aided and the aider (or perhaps merely to the view that the knowledge that someone or other voluntarily is not aiding produces unfraternal feelings).

Locke's Theory of Acquisition

Before we turn to consider another theory of justice in detail, we must introduce an additional bit of complexity into the structure of the entitlement theory. This is best approached by considering Locke's attempt to specify a principle of justice in acquisition. Locke views property rights in an unowned object as originating through someone's mixing his labour with it. This gives rise to many questions. What are the boundaries of what labour is mixed with? If a private astronaut clears a place on Mars, has he mixed his labour with (so that he comes to own) the whole planet, the whole uninhabited universe, or just a particular plot? Which plot does an act bring under ownership? The minimal (possibly disconnected) area such that an act decreases entropy in that area, and not elsewhere? Can virgin land (for the purposes of ecological investigation by high-flying airplanes) come under ownership by a Lockean process? Building a fence around a territory presumably would make one the owner of only the fence (and the land immediately underneath it).

Why does mixing one's labour with something make one the owner of it? Perhaps because one owns one's labour, and so one comes to own a previously unowned thing that becomes permeated with what one owns. Ownership seeps over into the rest. But why isn't mixing what I own with what I don't own a way of losing what I own rather than a way of gaining what I don't? If I own a can of tomato juice, and spill it in the sea so that its molecules (radioactive, so I can check this) mingle evenly throughout the sea, do I thereby come to own the sea, or have I foolishly dissipated my tomato juice? Perhaps the idea, instead, is that labouring on something improves it and makes it more valuable; and anyone is entitled to own a (thing whose) value he has created. (Reinforcing this, perhaps, is the view that labouring is unpleasant. If some people made things effortlessly, as the cartoon characters in *The Yellow Submarine* trail flowers in their wake, would they have lesser claim to their own products whose making didn't *cost* them anything?) Ignore the fact that labouring on something may make it less valuable (spraying pink enamel paint on a found piece of driftwood). Why should one's entitlement extend to the whole object rather than just to the *added value* one's labour has produced? (Such reference to value might also serve to delimit the extent of ownership; e.g. substitute 'increases the value of' for 'decreases entropy in' in the above entropy criterion.) No workable or coherent value-added property scheme has yet been devised, and any such scheme presumably would fall to objections (similar to those) that fell the theory of Henry George.

It will be implausible to view improving an object as giving full ownership to it, if the stock of unowned objects that might be improved is limited. For an object's coming under one person's ownership changes the situation of all others. Whereas previously they were at liberty (in Hohfeld's sense) to use the object, they now no longer are. This change in the situation of others (by removing their liberty to act on a previously unowned object) need not worsen their situation. If I appropriate a grain of sand from Coney Island, no one else may now do as they will with *that* grain of sand. But there are plenty of others left for them to do the same with. Or if not grains of sand, then other things. Alternatively, the things I do with the grain of sand I appropriate might improve the position of others, counterbalancing their loss of the liberty to use that grain. The crucial point is whether appropriation of an unowned object worsens the situation of others.

Locke's proviso that there be 'enough and as good left in common for others' (sect. 27) is meant to ensure that the situation of others is not worsened. (If this proviso is met, is there any motivation for his further condition of non-waste?) It is often said that this proviso once held but now no longer does. But there appears to be an argument for the conclusion that if the proviso no longer holds, then it cannot ever have held so as to yield permanent and inheritable property rights. Consider the first person Z for whom there is not enough and as good left to appropriate. The last person Y to appropriate left Z without his previous liberty to act on an object, and so worsened Z's situation. So Y's appropriation is not allowed under Locke's proviso. Therefore the next to last person X to appropriate left Y in a worse position, for X's act ended permissible appropriation. Therefore X's appropriation wasn't permissible. But then the appropriator two from last, W, ended permissible appropriation and so, since it worsened X's position, W's appropriation wasn't permissible. And so on back to the first appropriator A of a permanent property right.

This argument, however, proceeds too quickly. Someone may be made worse off by another's appropriation in two ways: first, by losing the opportunity to improve his situation by a particular appropriation or any one; and second, by no longer being able to use freely (without appropriation) what he previously could. A *stringent* requirement that another not be made worse off by an appropriation would exclude the first way if nothing else counterbalances the diminution in opportunity, as well as the second. A *weaker* requirement would exclude the second way though not the first. With the weaker requirement, we cannot zip back so quickly from Z to A, as in the above argument; for though person Z can no longer *appropriate*, there may remain some for him to *use* as before. In this case Y's appropriation would not violate the weaker Lockean condition. (With less remaining that people are at liberty to use, users might face more inconvenience, crowding, etc.: in that way the situation of others might be worsened, unless appropriation stopped far short of such a point.) It is arguable that no one legitimately can complain if the weaker provision is satisfied. However, since this is less clear than in the case of the more stringent proviso, Locke may have intended this stringent proviso by 'enough and as good' remaining, and perhaps he meant the non-waste condition to delay the end-point from which the argument zips back.

Is the situation of persons who are unable to appropriate (there being no more accessible and useful unowned objects) worsened by a system allowing appropriation and permanent property? Here enter the various familiar social considerations favouring private property: it increases the social product by putting means of production in the hands of those who can use them most efficiently (profitably); experimentation is encouraged, because with separate persons controlling resources, there is no one person or small group whom someone with a new idea must convince to try it out; private property enables people to decide on the pattern and types of risks they wish to bear, leading to specialized types of risk bearing; private property protects future persons by leading some to hold back resources from current consumption for future markets; it provides alternative sources of employment for unpopular persons who don't have to convince any one person or small group to hire them, and so on. These considerations enter a Lockean theory to support the claim that appropriation of private property satisfies the intent behind the 'enough and as good left over' proviso, *not* as a utilitarian justification of property. They enter to rebut the claim that because the proviso is violated, no natural right to private property can arise by a Lockean process. The difficulty in working such an argument to show the proviso is satisfied is in fixing the appropriate baseline for comparison. Lockean appropriation makes people no worse off than they would be *how*?[14] This question of fixing the baseline needs more detailed investigation than we are able to give it here. It would be desirable to have an estimate of the general economic importance of original appropriation for a society, in order to see how much leeway there is for differing theories of appropriation and of the location of the baseline. Perhaps this importance can be measured by the percentage of all income that is based upon untransformed raw materials and given resources (rather than human actions), mainly rental income representing the unimproved value of the land, and the price of raw materials *in situ*, and by the percentage of current wealth that represents such income in the past.[15]

[14] Compare sect. 2 of Robert Paul Wolff's 'A Refutation of Rawls' Theorem on Justice,' *Journal of Philosophy* 63 (Mar. 1966), 179–90. Wolff's criticism does not apply to Rawls's conception under which the baseline is fixed by the difference principle.

[15] I have not seen a precise estimate. David Friedman discusses this issue in *The Machinery of Freedom* (New York, 1973), pp. xiv, xv, and suggests one-twentieth (of national income) as an upper limit for the first two factors mentioned. However, he does not attempt to estimate the percentage of current wealth that is based upon such income in the past.

We should note that it is not only persons favouring *private* property who need a theory of how property rights legitimately originate. Those believing in collective property—for example, those believing that a group of persons living in an area jointly own the territory, or its mineral resources—also must provide a theory of how such property rights arise, of why the persons living there have rights to determine what is done with the land and resources there that persons living elsewhere don't have (with regard to the same land and resources).

8

'SOCIAL' OR DISTRIBUTIVE JUSTICE

F. A. VON HAYEK

So great is the uncertainty of merit, both from its natural obscurity, and from the self-conceit of each individual, that no determinate rule of conduct could ever follow from it.

David Hume

Welfare, however, has no principle, neither for him who receives it, nor for him who distributes it (one will place it here and another there); because it depends on the material content of the will, which is dependent upon particular facts and therefore incapable of a general rule.

Immanuel Kant[1]

THE CONCEPT OF 'SOCIAL JUSTICE'

While in the preceding chapter I had to defend the conception of justice as the indispensable foundation and limitation of all law, I must now turn against an abuse of the word which threatens to

F. A. von Hayek, ' "Social" or Distributive Justice', omitting appendix; from *Law, Legislation and Liberty, Vol. II: The Mirage of Social Justice* (Routledge: London, 1982). Reprinted by permission of Routledge.

[1] The first quotation is taken from David Hume, *An Enquiry Concerning the Principles of Morals*, sect. III, part II, *Works* iv. 187, and ought to be given here in its context: the

> most obvious thought would be, to assign the largest possessions to the most extensive virtue, and give every one the power of doing good proportioned to his inclination. . . . But were mankind to execute such a law; so great is the uncertainty of merit, both from its natural obscurity, and from the self-conceit of each individual, that no determinate rule of conduct would ever follow from it; and the total dissolution of society must be the immediate consequence.

The second quotation is translated from Immanuel Kant (*Der Streit der Fakultäten* (1798), sect. 2, para. 6, note 2) and reads in the original: 'Wohlfahrt aber hat kein Prinzip, weder für den der sie empfängt, noch für den der sie austeilt (der eine setzt sie hierin, der andere darin); weil es dabei auf das *Materiale* des Willens ankommt, welches empirisch und so einer allgemeinen Regel unfähig ist.' An English translation of this essay in which the passage is rendered somewhat differently will be found in *Kant's Political Writings*, ed. H. Reiss, tr. H. B. Nisbett (Cambridge, 1970), 183, note.

destroy the conception of law which made it the safeguard of individual freedom. It is perhaps not surprising that men should have applied to the joint effects of the actions of many people, even where these were never foreseen or intended, the conception of justice which they had developed with respect to the conduct of individuals towards each other. 'Social' justice (or sometimes 'economic' justice) came to be regarded as an attribute which the 'actions' of society, or the 'treatment' of individuals and groups by society, ought to possess. As primitive thinking usually does when first noticing some regular processes, the results of the spontaneous ordering of the market were interpreted as if some thinking being deliberately directed them, or as if the particular benefits or harm different persons derived from them were determined by deliberate acts of will, and could therefore be guided by moral rules. This conception of 'social' justice is thus a direct consequence of that anthropomorphism or personification by which naïve thinking tries to account for all self-ordering processes. It is a sign of the immaturity of our minds that we have not yet outgrown these primitive concepts and still demand from an impersonal process which brings about a greater satisfaction of human desires than any deliberate human organization could achieve, that it conform to the moral precepts men have evolved for the guidance of their individual actions.[2]

The use of the term 'social justice' in this sense is of comparatively recent date, apparently not much older than a hundred years. The expression was occasionally used earlier to describe the organized efforts to enforce the rules of just individual conduct,[3] and it is to the present day sometimes employed in learned discussion to evaluate the effects of the existing institutions of society.[4] But the sense in which it is now generally used and constantly appealed to in public discussion, and in which it will be examined in this chapter, is essentially the same as that in which the expression 'distributive justice' had long been employed. It seems to have become generally current in this sense at the time when (and perhaps partly because) John Stuart Mill explicitly treated the two terms as equivalent in such statements as that:

[2] Cf. P. H. Wicksteed, *The Common Sense of Political Economy* (London, 1910), 184: 'It is idle to assume that ethically desirable results will necessarily be produced by an ethically indifferent instrument.'

[3] Cf. G. del Vecchio, *Justice* (Edinburgh, 1952), 37. In the eighteenth century the expression 'social justice' was occasionally used to describe the enforcement of rules of just conduct within a given society, so e.g. by Edward Gibbon, *Decline and Fall of the Roman Empire*, ch. 41 (World's Classics edn. iv. 367).

[4] e.g. by John Rawls, *A Theory of Justice* (Cambridge, Mass., 1971).

society should treat all equally well who have deserved equally well of it, that is, who have deserved equally well absolutely. This is the highest abstract standard of social and distributive justice; towards which all institutions, and the efforts of all virtuous citizens should be made in the utmost degree to converge[5]

or that:

it is universally considered just that each person should obtain that (whether good or evil) which he deserves; and unjust that he should obtain a good, or be made to undergo an evil, which he does not deserve. This is perhaps the clearest and most emphatic form in which the idea of justice is conceived by the general mind. As it involves the idea of desert, the question arises of what constitutes desert.[6]

It is significant that the first of these two passages occurs in the description of one of five meanings of justice which Mill distinguishes, of which four refer to rules of just individual conduct while this one defines a factual state of affairs which may but need not have been brought about by deliberate human decision. Yet Mill appears to have been wholly unaware of the circumstance that in this meaning it refers to situations entirely different from those to which the four other meanings apply, or that this conception of 'social justice' leads straight to full-fledged socialism.

Such statements which explicitly connect 'social and distributive justice' with the 'treatment' by society of the individuals according to their 'deserts' bring out most clearly its difference from plain justice, and at the same time the cause of the vacuity of the concept: the demand for 'social justice' is addressed not to the individual but to society—yet society, in the strict sense in which it must be distinguished from the apparatus of government, is incapable of acting for a specific purpose, and the demand for 'social justice' therefore becomes a demand that the members of society should organize themselves in a manner which makes it possible to assign particular shares of the product of society to the different individuals or groups. The primary question then becomes whether there exists

---

[5] John Stuart Mill, *Utilitarianism* (London, 1861), ch. 5, p. 92; in J. P. Plamenatz, ed., *The English Utilitarians* (Oxford, 1949), 225.

[6] Ibid. 66 and 208 respectively. Cf. also J. S. Mill's review of F. W. Newman, *Lectures on Political Economy*, originally published in 1851 in the *Westminster Review* and republished in *Collected Works*, vol. v (Toronto and London, 1967), 444: 'the distinction between rich and poor, so slightly connected as it is with merit and demerit, or even with exertion and want of exertion, is obviously unjust.' Also *Principles of Political Economy* book II, ch. 1, §, ed. W. J. Ashley (London, 1909), 211 ff.: 'The proportioning of remuneration to work done is really just only in so far as the more or less of the work is a matter of choice: when it depends on natural differences of strength and capacity, this principle of remuneration is itself an injustice, it gives to those who have.'

a moral duty to submit to a power which can co-ordinate the efforts of the members of society with the aim of achieving a particular pattern of distribution regarded as just.

If the existence of such a power is taken for granted, the question of how the available means for the satisfaction of needs ought to be shared out becomes indeed a question of justice—though not a question to which prevailing morals provide an answer. Even the assumption from which most of the modern theorists of 'social justice' start, namely that it would require equal shares for all in so far as special considerations do not demand a departure from this principle, would then appear to be justified.[7] But the prior question is whether it is moral that men be subjected to the powers of direction that would have to be exercised in order that the benefits derived by the individuals could be meaningfully described as just or unjust.

It has of course to be admitted that the manner in which the benefits and burdens are apportioned by the market mechanism would in many instances have to be regarded as very unjust *if* it were the result of a deliberate allocation to particular people. But this is not the case. Those shares are the outcome of a process the effect of which on particular people was neither intended nor foreseen by anyone when the institutions first appeared—institutions which were then permitted to continue because it was found that they improve for all or most the prospects of having their needs satisfied. To demand justice from such a process is clearly absurd, and to single out some people in such a society as entitled to a particular share evidently unjust.

THE CONQUEST OF PUBLIC IMAGINATION BY 'SOCIAL JUSTICE'

The appeal to 'social justice' has nevertheless by now become the most widely used and most effective argument in political discussion. Almost every claim for government action on behalf of particular groups is advanced in its name, and if it can be made to appear that a certain measure is demanded by 'social justice', opposition to it will rapidly weaken. People may dispute whether or not the particular measure is required by 'social justice'. But that

---

[7] See e.g. A. M. Honoré, 'Social Justice' in *McGill Law Journal*, 8 (1962) and revised version in R. S. Summers (ed.), *Essays in Legal Philosophy* (Oxford, 1968), 62 of the reprint: 'The first [of the two propositions of which the principle of social justice consists] is the contention that *all men considered merely as men and apart from their conduct or choice have a claim to an equal share in all those things, here called advantages, which are generally desired and are in fact conducive to well-being.*' Also W. G. Runciman, *Relative Deprivation and Social Justice* (London, 1966), 261.

this is the standard which ought to guide political action, and that the expression has a definite meaning, is hardly ever questioned. In consequence, there are today probably no political movements or politicians who do not readily appeal to 'social justice' in support of the particular measures which they advocate.

It also can scarcely be denied that the demand for 'social justice' has already in a great measure transformed the social order and is continuing to transform it in a direction which those who called for it never foresaw. Though the phrase has undoubtedly helped occasionally to make the law more equal for all, whether the demand for justice in distribution has in any sense made society juster or reduced discontent must remain doubtful.

The expression of course described from the beginning the aspirations which were at the heart of socialism. Although classical socialism has usually been defined by its demand for the socialization of the means of production, this was for it chiefly a means thought to be essential in order to bring about a 'just' distribution of wealth; and since socialists have later discovered that this redistribution could in a great measure, and against less resistance, be brought about by taxation (and government services financed by it), and have in practice often shelved their earlier demands, the realization of 'social justice' has become their chief promise. It might indeed be said that the main difference between the order of society at which classical liberalism aimed and the sort of society into which it is now being transformed is that the former was governed by principles of just individual conduct while the new society is to satisfy the demands for 'social justice'—or, in other words, that the former demanded just action by the individuals while the latter more and more places the duty of justice on authorities with power to command people what to do.

The phrase could exercise this effect because it has gradually been taken over from the socialist not only by all the other political movements but also by most teachers and preachers of morality. It seems in particular to have been embraced by a large section of the clergy of all Christian denominations, who, while increasingly losing their faith in a supernatural revelation, appear to have sought a refuge and consolation in a new 'social' religion which substitutes a temporal for a celestial promise of justice, and who hope that they can thus continue their striving to do good. The Roman Catholic Church especially has made the aim of 'social justice' part of its official doctrine;[8] but the ministers of most Christian denominations

[8] Cf. especially the encyclicals *Quadragesimo anno* (1931) and *Divini redemptoris* (1937) and Johannes Messner, 'Zum Begriff der sozialen Gerechtigkeit' in the volume *Die soziale Frage und der Katholizismus* (Paderborn, 1931) issued to commemorate the fortieth anniversary of the encyclical *Rerum Novarum*.

appear to vie with each other with such offers of more mundane aims—which also seem to provide the chief foundation for renewed ecumenical efforts.

The various modern authoritarian or dictatorial governments have of course no less proclaimed 'social justice' as their chief aim. We have it on the authority of Mr Andrei Sakharov that millions of men in Russia are the victims of a terror that 'attempts to conceal itself behind the slogan of social justice'.

The commitment to 'social justice' has in fact become the chief outlet for moral emotion, the distinguishing attribute of the good man, and the recognized sign of the possession of a moral conscience. Though people may occasionally be perplexed to say which of the conflicting claims advanced in its name are valid, scarcely anyone doubts that the expression has a definite meaning, describes a high ideal, and points to grave defects of the existing social order which urgently call for correction. Even though until recently one would have vainly sought in the extensive literature for an intelligible definition of the term,[9] there still seems to exist little

[9] The term 'social justice' (or rather its Italian equivalent) seems to have been first used in its modern sense by Luigi Taparelli d'Azeglio, *Saggio teoretico di diritto naturale* (Palermo, 1840) and to have been made more generally known by Antonio Rosmini-Serbati, *La costitutione secondo la giustizia sociale* (Milan, 1848). For more recent discussions cf. N. W. Willoughby, *Social Justice* (New York, 1909); Stephen Leacock, *The Unsolved Riddle of Social Justice* (London and New York, 1920); John A. Ryan, *Distributive Justice* (New York, 1916); L. T. Hobhouse, *The Elements of Social Justice* (London and New York, 1922); T. N. Carver, *Essays in Social Justice* (Harvard, 1922); W. Shields, *Social Justice, The History and Meaning of the Term* (Notre Dame, Ind., 1941); Benevuto Donati 'Che cosa è giustizia sociale?', *Archivio giuridico*, 134 (1947); C. de Pasquier, 'La Notion de justice sociale', *Zeitschrift für Schweizerisches Recht* (1952); P. Antoine, 'Qu-est-ce la justice sociale?', *Archives de Philosophie*, 24 (1961); For a more complete list of this literature see G. del Vecchio, *Justice*, 37–9.

In spite of the abundance of writings on the subject, when about ten years ago I wrote the first draft of this chapter, I found it still very difficult to find any serious discussion of what people meant when they were using this term. But almost immediately afterwards a number of serious studies of the subject appeared, particularly the two works quoted in note 7 above as well as R. W. Baldwin, *Social Justice* (Oxford and London, 1966), and R. Rescher, *Distributive Justice* (Indianapolis, 1966). Much the most acute treatment of the subject is to be found in a German work by the Swiss economist Emil Küng, *Wirtschaft und Gerechtigkeit* (Tübingen, 1967) and many sensible comments in H. B. Acton, *The Morals of the Market* (London, 1971), particularly p. 71: 'Poverty and misfortune are evils but not injustices'. Very important is also Bertrand de Jouvenel, *The Ethics of Redistribution* (Cambridge, 1951) as well as certain passages in his *Sovereignty* (London, 1957), two of which may here be quoted. P. 140: 'The justice now recommended is a quality not of a man and man's actions, but of a certain configuration of things in social geometry, no matter by what means it is brought about. Justice is now something which exists independently of just men.' P. 164: 'No proposition is likelier to scandalise our contemporaries than this one: it is impossible to establish a just social order. Yet it flows logically from the very idea of justice, on which we have, not without difficulty, thrown light. To do justice is to apply, when making a share-out, the relevant serial order. But it is impossible for

doubt, either among ordinary people or among the learned, that the expression has a definite and well understood sense.

But the near-universal acceptance of a belief does not prove that it is valid or even meaningful any more than the general belief in witches or ghosts proved the validity of these concepts. What we have to deal with in the case of 'social justice' is simply a quasi-religious superstition of the kind which we should respectfully leave in peace so long as it merely makes those happy who hold it, but which we must fight when it becomes the pretext of coercing other men. And the prevailing belief in 'social justice' is at present probably the gravest threat to most other values of a free civilization.

Whether Edward Gibbon was wrong or not, there can be no doubt that moral and religious beliefs can destroy a civilization and that, where such doctrines prevail, not only the most cherished beliefs but also the most revered moral leaders, sometimes saintly figures whose unselfishness is beyond question, may become grave dangers to the values which the same people regard as unshakeable. Against this threat we can protect ourselves only by subjecting even our dearest dreams of a better world to ruthless rational dissection.

It seems to be widely believed that 'social justice' is just a new moral value which we must add to those that were recognized in the past, and that it can be fitted within the existing framework of moral rules. What is not sufficiently recognized is that in order to give this phrase meaning a complete change of the whole character of the social order will have to be effected, and that some of the values which used to govern it will have to be sacrificed. It is such a transformation of society into one of a fundamentally different type which is currently occurring piecemeal and without awareness of the outcome to which it must lead. It was in the belief that something like 'social justice' could thereby be achieved, that people have placed in the hands of government powers which it can now not refuse to employ in order to satisfy the claims of the ever-increasing number of special interests who have learnt to employ the open sesame of 'social justice'.

the human intelligence to establish a relevant serial order for all resources in all respects. Men have needs to satisfy, merits to reward, possibilities to actualize; even if we consider these three aspects only and assume that—what is not the case—there are precise *indicia* which we can apply to these aspects, we still could not weight correctly among themselves the three sets of *indicia* adopted.'

The at one time very famous and influential essay by Gustav Schmoller on 'Die Gerechtigkeit in der Volkswirtschaft' in that author's *Jahrbuch für Volkswirtschaft etc.*, vol. v (1895) is intellectually most disappointing—a pretentious statement of the characteristic muddle of the do-gooder foreshadowing some unpleasant later developments. We know now what it means if the great decisions are to be left to the 'jeweilige Volksbewusstsein nach der Ordnung der Zwecke, die im Augenblick als die richtige erscheint'!

I believe that 'social justice' will ultimately be recognized as a will-o'-the-wisp which has lured men to abandon many of the values which in the past have inspired the development of civilization—an attempt to satisfy a craving inherited from the traditions of the small group but which is meaningless in the Great Society of free men. Unfortunately, this vague desire which has become one of the strongest bonds spurring people of good will to action, not only is bound to be disappointed. This would be sad enough. But like most attempts to pursue an unattainable goal, the striving for it will also produce highly undesirable consequences, and in particular lead to the destruction of the indispensable environment in which the traditional moral values alone can flourish, namely personal freedom.

THE INAPPLICABILITY OF THE CONCEPT OF INJUSTICE TO THE RESULTS OF A SPONTANEOUS PROCESS

It is now necessary clearly to distinguish between two wholly different problems which the demand for 'social justice' raises in a market order.

The first is whether within an economic order based on the market the concept of 'social justice' has any meaning or content whatever.

The second is whether it is possible to preserve a market order while imposing upon it (in the name of 'social justice' or any other pretext) some pattern of remuneration based on the assessment of the performance or the needs of different individuals or groups by an authority possessing the power to enforce it.

The answer to each of these questions is a clear no.

Yet it is the general belief in the validity of the concept of 'social justice' which drives all contemporary societies into greater and greater efforts of the second kind and which has a peculiar self-accelerating tendency: the more dependent the position of the individuals or groups is seen to become on the actions of government, the more they will insist that the governments aim at some recognizable scheme of distributive justice; and the more governments try to realize some preconceived pattern of desirable distribution, the more they must subject the position of the different individuals and groups to their control. So long as the belief in 'social justice' governs political action, this process must progressively approach nearer and nearer to a totalitarian system.

We shall at first concentrate on the problem of the meaning, or rather lack of meaning, of the term 'social justice', and only later consider the effects which the efforts to impose *any* preconceived pattern of distribution must have on the structure of the society subjected to them.

The contention that in a society of free men (as distinct from any compulsory organization) the concept of social justice is strictly empty and meaningless will probably appear as quite unbelievable to most people. Are we not all constantly disquieted by watching how unjustly life treats different people and by seeing the deserving suffer and the unworthy prosper? And do we not all have a sense of fitness, and watch it with satisfaction, when we recognize a reward to be appropriate to effort or sacrifice?

The first insight which should shake this certainty is that we experience the same feelings also with respect to differences in human fates for which clearly no human agency is responsible and which it would therefore clearly be absurd to call injustice. Yet we do cry out against the injustice when a succession of calamities befalls one family while another steadily prospers, when a meritorious effort is frustrated by some unforeseeable accident, and particularly if of many people whose endeavours seem equally great, some succeed brilliantly while others utterly fail. It is certainly tragic to see the failure of the most meritorious efforts of parents to bring up their children, of young men to build a career, or of an explorer or scientist pursuing a brilliant idea. And we will protest against such a fate although we do not know anyone who is to blame for it, or any way in which such disappointments can be prevented.

It is no different with regard to the general feeling of injustice about the distribution of material goods in a society of free men. Though we are in this case less ready to admit it, our complaints about the outcome of the market as unjust do not really assert that somebody has been unjust; and there is no answer to the question of *who* has been unjust. Society has simply become the new deity to which we complain and clamour for redress if it does not fulfil the expectations it has created. There is no individual and no co-operating group of people against which the sufferer would have a just complaint, and there are no conceivable rules of just individual conduct which would at the same time secure a functioning order and prevent such disappointments.

The only blame implicit in those complaints is that we tolerate a system in which each is allowed to choose his occupation and therefore nobody can have the power and the duty to see that the results correspond to our wishes. For in such a system in which each is allowed to use his knowledge for his own purposes the concept of 'social justice' is necessarily empty and meaningless, because in it nobody's will can determine the relative incomes of the different people, or prevent that they be partly dependent on accident. 'Social justice' can be given a meaning only in a directed or 'command' economy (such as an army) in which the individuals are ordered what to do; and any particular conception of 'social justice' could be realized only in such a centrally directed system. It presupposes that people are guided by specific directions and not by rules of just individual conduct. Indeed, no system of rules of just individual conduct, and therefore no free action of the individuals, could produce results satisfying any principle of distributive justice.

We are of course not wrong in perceiving that the effects of the processes of a free society on the fates of the different individuals are not distributed according to some recognizable principle of justice. Where we go wrong is in concluding from this that they are unjust and that somebody is to be blamed for this. In a free society in which the position of the different individuals and groups is not the result of anybody's design—or could, within such a society, be altered in accordance with a generally applicable principle—the differences in reward simply cannot meaningfully be described as just or unjust. There are, no doubt, many kinds of individual action which are aimed at affecting particular remunerations and which might be called just or unjust. But there are no principles of individual conduct which would produce a pattern of distribution which as such could be called just, and therefore also no possibility for the individual to know what he would have to do to secure a just remuneration of his fellows.

THE RATIONALE OF THE ECONOMIC GAME IN WHICH ONLY THE
CONDUCT OF THE PLAYERS BUT NOT THE RESULT CAN BE JUST

We have seen earlier that justice is an attribute of human conduct which we have learnt to exact because a certain kind of conduct is required to secure the formation and maintenance of a beneficial order of actions. The attribute of justice may thus be predicated about the intended results of human action but not about circumstances which have not deliberately been brought about by men. Justice requires that in the 'treatment' of another person or persons, i.e. in the intentional actions affecting the well-being of other persons, certain uniform rules of conduct be observed. It clearly has no application to the manner in which the impersonal process of the market allocates command over goods and services to particular people: this can be neither just nor unjust, because the results are not intended or foreseen, and depend on a multitude of circumstances not known in their totality to anybody. The conduct of the individuals in that process may well be just or unjust; but since their wholly just actions will have consequences for others which were neither intended nor foreseen, these effects do not thereby become just or unjust.

The fact is simply that we consent to retain, and agree to enforce, uniform rules for a procedure which has greatly improved the chances of all to have their wants satisfied, but at the price of all individuals and groups incurring the risk of unmerited failure. With the acceptance of this procedure the recompense of different groups and individuals becomes exempt from deliberate control. It is the only procedure yet discovered in which information widely dispersed among millions of men can be effectively utilized for the benefit of all—and used by assuring to all an individual liberty desirable for itself on ethical grounds. It is a procedure which of course has never been 'designed' but which we have learnt gradually to improve after we had discovered how it increased the efficiency of men in the groups who had evolved it.

It is a procedure which, as Adam Smith (and apparently before him the ancient Stoics) understood[10] in all important respects (except that normally it is not pursued solely as a diversion) is wholly analogous to a game, namely a game partly of skill and partly of chance. We shall later describe it as the game of catallaxy. It proceeds, like all games, according to rules guiding the actions of individual participants whose aims, skills, and knowledge are different, with the consequence that the outcome will be unpredictable and that there will regularly be winners and losers. And while, as in a game, we are right in insisting that it be fair and that nobody cheat, it would be nonsensical to demand that the results for the different players be just. They will of necessity be determined partly by skill and partly by luck. Some of the circumstances which make the services of a person more or less valuable to his fellows, or which may make it desirable that he change the direction of his efforts, are not of human design or foreseeable by men.

We shall in the next chapter have to return to the rationale of the discovery procedure which the game of competition in a market in effect constitutes. Here we must content ourselves with emphasizing

---

[10] Cf. Adam Smith, *The Theory of Moral Sentiments* (London, 1801), vol. ii, part VII, sect. ii, ch. I, p. 198: 'Human life the Stoics appear to have considered as a game of great skill, in which, however, there was a mixture of chance or of what is vulgarly understood to be chance.' See also Adam Ferguson, *Principles of Moral and Political Science* (Edinburgh, 1792), i. 7: 'The Stoics conceived of human life under the image of a Game, at which the entertainment and merit of the players consisted in playing attentively and well whether the stake was great or small.' In a note Ferguson refers to the *Discourses of Epictetus* preserved by Arrian, book II, ch. 5.

that the results for the different individuals and groups of a procedure for utilizing more information than any one person or agency can possess, must themselves be unpredictable, and must often be different from the hopes and intentions which determined the direction and intensity of their striving; and that we can make effective use of that dispersed knowledge only if (as Adam Smith was also one of the first to see clearly)[11] we allow the principle of negative feedback to operate, which means that some must suffer unmerited disappointment.

We shall also see later that the importance for the functioning of the market order of particular prices or wages, and therefore of the incomes of the different groups and individuals, is not due chiefly to the effects of the prices on all of those who receive them, but to the effects of the prices on those for whom they act as signals to change the direction of their efforts. Their function is not so much to reward people for what they *have* done as to tell them what in their own as well as in general interest they *ought* to do. We shall then also see that, to hold out a sufficient incentive for those movements which are required to maintain a market order, it will often be necessary that the return of people's efforts do *not* correspond to recognizable merit, but should show that, in spite of the best efforts of which they were capable, and for reasons they could not have known, their efforts were either more or less successful than they had reason to expect. In a spontaneous order the question of whether or not someone has done the 'right' thing cannot always be a matter of merit, but must be determined independently of whether the persons concerned ought or could have known what was required.

The long and the short of it all is that men can be allowed to decide what work to do only if the remuneration they can expect to get for it corresponds to the value their services have to those of their fellows who receive them; and that *these values which their services will have to their fellows will often have no relations to their individual merits or needs*. Reward for merit earned and indication of what a person should do, both in his own and in his fellows' interest, are different things. It is not good intentions or needs but doing what in fact most benefits others, irrespective of motive, which will secure the best reward. Among those who try to climb Mount Everest or to reach

[11] Cf. G. Hardin, *Nature and Man's Fate* (New York, 1961), 55: 'In a free market, says Smith in effect, prices are regulated by negative feedback.' The much ridiculed 'miracle' that the pursuit of self-interest serves the general interest reduces to the self-evident proposition that an order in which the action of the elements is to be guided by effects of which they cannot know can be achieved only if they are induced to respond to signals reflecting the effects of those events. What was familiar to Adam Smith has belatedly been rediscovered by scientific fashion under the name of 'self-organizing systems'.

the Moon, we also honour not those who made the greatest efforts, but those who got there first.

The general failure to see that in this connection we cannot meaningfully speak of the justice or injustice of the results is partly due to the misleading use of the term 'distribution' which inevitably suggests a personal distributing agent whose will or choice determines the relative position of the different persons or groups.[12] There is of course no such agent, and we use an impersonal process to determine the allocation of benefits precisely because through its operation we can bring about a structure of relative prices and remunerations that will determine a size and composition of the total output which assures that the real equivalent of each individual's share that accident or skill assigns to him will be as large as we know to make it.

It would serve little purpose to enquire here at greater length into the relative importance of skill and luck in actually determining relative incomes. This will clearly differ a great deal between different trades, localities, and times, and in particular between highly competitive and less enterprising societies. I am on the whole inclined to believe that within any one trade or profession the correspondence between individual ability and industry is higher than is commonly admitted, but that the relative position of all the members of a particular trade or profession compared with others will more often be affected by circumstances beyond their control and knowledge. (This may also be one reason why what is called 'social' injustice is generally regarded as a graver fault of the existing order than the corresponding misfortunes of individuals.)[13] But the decisive point is not that the price mechanism does on the whole bring it about that rewards are proportioned to skill and effort, but that even where it is clear to us that luck plays a great part, and we have no idea why some are regularly luckier in guessing than others, it is still in the general interest to proceed on the presumption that the past success of some people in picking winners makes it probable that they will also do so in the future, and that it is therefore worthwhile to induce them to continue their attempts.

[12] See L. von Mises, *Human Action* (Yale, 1949), 255 note: 'There is in the operation of the market economy nothing which could properly be called distribution. Goods are not first produced and then distributed, as would be the case in a socialist state.' Cf. also M. R. Rothbard, 'Towards a Reconstruction of Utility and Welfare Economics' in M. Sennholz (ed.), *On Freedom and Free Enterprise* (New York, 1965), 231.

[13] Cf. W. G. Runciman, *Relative Deprivation*, 274: 'Claims for social justice are claims on behalf of a group, and the person relatively deprived within an individual category will, if he is the victim of an unjust inequality, be a victim only of individual injustice.'

THE ALLEGED NECESSITY OF A BELIEF IN THE JUSTICE OF
REWARDS

It has been argued persuasively that people will tolerate major inequalities of the material positions only if they believe that the different individuals get on the whole what they deserve, that they did in fact support the market order only because (and so long as) they thought that the differences of remuneration corresponded roughly to differences of merit, and that in consequence the maintenance of a free society presupposes the belief that some sort of 'social justice' is being done.[14] The market order, however, does not in fact owe its origin to such beliefs, nor was originally justified in this manner. This order could develop, after its earlier beginnings had decayed during the Middle Ages and to some extent been destroyed by the restrictions imposed by authority, when a thousand years of vain efforts to discover substantively just prices or wages were abandoned and the late schoolmen recognized them to be empty formulae and taught instead that the prices determined by just conduct of the parties in the market, i.e. the competitive prices arrived at without fraud, monopoly, and violence, was all that justice required.[15] It was from this tradition that John Locke and his

[14] See Irving Kristol, 'When Virtue Loses all her Loveliness—Some Reflections on Capitalism and "The Free Society" ', *The Public Interest*, 21 (1970), reprinted in the author's *On the Democratic Idea in America* (New York, 1972), as well as in Daniel Bell and Irving Kristol (eds.), *Capitalism Today* (New York, 1970).

[15] Cf. J. Höffner, *Wirtschaftsethik und Monopole im 15. und 16. Jahrhundert* (Jena, 1941) und 'Der Wettbewerb in der Scholastik', *Ordo*, 5 (1953); also Max Weber, *On Law in Economy and Society*, ed. Max Rheinstein (Harvard, 1954), 295 ff., but on the latter also H. M. Robertson, *Aspects on the Rise of Economic Individualism* (Cambridge, 1933) and B. Groethuysen, *Origines de l'esprit bourgeois en France* (Paris, 1927). For the most important expositions of the conception of a just price by the late sixteenth-century Spanish Jesuits see particularly L. Molina, *De iustitia et de iure*, vol. ii, *De contractibus* (Cologne, 1594), disp. 347, no. 3 and especially disp. 348, no. 3, where the just price is defined as that which will form 'quando absque fraude, monopoliis, atque aliis versutiis, communiter res aliqua vendi consuevit pretio in aliqua regione, aut loco, it habendum est pro mensura et regula judicandi pretium iustum rei illius in ea regione'. About man's inability to determine beforehand what a just price would be see also particularly Johannes de Salas, *Commentarii in secundum secundae D. Thomas de contractibus* (Lyon, 1617), *Tr. de empt. et Vend.* IV, n. 6, p. 9: '. . . quas exacte comprehendere, et ponderare Dei est, not hominum'; and J. de Lugo, *Disputationes de iustitia et iure* (Lyon, 1643), vol. ii, d. 26, s. 4, n. 40; 'pretium iustum matematicum, licet soli Deo notum.' See also L. Molina, *De iustitia*, disp. 365, no. 9: 'omnesque rei publicae partes ius habent conscendendi ad gradum superiorem, si cuiusque sors id tulerit, neque cuiquam certus quidam gradus debitur, qui descendere et conscendere possit.' It would seem that H. M. Robertson (*Aspects*, 164) hardly exaggerates when he writes 'It would not be difficult to claim that the religion which favoured the spirit of capitalism was Jesuitry, not Calvinism.'

contemporaries derived the classical liberal conception of justice for which, as has been rightly said, it was only 'the way in which competition was carried on, not its results',[16] that could be just or unjust.

It is unquestionably true that, particularly among those who were very successful in the market order, a belief in a much stronger moral justification of individual success developed, and that, long after the basic principles of such an order had been fully elaborated and approved by Catholic moral philosophers, it had in the Anglo-Saxon world received strong support from Calvinist teaching. It certainly is important in the market order (or free enterprise society, misleadingly called 'capitalism') that the individuals believe that their well-being depends primarily on their own efforts and decisions. Indeed, few circumstances will do more to make a person energetic and efficient than the belief that it depends chiefly on him whether he will reach the goals he has set himself. For this reason this belief is often encouraged by education and governing opinion—it seems to me, generally much to the benefit of most of the members of the society in which it prevails, who will owe many important material and moral improvements to persons guided by it. But it leads no doubt also to an exaggerated confidence in the truth of this generalization which to those who regard themselves (and perhaps are) equally able but have failed must appear as a bitter irony and severe provocation.

It is probably a misfortune that, especially in the USA, popular writers like Samuel Smiles and Horatio Alger, and later the sociologist W. G. Sumner, have defended free enterprise on the ground that it regularly rewards the deserving, and it bodes ill for the future of the market order that this seems to have become the only defence of it which is understood by the general public. That it has largely become the basis of the self-esteem of the businessman often gives him an air of self-righteousness which does not make him more popular.

It is therefore a real dilemma to what extent we ought to encourage in the young the belief that when they really try they will succeed, or should rather emphasize that inevitably some unworthy

[16] John W. Chapman, 'Justice and Fairness', *Nomos VI, Justice* (New York, 1963), 153. This Lockean conception has been preserved even by John Rawls, at least in his earlier work, 'Constitutional Liberty and the Concept of Justice', *Nomos VI, Justice* (New York, 1963), 117, note: 'If one assumes that law and government effectively act to keep markets competitive, resources fully employed, property and wealth widely distributed over time, and maintains a reasonable social minimum, then, if there is equality of opportunity, the resulting distribution will be just or at least not unjust. It will have resulted from the working of a just system . . . a social minimum is simply a form of rational insurance and prudence.'

will succeed and some worthy fail—whether we ought to allow the views of those groups to prevail with whom the over-confidence in the appropriate reward of the able and industrious is strong and who in consequence will do much that benefits the rest, and whether without such partly erroneous beliefs the large numbers will tolerate actual differences in rewards which will be based only partly on achievement and partly on mere chance.

THERE IS NO 'VALUE TO SOCIETY'

The futile medieval search for the just price and just wage, finally abandoned when it was recognized that only that 'natural' price could be regarded as just which would be arrived at in a competitive market where it would be determined not by any human laws or decrees but would depend on so many circumstances that it could be known beforehand only by God,[17] was not the end of the search for that philosophers' stone. It was revived in modern times, not only by the general demand for 'social justice', but also by the long and equally abortive efforts to discover criteria of justice in connection with the procedures for reconciliation or arbitration in wage disputes. Nearly a century of endeavours by public spirited men and women in many parts of the world to discover principles by which just wage rates could be determined have, as more and more of them acknowledge, produced not a single rule which would do this.[18] It is somewhat surprising in view of this when we find an experienced arbitrator like Lady Wootton, after admitting that arbitrators are 'engaged in the impossible task of attempting to do justice in an ethical vacuum', because 'nobody knows in this context what justice is', drawing from it the conclusion that the criteria should be determined by legislation, and explicitly demand a political determination of all wages and incomes.[19] One can hardly carry any further the illusion that Parliament can determine what is just, and I don't suppose the writer would really wish to defend the atrocious principle implied that all rewards should be determined by political power.

Another source of the conception that the categories of just and unjust can be meaningfully applied to the remunerations determined by the market is the idea that the different services have a determined and ascertainable 'value to society', and that the actual

[17] See passages quoted in note 15 above.
[18] See M. Fogarty, *The Just Wage* (London, 1961).
[19] Barbara Wootton, *The Social Foundation of Wage Policy* (London, 1962, 120 and 162, and now also her *Incomes Policy, An Inquest and a Proposal* (London, 1974).

remuneration frequently differs from the value. But though the conception of a 'value to society' is sometimes carelessly used even by economists, there is strictly no such thing and the expression implies the same sort of anthropomorphism or personification of society as the term 'social justice'. Services can have value only to particular people (or an organization), and any particular service will have very different values for different members of the same society. To regard them differently is to treat society not as a spontaneous order of free men but as an organization whose members are all made to serve a single hierarchy of ends. This would necessarily be a totalitarian system in which personal freedom would be absent.

Although it is tempting to speak of a 'value to society' instead of a man's value to his fellows, it is in fact highly misleading if we say, e.g., that a man who supplies matches to millions and thereby earns $200,000 a year is worth more 'to society' than a man who supplies great wisdom or exquisite pleasure to a few thousand and thereby earns $20,000 a year. Even the performance of a Beethoven sonata, a painting by Leonardo or a play by Shakespeare have no 'value to society' but a value only to those who know and appreciate them. And it has little meaning to assert that a boxer or a crooner is worth more to society than a violin virtuoso or a ballet dancer if the former renders services to millions and the latter to a much smaller group. The point is not that the true values are different, but that the values attached to the different services by different groups of people are incommensurable; all that these expressions mean is merely that one in fact receives a larger aggregate sum from a larger number of people than the other.[20]

Incomes earned in the market by different persons will normally not correspond to the relative values of their services to any one person. Although, in so far as any one of a given group of different commodities is consumed by any one person, he or she will buy so much of each that the relative values to them of the last units bought will correspond to their relative prices, many pairs of commodities will never be consumed by the same person: the relative price of articles consumed only by men and of articles consumed only by women will not correspond to the relative values of these articles to anybody.

The remunerations which the individuals and groups receive in the market are thus determined by what these services are worth to

[20] Surely Samuel Butler (*Hudibras*, II, 1) was right when he wrote

> For what is worth in any thing
> But so much money as 'twill bring.

those who receive them (or, strictly speaking, to the last pressing demand for them which can still be satisfied by the available supply) and not by some fictitious 'value to society'.

Another source of the complaint about the alleged injustice of this principle of remuneration is that the remuneration thus determined will often be much higher than would be necessary to induce the recipient to render those services. This is perfectly true but necessary if all who render the same service are to receive the same remuneration, if the kind of service in question is to be increased so long as the price still exceeds costs, and if anyone who wishes to buy or sell it at the current price is to be able to do so. The consequence must be that all but the marginal sellers make a gain in excess of what was necessary to induce them to render the services in question—just as all but the marginal buyers will get what they buy for less than they were prepared to pay. The remuneration of the market will therefore hardly ever seem just in the sense in which somebody might endeavour justly to compensate others for the efforts and sacrifice incurred for his benefit.

The consideration of the different attitudes which different groups will take to the remuneration of different services incidentally also shows that the large numbers by no means grudge all the incomes higher than theirs, but generally only those earned by activities the functions of which they do not understand or which they even regard as harmful. I have never known ordinary people grudge the very high earnings of the boxer or torero, the football idol or the cinema star or the jazz king—they seem often even to revel vicariously in the display of extreme luxury and waste of such figures compared with which those of industrial magnates or financial tycoons pale. It is where most people do not comprehend the usefulness of an activity, and frequently because they erroneously regard it as harmful (the 'speculator'—often combined with the belief that only dishonest activities can bring so much money), and especially where the large earnings are used to accumulate a fortune (again out of the erroneous belief that it would be desirable that it should be spent rather than invested) that the outcry about the injustice of it arises. Yet the complex structure of the modern Great Society would clearly not work if the remunerations of all the different activities were determined by the opinion which the majority holds of their value—or indeed if they were dependent on any one person's understanding or knowledge of the importance of all the different activities required for the functioning of the system.

The main point is not that the masses have in most instances no idea of the values which a man's activities have to his fellows, and that it is necessarily their prejudices which would determine the use of the government's power. It is that nobody knows except in so far as the market tells him. It is true enough that our esteem of particular activities often differs from the value given to them by the market; and we express this feeling by an outcry about the injustice of it. But when we ask what ought to be the relative remunerations of a nurse and a butcher, of a coal miner and a judge at a high court, of the deep sea diver or the cleaner of sewers, of the organizer of a new industry and a jockey, of the inspector of taxes and the inventor of a life-saving drug, of the jet pilot or the professor of mathematics, the appeal to 'social justice' does not give us the slightest help in deciding—and if we use it it is no more than an insinuation that the others ought to agree with our view without giving any reason for it.

It might be objected that, although we cannot give the term 'social justice' a precise meaning, this need not be a fatal objection because the position may be similar to that which I have earlier contended exists with regard to justice proper: we might not know what is 'socially just' yet know quite well what is 'socially unjust'; and by persistently eliminating 'social injustice' whenever we encounter it, gradually approach 'social justice'. This, however, does not provide a way out of the basic difficulty. There can be no test by which we can discover what is 'socially unjust' because there is no subject by which such an injustice can be committed, and there are no rules of individual conduct the observance of which in the market order would secure to the individuals and groups the position which as such (as distinguished from the procedure by which it is determined) would appear just to us.[21] It does not belong to the category of error but to that of nonsense, like the term 'a moral stone'.

THE MEANING OF 'SOCIAL'

One might hope to get some help in the search for the meaning of 'social justice' by examining the meaning of the attribute 'social';

[21] On the general problem of remuneration according to merit, apart from the passages by David Hume and Immanuel Kant placed at the head of this chapter, see chapter 6 of my book *The Constitution of Liberty* (London and Chicago, 1960) and cf. also Maffeo Pantaleoni, 'L'atto economico' in *Erotemi di Economia* (2 vols., Padua, 1963), i. 101:

E tre sono le proposizioni che conviene comprendere bene:
La prima è che il merito è una parola vuota di senso.
La seconda è che il concetto di giustizia è un polisenso che si presta a quanti paralogismi si vogliono ex amphibologia.
La terza è che la remunerazione non può essere commisurata da una produttivià (marginale) capace di determinazione isolatamente, cioè senza la simultanea determinazione della produttività degli altri fattori con i quali entra in una combinazione di complimentarità.

but the attempt to do so soon leads into a quagmire of confusion nearly as bad as that which surrounds 'social justice' itself.[22] Originally 'social' had of course a clear meaning (analogous to formations like 'national', 'tribal', or 'organizational'), namely that of pertaining to, or characteristic of the structure and operations of society. In this sense justice clearly is a social phenomenon and the addition of 'social' to the noun a pleonasm[23] such as if we spoke of 'social language'—though in occasional early uses it might have been intended to distinguish the generally prevailing views of justice from that held by particular persons or groups.

But 'social justice' as used today is not 'social' in the sense of 'social norms', i.e. something which has developed as a practice of individual action in the course of social evolution, not a product of society or of a social process, but a conception to be imposed upon society. It was the reference of 'social' to the whole of society, or to the interests of all its members, which led to its gradually acquiring a predominant meaning of moral approbation. When it came into general use during the third quarter of the last century it was meant to convey an appeal to the still ruling classes to concern themselves more with the welfare of the much more numerous poor whose interests had not received adequate consideration.[24] The 'social question' was posed as an appeal to the conscience of the upper classes to recognize their responsibility for the welfare of the neglected sections of society whose voices had till then carried little weight in the councils of government. 'Social policy' (or *Socialpolitik* in the language of the country then leading in the movement) became the order of the day, the chief concern of all progressive and good people, and 'social' came increasingly to displace such terms as 'ethical' or simply 'good'.

But from such an appeal to the conscience of the public to concern themselves with the unfortunate ones and recognize them as members of the same society, the conception gradually came to mean that 'society' ought to hold itself responsible for the particular

[22] On the history of the term 'social' see Karl Wasserrab, *Sozialwissenschaft und soziale Frage* (Leipzig, 1903); Leopold von Wiese, *Der Liberalismus in Vergangenheit und Zukunft* (Berlin, 1917), and *Sozial Geistig, Kulturell* (Cologne, 1936); Waldemar Zimmermann, 'Das "Soziale" im geschichtlichen Sinn- und Begriffswandel' in *Studien zur Soziologie, Festgabe für L. von Wiese* (Mainz, 1948); L. H. A. Geck, *Über das Eindringen des Wortes 'sozial' in die deutsche Sprache* (Göttingen, 1963); and Ruth Crummenerl, 'Zur Wortgeschichte von "sozial" bis zur englischen Aufklärung', unpublished essay for the State examination in philology (Bonn, 1963). Cf. also my essay 'What is "Social"? What does it Mean?' in a corrected English version in my *Studies in Philosophy, Politics and Economics* (London and Chicago, 1967).

[23] Cf. G. del Vecchio, *Justice*, 37.

[24] Very instructive on this is Leopold von Wiese, *Der Liberalismus in Vergangenheit und Zukunft* (Berlin, 1917), 115 ff.

material position of all its members, and for assuring that each received what was 'due' to him. It implied that the processes of society should be deliberately directed to particular results and, by personifying society, represented it as a subject endowed with a conscious mind, capable of being guided in its operation by moral principles.[25] 'Social' became more and more the description of the pre-eminent virtue, the attribute in which the good man excelled and the ideal by which communal action was to be guided.

But while this development indefinitely extended the field of application of the term 'social', it did not give it the required new meaning. It even so much deprived it of its original descriptive meaning that American sociologists have found it necessary to coin the new term 'societal' in its place. Indeed, it has produced a situation in which 'social' can be used to describe almost any action as publicly desirable and has at the same time the effect of depriving any terms with which it is combined of clear meaning. Not only 'social justice' but also 'social democracy', 'social market economy'[26] or the 'social state of law' (or rule of law—in German *sozialer Rechtsstaat*) are expressions which, though justice, democracy, the market economy or the *Rechtsstaat* have by themselves perfectly good meanings, the addition of the adjective 'social' makes them capable of meaning almost anything one likes. The word has indeed become one of the chief sources of confusion of political discourse and can probably no longer be reclaimed for a useful purpose.

There is apparently no end to the violence that will be done to language to further some ideal and the example of 'social justice' has recently given rise to the expression 'global justice'! Its negative, 'global injustice', was defined by an ecumenical gathering of American religious leaders as 'characterized by a dimension of sin in the economic, political, social, sexual, and class structures and systems of global society'![27] It would seem as if the conviction that

[25] Characteristic for many discussions of the issue by social philosophers is W. A. Frankena, 'The Concept of Social Justice', in R. B. Brandt (ed.), *Social Justice* (New York, 1962), 4, whose argument rests on the assumption that 'society' *acts*, which is a meaningless term if applied to a spontaneous order. Yet this anthropomorphic interpretation of society seems to be one to which utilitarians are particularly prone . . .

[26] I regret this usage though by means of it some of my friends in Germany (and more recently also in England) have apparently succeeded in making palatable to wider circles the sort of social order for which I am pleading.

[27] Cf. the 'Statement of Conscience' received by the 'Aspen Consultation on Global Justice', an 'ecumenical gathering of American religious leaders' at Aspen, Colorado, 4–7 June 1974, which recognized that 'global injustice is characterised by a dimension of sin in the economic, political, social, racial, sexual and class structures and systems of global society'. *Aspen Institute Quarterly* (New York), no. 7, third quarter (1974), 4.

one is arguing in a good cause produced more sloppy thinking and even intellectual dishonesty than perhaps any other cause.

'SOCIAL JUSTICE' AND EQUALITY

The most common attempts to give meaning to the concept of 'social justice' resort to egalitarian considerations and argue that every departure from equality of material benefits enjoyed has to be justified by some recognizable common interest which these differences serve.[28] This is based on a specious analogy with the situation in which some human agency has to distribute rewards, in which case indeed justice would require that these rewards be determined in accordance with some recognizable rule of general applicability. But earnings in a market system, though people tend to regard them as rewards, do not serve such a function. Their rationale (if one may use this term for a role which was not designed but developed because it assisted human endeavour without people understanding how), is rather to indicate to people what they ought to do if the order is to be maintained on which they all rely. The prices which must be paid in a market economy for different kinds of labour and other factors of production if individual efforts are to match, although they will be affected by effort, diligence, skill, need, etc., cannot conform to any one of these magnitudes; and considerations of justice just do not make sense[29] with respect to the determination of a magnitude which does not depend on anyone's will or desire, but on circumstances which nobody knows in their totality.

The contention that all differences in earnings must be justified by some corresponding difference in deserts is one which would certainly not have been thought to be obvious in a community of farmers or merchants or artisans, that is, in a society in which success or failure were clearly seen to depend only in part on skill and industry, and in part on pure accident which might hit any

[28] See particularly A. M. Honoré, 'Social Justice'. The absurdity of the contention that in a Great Society it needs moral justification if A has more than B, as if this were the result of some human artifice, becomes obvious when we consider not only the elaborate and complex apparatus of government which would be required to prevent this, but also that this apparatus would have to possess power to direct the efforts of all citizens and to claim the products of those efforts.

[29] One of the few modern philosophers to see this clearly and speak out plainly was R. G. Collingwood. See his essay on 'Economics as a philosophical science,' *Ethics* 36 (1926), esp. p. 74: 'A just price, a just wage, a just rate of interest, is a contradiction in terms. The question of what a person ought to get in return for his goods and labour is a question absolutely devoid of meaning.'

one—although even in such societies individuals were known to complain to God or fortune about the injustice of their fate. But, though people resent that their remuneration should in part depend on pure accident, that is in fact precisely what it must if the market order is to adjust itself promptly to the unavoidable and unforeseen changes in circumstances, and the individual is to be allowed to decide what to do. The now prevalent attitude could arise only in a society in which large numbers worked as members of organizations in which they were remunerated at stipulated rates for time worked. Such communities will not ascribe the different fortunes of its members to the operation of an impersonal mechanism which serves to guide the directions of efforts, but to some human power that ought to allocate shares according to merit.

The postulate of material equality would be a natural starting-point only if it were a necessary circumstance that the shares of the different individuals or groups were in such a manner determined by deliberate human decision. In a society in which this were an unquestioned fact, justice would indeed demand that the allocation of the means for the satisfaction of human needs were effected according to some uniform principle such as merit or need (or some combination of these), and that, where the principle adopted did not justify a difference, the shares of the different individuals should be equal. The prevalent demand for material equality is probably often based on the belief that the existing inequalities are the effect of somebody's decision—a belief which would be wholly mistaken in a genuine market order and has still only very limited validity in the highly interventionist 'mixed' economy existing in most countries today. This now prevalent form of economic order has in fact attained its character largely as a result of governmental measures aiming at what was thought to be required by 'social justice'.

When the choice, however, is between a genuine market order, which does not and cannot achieve a distribution corresponding to any standard of material justice, and a system in which government uses its powers to put some such standard into effect, the question is not whether government ought to exercise, justly or unjustly, powers it must exercise in any case, but whether government should possess and exercise additional powers which can be used to determine the shares of the different members of society. The demand for 'social justice', in other words, does not merely require government to observe some principle of action according to uniform rules in those actions which it must perform in any case, but demands that it undertake additional activities, and thereby assume new respon-sibilities—tasks which are not necessary for maintaining law and order and providing for certain collective needs which the market could not satisfy.

The great problem is whether this new demand for equality does not conflict with the equality of the rules of conduct which government must enforce on all in a free society. There is, of course, a great difference between government treating all citizens according to the same rules in all the activities it undertakes for other purposes, and government doing what is required in order to place the different citizens in equal (or less unequal) material positions. Indeed, there may arise a sharp conflict between these two aims. Since people will differ in many attributes which government cannot alter, to secure for them the same material position would require that government treat them very differently. Indeed, to assure the same material position to people who differ greatly in strength, intelligence, skill, knowledge, and perseverance as well as in their physical and social environment, government would clearly have to treat them very differently to compensate for those disadvantages and deficiencies it could not directly alter. Strict equality of those benefits which government could provide for all, on the other hand, would clearly lead to inequality of the material positions.

This, however, is not the only and not even the chief reason why a government aiming to secure for its citizens equal material positions (or any determined pattern of material welfare) would have to treat them very unequally. It would have to do so because under such a system it would have to undertake to tell people what to do. Once the rewards the individual can expect are no longer an appropriate indication of how to direct their efforts to where they are most needed, because these rewards correspond not to the value which their services have for their fellows, but to the moral merit or desert the persons are deemed to have earned, they lose the guiding function they have in the market order and would have to be replaced by the commands of the directing authority. A central planning office would, however, have to decide on the tasks to be allotted to the different groups or individuals wholly on grounds of expediency or efficiency and, in order to achieve its ends, would have to impose upon them very different duties and burdens. The individuals might be treated according to uniform rules so far as their rewards were concerned, but certainly not with respect to the different kinds of work they would have to be made to do. In assigning people to their different tasks, the central planning authority would have to be guided by considerations of efficiency and expediency and not by principles of justice or equality. No less than in the market order would the individuals in the common interest have to submit to great inequality—only these inequalities would be determined not by the interaction of individual skills in an impersonal process, but by the uncontradictable decision of authority.

As is becoming clear in ever-increasing fields of welfare policy, an authority instructed to achieve particular results for the individuals must be given essentially arbitrary powers to make the individuals do what seems necessary to achieve the required result. Full equality for most cannot but mean the equal submission of the great masses under the command of some élite who manages their affairs. While an equality of rights under a limited government is possible and an essential condition of individual freedom, a claim for equality of material position can be met only by a government with totalitarian powers.[30]

We are of course not wrong when we perceive that the effects on the different individuals and groups of the economic processes of a free society are not distributed according to some recognizable principle of justice. Where we go wrong is in concluding from this that they are unjust and that somebody is responsible and to be blamed for this. In a free society in which the position of the different individuals and groups is not the result of anybody's design—or could within such a society not be altered in accordance with a principle of general applicability—the differences in rewards cannot meaningfully be described as just or unjust. There are, no doubt, many kinds of individual actions which are aimed at affecting particular remunerations and which might be regarded as unjust. But there are no principles of individual conduct which would produce a pattern of distribution which as such could be called just, and therefore also no possibility for the individual to know what he would have to do to secure a just remuneration of his fellows.

Our whole system of morals is a system of rules of individual conduct, and in a Great Society no conduct guided by such rules, or by decisions of the individuals guided by such rules, could produce for the individuals results which would appear to us as just in the sense in which we regard designed rewards as just or unjust: simply

[30] If there is any one fact which all serious students of the claims for equality have recognized it is that material equality and liberty are irreconcilable. Cf. A. de Tocqueville, *Democracy in America*, book II, ch. 1 (New York, 1946 edn., vol. 11, 87): democratic communities 'call for equality in freedom, and if they cannot obtain that, they still call for equality in slavery'; William S. Sorley, *The Moral Life and the Moral Worth* (Cambridge, 1911), 110: 'Equality is gained only by constant interference with liberty'; or more recently Gerhard Leibholz, 'Die Bedrohung der Freiheit durch die Macht der Gesetzgeber', in *Freiheit der Persönlichkeit* (Stuttgart, 1958), 80: 'Freiheit erzeugt notwendig Ungleichheit und Gleichheit notwendig Unfreiheit', are merely a few instances which I readily find in my notes. Yet people who claim to be enthusiastic supporters of liberty still clamour constantly for material equality.

because in such a society nobody has the power or the knowledge which would enable him to ensure that those affected by his actions will get what he thinks right for them to get. Nor could anyone who is assured remuneration according to some principle which is accepted as constituting 'social justice' be allowed to decide what he is to do: remuneration indicating how urgent it was that a certain work should be done could not be just in this sense, because the need for work of a particular kind would often depend on unforeseeable accidents and certainly not on the good intentions or efforts of those able to perform it. And an authority that fixed remunerations with the intention of thereby reducing the kind and number of people thought necessary in each occupation could not make these remunerations 'just', i.e. proportionate to desert, or need, or the merits of any other claim of the persons concerned, but would have to offer what was necessary to attract or retain the number of people wanted in each kind of activity.

'EQUALITY OF OPPORTUNITY'

It is of course not to be denied that in the existing market order not only the results but also the initial chances of different individuals are often very different; they are affected by circumstances of their physical and social environment which are beyond their control but in many particular respects might be altered by some governmental action. The demand for equality of opportunity or equal starting conditions (*Startgerechtigkeit*) appeals to, and has been supported by, many who in general favour the free market order. So far as this refers to such facilities and opportunities as are of necessity affected by governmental decisions (such as appointments to public office and the like), the demand was indeed one of the central points of classical liberalism, usually expressed by the French phrase 'la carrière ouverte aux talents'. There is also much to be said in favour of the government providing on an equal basis the means for the schooling of minors who are not yet fully responsible citizens, even though there are grave doubts whether we ought to allow government to administer them.

But all this would still be very far from creating real equality of opportunity, even for persons possessing the same abilities. To achieve this government would have to control the whole physical and human environment of all persons, and have to endeavour to provide at least equivalent chances for each; and the more government succeeded in these endeavours, the stronger would become the legitimate demand that, on the same principle, any still remaining handicaps must be removed—or compensated for by putting extra burden on the still relatively favoured. This would have to go on until government literally controlled every circumstance which could affect any person's well-being. Attractive as the phrase of equality of opportunity at first sounds, once the idea is extended beyond the facilities which for other reasons have to be provided by government, it becomes a wholly illusory ideal, and any attempt concretely to realize it apt to produce a nightmare.

'SOCIAL JUSTICE' AND FREEDOM UNDER THE LAW

The idea that men ought to be rewarded in accordance with the assessed merits or deserts of their services 'to society' presupposes an authority which not only distributes these rewards but also assigns to the individuals the tasks for the performance of which they will be rewarded. In other words, if 'social justice' is to be brought about, the individuals must be required to obey not merely general rules but specific demands directed to them only. The type of social order in which the individuals are directed to serve a single system of ends is the organization and not the spontaneous order of the market, that is, not a system in which the individual is free because bound only by general rules of just conduct, but a system in which all are subject to specific directions by authority.

It appears sometimes to be imagined that a mere alteration of the rules of individual conduct could bring about the realization of 'social justice'. But there can be no set of such rules, no principles by which the individuals could so govern their conduct that in a Great Society the joint effect of their activities would be a distribution of benefits which could be described as materially just, or any other specific and intended allocation of advantages and disadvantages among particular people or groups. In order to achieve *any* particular pattern of distribution through the market process, each producer would have to know, not only whom his efforts will benefit (or harm), but also how well off all the other people (actually or potentially) affected by his activities will be as the result of the services they are receiving from other members of the society. As we have seen earlier, appropriate rules of conduct can determine only the formal character of the order of activities that will form itself, but not the specific advantages particular groups or individuals will derive from it.

This rather obvious fact still needs to be stressed since even eminent jurists have contended that the substitution of 'social' or distributive for individual or commutative justice need not destroy the freedom under the law of the individual. Thus the distinguished German legal philosopher Gustav Radbruch explicitly maintained that 'the socialist community would also be a *Rechtsstaat* [i.e. the Rule of Law would prevail there], although a *Rechtsstaat* governed not by commutative but by distributive justice'.[31] And of France it is reported that 'it has been suggested that some highly placed administrators should be given the permanent task of "pronouncing" on the distribution of national income, as judges pronounce on legal matters'.[32] Such beliefs, however, overlook the fact that no specific pattern of distribution can be achieved by making the individuals obey rules of conduct, but that the achievement of such particular predetermined results requires deliberate co-ordination of all the different activities in accordance with the concrete circumstances of time and place. It precludes, in other words, that the several individuals act on the basis of their own knowledge and in the service of their own ends, which is the essence of freedom, but requires that they be made to act in the manner which according to the knowledge of the directing authority is required for the realization of the ends chosen by that authority.

The distributive justice at which socialism aims is thus irreconcilable with the rule of law, and with that freedom under the law which the rule of law is intended to secure. The rules of distributive justice cannot be rules for the conduct towards equals, but must be rules for the conduct of superiors towards their subordinates. Yet though some socialists have long ago themselves drawn the inevitable conclusion that 'the fundamental principles of formal law by which every case must be judged according to general rational principles . . . obtains only for the competitive phase of capitalism,'[33] and the communists, so long as they took socialism seriously, had even proclaimed that 'communism means not the victory of socialist law, but the victory of socialism over any law, since with the abolition of classes with antagonistic interests, law will disappear altogether',[34] when, more than thirty years ago, the present author made this the

---

[31] Gustav Radbruch, *Rechtsphilosophie* (Stuttgart, 1956), 87: 'Auch das sozialistische Gemeinwesen wird also ein Rechtsstaat sein, ein Rechtsstaat freilich, der statt von der ausgleichenden von der austeilenden Gerechtigkeit beherrscht wird.'

[32] See M. Duverger, *The Idea of Politics* (Indianapolis, 1966), 201.

[33] Karl Mannheim, *Man and Society in an Age of Reconstruction* (London, 1940), 180.

[34] P. J. Stuchka (President of the Soviet Supreme Court) in *Encyclopedia of State and Law* (in Russian, Moscow, 1927), quoted by V. Gsovski, *Soviet Civil Law* (Ann Arbor, Mich., 1948), i. 70. The work of E. Paschukanis the Soviet author who has most consistently developed the idea of the disappearance of law under socialism, has been described by Karl Korsch in *Archiv sozialistischer Literatur*, iii (Frankfurt, 1966) as the only consistent development of the teaching of Karl Marx.

central point of a discussion of the political effects of socialist economic policies,[35] it evoked great indignation and violent protests. But the crucial point is implied even in Radbruch's own emphasis on the fact that the transition from commutative to distributive justice means a progressive displacement of private by public law,[36] since public law consists not of rules of conduct for private citizens but of rules of organization for public officials. It is, as Radbruch himself stresses, a law that subordinates the citizens to authority.[37] Only if one understands by law not the general rules of just conduct only but any command issued by authority (or any authorization of such commands by a legislature), can the measures aimed at distributive justice be represented as compatible with the rule of law. But this concept is thereby made to mean mere legality and ceases to offer the protection of individual freedom which it was originally intended to serve.

There is no reason why in a free society government should not assure to all protection against severe deprivation in the form of an assured minimum income, or a floor below which nobody need to descend. To enter into such an insurance against extreme misfortune may well be in the interest of all; or it may be felt to be a clear moral duty of all to assist, within the organized community, those who cannot help themselves. So long as such a uniform minimum income is provided outside the market to all those who, for any reason, are unable to earn in the market an adequate maintenance, this need not lead to a restriction of freedom, or conflict with the Rule of Law. The problems with which we are here concerned arise only when the remuneration for services rendered is determined by

---

[35] *The Road to Serfdom* (London and Chicago, 1944), ch. 4. For discussions of the central thesis of that book by lawyers see W. Friedmann, *The Planned State and the Rule of Law* (Melbourne, 1948), reprinted in the same author's *Law and Social Change in Contemporary Britain* (London, 1951): Hans Kelsen, 'The Foundations of Democracy', *Ethics* 66 (1955); Roscoe Pound, 'The Rule of Law and the Modern Welfare State', *Vanderbilt Law Review*, 7 (1953); Harry W. Jones, 'The Rule of Law and the Modern Welfare State', *Columbia Law Review*, 58 (1958); A. L. Goodhart, 'The Rule of Law and Absolute Sovereignty', *University of Pennsylvania Law Review*, 106 (1958).

[36] G. Radbruch, *Rechtsphilosophie*, 126.

[37] Radbruch's conceptions of these matters are concisely summed up by Roscoe Pound (in his introduction to R. H. Graves, *Status in the Common Law* (London, 1953), p. xl): Radbruch 'starts with a distinction between commutative justice, a correcting justice which gives back to one what has been taken away from him or gives him a substantial substitute, and distributive justice, a distribution of the goods of existence not equally but according to a scheme of values. Thus there is a contrast between co-ordinating law, which secures interests by reparation and the like, treating all individuals as equal, and subordinating law, which prefers some or the interests of some according to its measure of value. Public law, he says, is a law of subordination, subordinating individual to public interests but not the interests of other individuals with those public interests.'

authority, and the impersonal mechanism of the market which guides the direction of individual efforts is thus suspended.

Perhaps the acutest sense of grievance about injustice inflicted on one, not by particular persons but by the 'system', is that about being deprived of opportunities for developing one's abilities which others enjoy. For this any difference of environment, social or physical, may be responsible, and at least some of them may be unavoidable. The most important of these is clearly inseparable from the institution of the family. This not only satisfies a strong psychological need but in general serves as an instrument for the transmission of important cultural values. There can be no doubt that those who are either wholly deprived of this benefit, or grew up in unfavourable conditions, are gravely handicapped; and few will question that it would be desirable that some public institution so far as possible should assist such unfortunate children when relatives and neighbours fail. Yet few will seriously believe (although Plato did) that we can fully make up for such a deficiency, and I trust even fewer that, because this benefit cannot be assured to all, it should, in the interest of equality, be taken from those who now enjoy it. Nor does it seem to me that even material equality could compensate for those differences in the capacity of enjoyment and of experiencing a lively interest in the cultural surroundings which a suitable upbringing confers.

There are of course many other irremediable inequalities which must seem as unreasonable as economic inequalities but which are less resented than the latter only because they do not appear to be man-made or the consequence of institutions which could be altered.

THE SPATIAL RANGE OF 'SOCIAL JUSTICE'

There can be little doubt that the moral feelings which express themselves in the demand for 'social justice' derive from an attitude which in more primitive conditions the individual developed towards the fellow members of the small group to which he belonged. Towards the personally known member of one's own group it may well have been a recognized duty to assist him and to adjust one's actions to his needs. This is made possible by the knowledge of his person and his circumstances. The situation is wholly different in the Great or Open Society. Here the products and services of each benefit mostly persons he does not know. The greater productivity of such a society rests on a division of labour extending far beyond the range any one person can survey. This extension of the process of exchange beyond relatively small groups, and including large numbers of persons not known to each other, has been made possible by conceding to the stranger and even the foreigner the same protection of rules of just conduct which apply to the relations to the known members of one's own small group.

This application of the same rules of just conduct to the relations to all other men is rightly regarded as one of the great achievements of a liberal society. What is usually not understood is that this extension of the same rules to the relations to all other men (beyond the most intimate group such as the family and personal friends) requires an attenuation at least of some of the rules which are enforced in the relations to other members of the smaller group. If the legal duties towards strangers or foreigners are to be the same as those towards the neighbours or inhabitants of the same village or town, the latter duties will have to be reduced to such as can also be applied to the stranger. No doubt men will always wish to belong also to smaller groups and be willing voluntarily to assume greater obligations towards self-chosen friends or companions. But such moral obligations towards some can never become enforced duties in a system of freedom under the law, because in such a system the selection of those towards whom a man wishes to assume special moral obligations must be left to him and cannot be determined by law. A system of rules intended for an Open Society and, at least in principle, meant to be applicable to all others, must have a somewhat smaller content than one to be applied in a small group.

Especially a common agreement on what is the due status or material position of the different members is likely to develop only in the relatively small group in which the members will be familiar with the character and importance of each other's activities. In such small communities the opinion about appropriate status will also still be associated with a feeling about what one self owes to the other, and not be merely a demand that somebody provide the appropriate reward. Demands for the realization of 'social justice' are usually as a matter of course, though often only tacitly, addressed to national governments as the agencies which possess the necessary powers. But it is doubtful whether in any but the smallest countries standards can be applied nationally which are derived from the condition of the particular locality with which the individual is familiar, and fairly certain that few men would be willing to concede to foreigners the same right to a particular income that they tend to recognize in their fellow citizens.

It is true that in recent years concern about the suffering of large numbers in the poor countries has induced the electorates of the wealthier nations to approve substantial material aid to the former; but it can hardly be said that in this considerations of justice played a significant role. It is indeed doubtful whether any substantial help would have been rendered if competing power groups had not striven to draw as many as possible of the developing countries into their orbit. And it deserves notice that the modern technology which has made such assistance possible could develop only because some countries were able to build up great wealth while most of the world saw little change.

Yet the chief point is that, if we look beyond the limits of our national states, and certainly if we go beyond the limits of what we regard as our civilization, we no longer even deceive ourselves that we know what would be 'socially just', and that those very groups within the existing states which are loudest in their demands for 'social justice', such as the trade unions, are regularly the first to reject such claims raised on behalf of foreigners. Applied to the international sphere, the complete lack of a recognized standard of 'social justice', or of any known principles on which such a standard could be based, becomes at once obvious; while on a national scale most people still think that what on the level of the face-to-face society is to them a familiar idea must also have some validity for national politics or the use of the powers of government. In fact, it becomes on this level a humbug—the effectiveness of which with well-meaning people the agents of organized interests have learnt successfully to exploit.

There is in this respect a fundamental difference between what is possible in the small group and in the Great Society. In the small group the individual can know the effects of his actions on his several fellows, and the rules may effectively forbid him to harm them in any manner and even require him to assist them in specific ways. In the Great Society many of the effects of a person's actions on various fellows must be unknown to him. It can, therefore, not be the specific effects in the particular case, but only rules which define kinds of actions as prohibited or required, which must serve as guides to the individual. In particular, he will often not know who the individual people will be who will benefit by what he does, and therefore not know whether he is satisfying a great need or adding to abundance. He cannot aim at just results if he does not know who will be affected.

Indeed the transition from the small group to the Great or Open Society—and the treatment of every other person as a human being rather than as either a known friend or an enemy—requires a reduction of the range of duties we owe to all others.

If a person's legal duties are to be the same towards all, including the stranger and even the foreigner (and greater only where he has voluntarily entered into obligations, or is connected by physical ties as between parents and children), the legally enforceable duties to neighbour and friend must not be more than those towards the stranger. That is, all those duties which are based on personal acquaintance and familiarity with individual circumstances must cease to be enforceable. The extension of the obligation to obey certain rules of just conduct to wider circles and ultimately to all men must thus lead to an attenuation of the obligation towards fellow members of the same small group. Our inherited or perhaps in part even innate moral emotions are in part inapplicable to Open Society (which is an abstract society), and the kind of 'moral socialism' that is possible in the small group and often satisfies a deeply ingrained instinct may well be impossible in the Great Society. Some altruistic conduct aimed at the benefit of some known friend that in the small group might be highly desirable, need not be so in the Open Society, and may there even be harmful (as e.g. the requirement that members of the same trade refrain from competing with each other).[38]

It may at first seem paradoxical that the advance of morals should lead to a reduction of specific obligations towards others: yet whoever believes that the principle of equal treatment of all men, which is probably the only chance for peace, is more important than special help to visible suffering, must wish it. It admittedly means that we make our rational insight dominate over our inherited instincts. But the great moral adventure on which modern man has embarked when he launched into the Open Society is threatened when he is required to apply to all his fellow men rules which are appropriate only to the fellow members of a tribal group.

CLAIMS FOR COMPENSATION FOR DISTASTEFUL JOBS

The reader will probably expect me now to examine in greater detail the particular claims usually justified by the appeal to 'social justice'. But this, as bitter experience has taught me, would be not only an endless but also a bootless task. After what has been said already, it should be obvious that there are no practicable standards of merit, deserts, or needs, on which in a market order the

---

[38] Cf. Bertrand de Jouvenel, *Sovereignty* (Chicago, 1957), 136: 'The small society, as the milieu in which man is first found, retains for him an infinite attraction; he undoubtedly goes to it to renew his strength; but . . . any attempt to graft the same features on a large society is utopian and leads to tyranny. With that admitted, it is clear that as social relations become wider and more various, the common good conceived as reciprocal trustfulness cannot be sought in methods which the model of the small, closed society inspires; such a model is, in the contrary, entirely misleading.'

distribution of material benefits could be based, and still less any principle by which these different claims could be reconciled. I shall therefore confine myself to considering two arguments in which the appeal to 'social justice' is very commonly used. The first case is usually quoted in theoretical argument to illustrate the injustice of the distribution by the market process, though little is done about it in practice, while the second is probably the most frequent type of situation in which the appeal to social justice leads to government action.

The circumstance which is usually pointed out to demonstrate the injustice of the existing market order is that the most unpleasant jobs are commonly also the worst paid. In a just society, it is contended, those who have to dig coal underground or to clean chimneys or sewers, or who perform other unclean or menial tasks, should be remunerated more highly than those whose work is pleasurable.

It is of course true that it would be unjust if persons, although equally able as others to perform other tasks, were without special compensation assigned by a superior to such distasteful duties. If, e.g., in such an organization as an army, two men of equal capacity were made to perform different tasks, one of which was attractive and the other very unpleasant, justice would clearly require that the one who had regularly to perform the unpleasant duty should in some way be specially compensated for it.

The situation is entirely different, however, where people earn their living by selling their services to whoever pays best for them. Here the sacrifice brought by a particular person in rendering the service is wholly irrelevant and all that counts is the (marginal) value the services have to those to whom they are rendered. The reason for this is not only that the sacrifices different people bring in rendering the same kind of service will often be very different, or that it will not be possible to take account of the reason why some will be capable of rendering only less valuable services than others. But those whose aptitudes, and therefore also remunerations, will be small in the more attractive occupations will often find that they can earn more than they could otherwise by undertaking unpleasant tasks that are scorned by their more fortunate fellows. The very fact that the more unpleasant occupations will be avoided by those who can render services that are valued more highly by the buyers, will open to those whose skills are little valued opportunities to earn more than they otherwise could.

That those who have to offer to their fellows little that is valuable may have to incur more pain and effort to earn even a pittance than others who perhaps actually enjoy rendering services for which they are well paid, is a necessary concomitant of any system in which remuneration is based on the values the services have to the user and not on an assessment of merit earned. It must therefore prevail in any social order in which the individual is free to choose whatever occupation he can find and is not assigned to one by authority.

The only assumption on which it could be represented as just that the miner working underground, or the scavenger, or slaughter-house workers, should be paid more highly than those engaged in more pleasant occupations, would thus be that this was necessary to induce a sufficient number of persons to perform these tasks, or that they are by some human agency deliberately assigned to these tasks. But while in a market order it may be a misfortune to have been born and bred in a village where for most the only chance of making a living is fishing (or for the women the cleaning of fish), it does not make sense to describe this as unjust. Who is supposed to have been unjust?—especially when it is considered that, if these local opportunities had not existed, the people in question would probably never have been born at all, as most of the population of such a village will probably owe its existence to the opportunities which enabled their ancestors to produce and rear children.

THE RESENTMENT OF THE LOSS OF ACCUSTOMED POSITIONS

The appeal to 'social justice' which in practice has probably had the greatest influence is not one which has been much considered in literary discussion. The considerations of a supposed 'social injustice' which have led to the most far-reaching interference with the functioning of the market order are based on the idea that people are to be protected against an unmerited descent from the material position to which they have become accustomed. No other consideration of 'social justice' has probably exercised as widespread an influence as the 'strong and almost universal belief that it is unjust to disappoint legitimate expectations of wealth. When differences of opinion arise, it is always on the question of what expectations are legitimate.' It is believed, as the same author says, 'that it is legitimate even for the largest classes to expect that no very great and sudden changes will be made to their detriment'.[39]

The opinion that long-established positions create a just expectation that they will continue serves often as a substitute for more substantial criteria of 'social justice'. Where expectations are disappointed, and in consequence the rewards of effort often

[39] Edwin Cannan, *The History of Local Rates in England*, 2nd edn. (London, 1912), 162.

disproportionate to the sacrifice incurred, this will be regarded as an injustice without any attempt to show that those affected had a claim in justice to the particular income which they expected. At least when a large group of people find their income reduced as a result of circumstances which they could not have altered or foreseen, this is commonly regarded as unjust.

The frequent recurrence of such undeserved strokes of misfortune affecting some group is, however, an inseparable part of the steering mechanism of the market: it is the manner in which the cybernetic principle of negative feedback operates to maintain the order of the market. It is only through such changes which indicate that some activities ought to be reduced, that the efforts of all can be continuously adjusted to a greater variety of facts than can be known to any one person or agency, and that the utilization of dispersed knowledge is achieved on which the well-being of the Great Society rests. We cannot rely on a system in which the individuals are induced to respond to events of which they do not and cannot know without changes of the values of the services of different groups occurring which are wholly unrelated to the merits of their members. It is a necessary part of that process of constant adaptation to changing circumstances on which the mere maintenance of the existing level of wealth depends that some people should have to discover by bitter experience that they have misdirected their efforts and are forced to look elsewhere for a remunerative occupation. And the same applies to the resentment of the corresponding undeserved gains that will accrue to others for whom things have turned out better than they had reason to expect.

The sense of injury which people feel when an accustomed income is reduced or altogether lost is largely the result of a belief that they have morally deserved that income and that, therefore, so long as they work as industriously and honestly as they did before, they are in justice entitled to the continuance of that income. But the idea that we have morally deserved what we have honestly earned in the past is largely an illusion. What is true is only that it would have been unjust if anybody had taken from us what we have in fact acquired while observing the rules of the game.

It is precisely because in the cosmos of the market we all constantly receive benefits which we have not deserved in any moral sense that we are under an obligation also to accept equally undeserved diminutions of our incomes. Our only moral title to what the market gives us we have earned by submitting to those rules which makes the formation of the market order possible. These rules imply that nobody is under an obligation to supply us with a particular income unless he has specifically contracted to do so. If we were all to be consistently deprived, as the socialists propose to do, of all 'unearned benefits' which the market confers upon us, we would have to be deprived of most of the benefits of civilization.

It is clearly meaningless to reply, as is often done, that, since we owe these benefits to 'society', 'society' should also be entitled to allocate these benefits to those who in its opinion deserve them. Society, once more, is not an acting person but an orderly structure of actions resulting from the observation of certain abstract rules by its members. We all owe the benefits we receive from the operation of this structure not to anyone's intention to confer them on us, but to the members of society generally obeying certain rules in the pursuit of their interests, rules which include the rule that nobody is to coerce others in order to secure for himself (or for third persons) a particular income. This imposes upon us the obligation to abide by the results of the market also when it turns against us.

The chance which any individual in our society has of earning an income approximating that which he has now is the consequence of most individuals obeying the rules which secure the formation of that order. And though this order provides for most good prospects for the successful employment of their skills, this success must remain dependent also on what from the point of view of the individual must appear as mere luck. The magnitude of the chances open to him are not of his making but the result of others submitting to the same rules of the game. To ask for protection against being displaced from a position one has long enjoyed, by others who are now favoured by new circumstances, means to deny to them the chances to which one's own present position is due.

Any protection of an accustomed position is thus necessarily a privilege which cannot be granted to all and which, if it had always been recognized, would have prevented those who now claim it from ever reaching the position for which they now demand protection. There can, in particular, be no right to share equally in a general increase of incomes if this increase (or perhaps even their maintenance at the existing level) is dependent on the continuous adjustment of the whole structure of activities to new and unforeseen circumstances that will alter and often reduce the contributions some groups can make to the needs of their fellows. There can thus be in justice no such claims as, e.g., those of the American farmer for 'parity', or of any other group to the preservation of their relative or absolute position.

The satisfaction of such claims by particular groups would thus not be just but eminently unjust, because it would involve the denial to some of the chances to which those who make this claim owe their position. For this reason it has always been conceded only to some powerfully organized groups who were in the position to enforce their demands. Much of what is today done in the name of 'social justice' is thus not only unjust but also highly unsocial in the true sense of the word: it amounts simply to the protection of entrenched interests. Though it has come to be regarded as a 'social problem' when sufficiently large numbers clamour for protection of their accustomed position, it becomes a serious problem chiefly because, camouflaged as a demand for 'social justice', it can engage the sympathy of the public. . . . under the existing type of democratic institutions, it is in practice inevitable that legislatures with unlimited powers yield to such demands when made by sufficiently large groups. This does not alter the fact that to represent such measures as satisfying 'social justice' is little more than a pretext for making the interest of the particular groups prevail over the general interest of all. Though it is now usual to regard every claim of an organized group as a 'social problem', it would be more correct to say that, though the long run interests of the several individuals mostly agree with the general interest, the interests of the organized groups almost invariably are in conflict with it. Yet it is the latter which are commonly represented as 'social'.

CONCLUSIONS

The basic contention of this chapter, namely that in a society of free men whose members are allowed to use their own knowledge for their own purposes the term 'social justice' is wholly devoid of meaning or content, is one which by its very nature cannot be *proved*. A negative assertion never can. One may demonstrate for any number of particular instances that the appeal to 'social justice' in no way assists the choices we have to make. But the contention that in a society of free men the term has no meaning whatever can only be issued as a challenge which will make it necessary for others to reflect on the meaning of the words they use, and as an appeal not to use phrases the meaning of which they do not know.

So long as one assumes that a phrase so widely used must have some recognizable meaning one may endeavour to prove that attempts to enforce it in a society of free individuals must make that society unworkable. But such efforts become redundant once it is recognized that such a society lacks the fundamental precondition for the application of the concept of justice to the manner in which material benefits are shared among its members, namely that this is determined by a human will—or that the determination of rewards by human will could produce a viable market order. One does not have to prove that something is impracticable which cannot exist.

What I hope to have made clear is that the phrase 'social justice' is not, as most people probably feel, an innocent expression of good will towards the less fortunate, but that it has become a dishonest insinuation that one ought to agree to a demand of some special interest which can give no real reason for it. If political discussion is to become honest it is necessary that people should recognize that the term is intellectually disreputable, the mark of demagogy or cheap journalism which responsible thinkers ought to be ashamed to use because, once its vacuity is recognized, its use is dishonest. I may, as a result of long endeavours to trace the destructive effect which the invocation of 'social justice' has had on our moral sensitivity, and of again and again finding even eminent thinkers thoughtlessly using the phrase,[40] have become unduly allergic to it, but I have come to feel strongly that the greatest service I can still render to my fellow men would be that I could make the speakers and writers among them thoroughly ashamed ever again to employ the term 'social justice'.

That in the present state of the discussion the continued use of the term is not only dishonest and the source of constant political confusion, but destructive of moral feeling, is shown by the fact that again and again thinkers, including distinguished philosophers,[41] after rightly recognizing that the term justice in its now predominant meaning of distributive (or retributive) justice is meaningless, draw from this the conclusion that the concept of justice itself is empty,

[40] While one has become used to finding the confused minds of social philosophers talking about 'social justice', it greatly pains me if I find a distinguished thinker like the historian Peter Geyl (*Encounters in History* (London, 1963), 358) thoughtlessly using the term. J. M. Keynes (*The Economic Consequences of Mr. Churchill* (London, 1925), *Collected Writings*, ix. 223) also writes unhesitatingly that 'on grounds of social justice no case can be made for reducing the wages of the miners.'

[41] Cf. e.g. Walter Kaufmann, *Without Guilt and Justice* (New York, 1973), who, after rightly rejecting the concepts of distributive and retributive justice, believes that this must lead him to reject the concept of justice altogether. But this is not surprising after even *The Times* (London) in a thoughtful leading article (1 Mar. 1957) apropos the appearance of an English translation of Josef Pieper's *Justice* (London, 1957) had observed that 'roughly, it may be said that in so far as the notion of justice continues to influence political thinking, it has been reduced to the meaning of the phrase "distributive justice" and that the idea of commutative justice has almost entirely ceased to influence our calculations except in so far it is embodied in laws and customs—in the maxims for instance of the Common Law—which are preserved from sheer conservatism.' Some contemporary social philosophers indeed beg the whole issue by so *defining* 'justice' that it includes *only* distributive justice. See e.g. Brian M. Barry, 'Justice and the Common Good', *Analysis*, 19 (1961), 80: 'although Hume uses the expression "rules of justice" to cover such things as property rules, "*justice*" *is now analytically tied to* "*desert*" *and* "*need*", so that one could quite properly say that some of what Hume calls "rules of justice" were unjust' (italics added). Cf. ibid. 89.

and who in consequence jettison one of the basic moral conceptions on which the working of a society of free men rests. But it is justice in this sense which courts of justice administer and which is the original meaning of justice and must govern men's conduct if peaceful coexistence of free men is to be possible. While the appeal to 'social justice' is indeed merely an invitation to give moral approval to demands that have no moral justification, and which are in conflict with that basic rule of a free society that only such rules as can be applied equally to all should be enforced, justice in the sense of rules of just conduct is indispensable for the intercourse of free men.

We are touching here upon a problem which with all its ramifications is much too big to try to be examined here systematically, but which must at least be mentioned briefly. It is that we can't have any morals we like or dream of. Morals, to be viable, must satisfy certain requirements, requirements which we may not be able to specify but may only be able to find out by trial and error. What is required is not merely consistency, or compatibility of the rules as well as the acts demanded by them. A system of morals also must produce a functioning order, capable of maintaining the apparatus of civilization which it presupposes.

We are not familiar with the concept of non-viable systems of morals and certainly cannot observe them anywhere in practice since societies which try them rapidly disappear. But they are being preached, often by widely revered saintly figures, and the societies in decay which we can observe are often societies which have been listening to the teaching of such moral reformers and still revere the destroyers of their society as good men. More often, however, the gospel of 'social justice' aims at much more sordid sentiments: the dislike of people who are better off than oneself, or simply envy, that 'most anti-social and evil of all passions' as John Stuart Mill called it,[42] that animosity towards great wealth which represents it as a 'scandal' that some should enjoy riches while others have basic needs unsatisfied, and camouflages under the name of justice what has nothing to do with justice. At least all those who wish to despoil the rich, not because they expect that some more deserving might enjoy that wealth, but because they regard the very existence of the rich as an outrage, not only cannot claim any moral justification for their demands, but indulge in a wholly irrational passion and in fact harm those to whose rapacious instincts they appeal.

There can be no moral claim to something that would not exist but for the decision of others to risk their resources on its creation. What those who attack great private wealth do not understand is that it is neither by physical effort nor by the mere act of saving and

[42] J. S. Mill, *On Liberty*, ed. McCallum (Oxford, 1946), 70.

investing, but by directing resources to the most productive uses that wealth is chiefly created. And there can be no doubt that most of those who have built up great fortunes in the form of new industrial plants and the like have thereby benefited more people through creating opportunities for more rewarding employment than if they had given their superfluity away to the poor. The suggestion that in these cases those to whom in fact the workers are most indebted do wrong rather than greatly benefit them is an absurdity. Though there are undoubtedly also other and less meritorious ways of acquiring large fortunes (which we can hope to control by improving the rules of the game), the most effective and important is by directing investment to points where they most enhance the productivity of labour—a task in which governments notoriously fail, for reasons inherent in non-competitive bureaucratic organizations.

But it is not only by encouraging malevolent and harmful prejudices that the cult of 'social justice' tends to destroy genuine moral feelings. It also comes, particularly in its more egalitarian forms, into constant conflict with some of the basic moral principles on which any community of free men must rest. This becomes evident when we reflect that the demand that we should equally esteem all our fellow men is irreconcilable with the fact that our whole moral code rests on the approval or disapproval of the conduct of others; and that similarly the traditional postulate that each capable adult is primarily responsible for his own and his dependants' welfare, meaning that he must not through his own fault become a charge to his friends or fellows, is incompatible with the idea that 'society' or government owes each person an appropriate income.

Though all these moral principles have also been seriously weakened by some pseudo-scientific fashions of our time which tend to destroy all morals—and with them the basis of individual freedom—the ubiquitous dependence on other people's power, which the enforcement of any image of 'social justice' creates, inevitably destroys that freedom of personal decisions on which all morals must rest.[43] In fact, that systematic pursuit of the *ignis fatuus* of 'social justice' which we call socialism is based throughout on the atrocious idea that political power ought to determine the material position of the different individuals and groups—an idea defended by the false assertion that this must always be so and socialism

---

[43] On the destruction of moral values by scientific error see my discussion in my inaugural lecture as Visiting Professor at the University of Salzburg, *Die Irrtümer des Konstruktivismus und die Grundlagen legitimer Kritik gesellschaftlicher Gebilde* (Munich, 1970, now reprinted for the Walter Eucken Institute at Freiburg i. Brg. by J. C. B. Mohr, Tübingen, 1975).

merely wishes to transfer this power from the privileged to the most numerous class. It was the great merit of the market order as it has spread during the last two centuries that it deprived everyone of such power which can be used only in arbitrary fashion. It had indeed brought about the greatest reduction of arbitrary power ever achieved. This greatest triumph of personal freedom the seduction of 'social justice' threatens again to take from us. And it will not be long before the holders of the power to enforce 'social justice' will entrench themselves in their position by awarding the benefits of 'social justice' as the remuneration for the conferment of that power and in order to secure to themselves the support of a praetorian guard which will make it certain that their view of what is 'social justice' will prevail.

Before leaving the subject I want to point out once more that the recognition that in such combinations as 'social', 'economic', 'distributive', or 'retributive' justice the term 'justice', is wholly empty should not lead us to throw the baby out with the bath water. Not only as the basis of the legal rules of just conduct is the justice which the courts of justice administer exceedingly important; there unquestionably also exists a genuine problem of justice in connection with the deliberate design of political institutions, the problem to which Professor John Rawls has recently devoted an important book. The fact which I regret and regard as confusing is merely that in this connection he employs the term 'social justice'. But I have no basic quarrel with an author who, before he proceeds to that problem, acknowledges that the task of selecting specific systems or distributions of desired things as just must be 'abandoned as mistaken in principle, and it is, in any case, not capable of a definite answer. Rather, the principles of justice define the crucial constraints which institutions and joint activities must satisfy if persons engaging in them are to have no complaints against them. If these constraints are satisfied, the resulting distribution, whatever it is, may be accepted as just (or at least not unjust).'[44] This is more or less what I have been trying to argue in this chapter.

[44] John Rawls, 'Constitutional Liberty and the Concept of Justice', *Nomos IV, Justice* (New York, 1963), 102, where the passage quoted is preceded by the statement that 'It is the system of institutions which has to be judged and judged from a general point of view.' I am not aware that Professor Rawls's later more widely read work *A Theory of Justice* contains a comparatively clear statement of the main point, which may explain why this work seems often, but as it appears to me wrongly, to have been interpreted as lending support to socialist demands, e.g. by Daniel Bell, 'On Meritocracy and Equality', *Public Interest* (Autumn 1972), 72, who describes Rawls's theory as 'the most comprehensive effort in modern philosophy to justify a socialistic ethic'.

9

CRITIQUE OF THE GOTHA PROGRAMME

KARL MARX

'The emancipation of labour demands the promotion of the instruments of labour to the common property of society and the co-operative regulation of the total labour with a fair distribution of the proceeds of labour.'

'Promotion of the instruments of labour to the common property' ought obviously to read their 'conversion into the common property'; but this only in passing.

What are 'proceeds of labour'? The product of labour or its value? And in the latter case, is it the total value of the product or only that part of the value which labour has newly added to the value of the means of production consumed?

'Proceeds of labour' is a loose notion which Lassalle has put in the place of definite economic conceptions.

What is 'a fair distribution'?

Do not the bourgeois assert that the present-day distribution is 'fair'? And is it not, in fact, the only 'fair' distribution on the basis of the present-day mode of production? Are economic relations regulated by legal conceptions or do not, on the contrary, legal relations arise from economic ones? Have not also the socialist sectarians the most varied notions about 'fair' distribution?

To understand what is implied in this connection by the phrase 'fair distribution', we must take the first paragraph and this one together. The latter presupposes a society wherein 'the instruments of labour are common property and the total labour is co-operatively regulated', and from the first paragraph we learn that 'the proceeds of labour belong undiminished with equal right to all members of society'.

'To all members of society'? To those who do not work as well? What remains then of the 'undiminished proceeds of labour'? Only to those members of society who work? What remains then of the 'equal right' of all members of society?

Karl Marx, *Critique of the Gotha Programme* from R. C. Tucker, *Marx–Engels Reader* (Norton: New York, 1978). Reprinted by permission of the publishers.

But 'all members of society' and 'equal right' are obviously mere phrases. The kernel consists in this, that in this communist society every worker must receive the 'undiminished' Lassallean 'proceeds of labour'.

Let us take first of all the words 'proceeds of labour' in the sense of the product of labour; then the co-operative proceeds of labour are the *total social product*.

From this must now be deducted:

First, cover for replacement of the means of production used up.

Secondly, additional portion for expansion of production.

Thirdly, reserve or insurance funds to provide against accidents, dislocations caused by natural calamities, etc.

These deductions from the 'undiminished proceeds of labour' are an economic necessity and their magnitude is to be determined according to available means and forces, and partly by computation of probabilities, but they are in no way calculable by equity.

There remains the other part of the total product, intended to serve as means of consumption.

Before this is divided among the individuals, there has to be deducted again, from it:

First, the general costs of administration not belonging to production.

This part will, from the outset, be very considerably restricted in comparison with present-day society and it diminishes in proportion as the new society develops.

Secondly, that which is intended for the common satisfaction of needs, such as schools, health services, etc.

From the outset this part grows considerably in comparison with present-day society and it grows in proportion as the new society develops.

Thirdly, funds for those unable to work, etc., in short, for what is included under so-called official poor relief today.

Only now do we come to the 'distribution' which the programme, under Lassallean influence, alone has in view in its narrow fashion, namely, to that part of the means of consumption which is divided among the individual producers of the co-operative society.

The 'undiminished proceeds of labour' have already unnoticeably become converted into the 'diminished' proceeds, although what the producer is deprived of in his capacity as a private individual benefits him directly or indirectly in his capacity as a member of society.

Just as the phrase of the 'undiminished proceeds of labour' has disappeared, so now does the phrase of the 'proceeds of labour' disappear altogether.

Within the co-operative society based on common ownership of the means of production, the producers do not exchange their products; just as little does the labour employed on the products appear here *as the value* of these products, as a material quality possessed by them, since now, in contrast to capitalist society, individual labour no longer exists in an indirect fashion but directly as a component part of the total labour. The phrase 'proceeds of labour', objectionable also today on account of its ambiguity, thus loses all meaning.

What we have to deal with here is a communist society, not as it has *developed* on its own foundations, but, on the contrary, just as it *emerges* from capitalist society; which is thus in every respect, economically, morally, and intellectually, still stamped with the birth marks of the old society from whose womb it emerges. Accordingly, the individual producer receives back from society—after the deductions have been made—exactly what he gives to it. What he has given to it is his individual quantum of labour. For example, the social working day consists of the sum of the individual hours of work; the individual labour time of the individual producer is the part of the social working day contributed by him, his share in it. He receives a certificate from society that he has furnished such and such an amount of labour (after deducting his labour for the common funds), and with this certificate he draws from the social stock of means of consumption as much as costs the same amount of labour. The same amount of labour which he has given to society in one form he receives back in another.

Here obviously the same principle prevails as that which regulates the exchange of commodities, as far as this is exchange of equal values. Content and form are changed, because under the altered circumstances no one can give anything except his labour, and because, on the other hand, nothing can pass to the ownership of individuals except individual means of consumption. But, as far as the distribution of the latter among the individual producers is concerned, the same principle prevails as in the exchange of commodity equivalents: a given amount of labour in one form is exchanged for an equal amount of labour in another form.

Hence, *equal right* here is still in principle—*bourgeois right*, although principle and practice are no longer at loggerheads, while the exchange of equivalents in commodity exchange only exists *on the average* and not in the individual case.

In spite of this advance, this *equal right* is still constantly stigmatized by a bourgeois limitation. The right of the producers is *proportional* to the labour they supply; the equality consists in the fact that measurement is made with an *equal standard*, labour.

But one man is superior to another physically or mentally and so supplies more labour in the same time, or can labour for a longer time; and labour, to serve as a measure, must be defined by its duration or intensity, otherwise it ceases to be a standard of measurement. This *equal* right is an unequal right for unequal labour. It recognizes no class differences, because everyone is only a worker like everyone else; but it tacitly recognizes unequal individual endowment and thus productive capacity as natural privileges. *It is, therefore, a right of inequality, in its content, like every right.* Right by its very nature can consist only in the application of an equal standard; but unequal individuals (and they would not be different individuals if they were not unequal) are measurable only by an equal standard in so far as they are brought under an equal point of view, are taken from one *definite* side only, for instance, in the present case, are regarded *only as workers* and nothing more is seen in them, everything else being ignored. Further, one worker is married, another not; one has more children than another, and so on and so forth. Thus, with an equal performance of labour, and hence an equal share in the social consumption fund, one will in fact receive more than another, one will be richer than another, and so on. To avoid all these defects, right instead of being equal would have to be unequal.

But these defects are inevitable in the first phase of communist society as it is when it has just emerged after prolonged birth pangs from capitalist society. Right can never be higher than the economic structure of society and its cultural development conditioned thereby.

In a higher phase of communist society, after the enslaving subordination of the individual to the division of labour, and therewith also the antithesis between mental and physical labour, has vanished; after labour has become not only a means of life but life's prime want; after the productive forces have also increased with the all-round development of the individual, and all the springs of co-operative wealth flow more abundantly—only then can the narrow horizon of bourgeois right be crossed in its entirety and society inscribe on its banner: from each according to his ability, to each according to his needs!

I have dealt more at length with the 'undiminished proceeds of labour', on the one hand, and with 'equal right' and 'fair distribution', on the other, in order to show what a crime it is to attempt, on the one hand, to force on our Party again, as dogmas, ideas which in a certain period had some meaning but have now become obsolete verbal rubbish, while again perverting, on the other, the realistic outlook, which it cost so much effort to instil into the Party but which has now taken root in it, by means of ideological nonsense about right and other trash so common among the democrats and French Socialists.

Quite apart from the analysis so far given, it was in general a mistake to make a fuss about so-called *distribution* and put the principal stress on it.

Any distribution whatever of the means of consumption is only a consequence of the distribution of the conditions of production themselves. The latter distribution, however, is a feature of the mode of production itself. The capitalist mode of production, for example, rests on the fact that the material conditions of production are in the hands of non-workers in the form of property in capital and land, while the masses are only owners of the personal condition of production, of labour power. If the elements of production are so distributed, then the present-day distribution of the means of consumption results automatically. If the material conditions of production are the co-operative property of the workers themselves, then there likewise results a distribution of the means of consumption different from the present one. Vulgar socialism (and from it in turn a section of the democracy) has taken over from the bourgeois economists the consideration and treatment of distribution as independent of the mode of production and hence the presentation of socialism as turning principally on distribution. After the real relation has long been made clear, why retrogress again?

10

JUSTICE AND RIGHTS

STEVEN LUKES

JUSTICE

Did Marx think that capitalism, and more particularly the wage relation between capitalist and worker, was unjust? A lively debate on this question has recently flourished, and by now all the logically possible positions on the issue have been ably and convincingly defended, viz.:

(1) Marx thought the relation between capitalist and worker was just
(2) he thought it was unjust
(3) he thought it was both just and unjust—that is, just in one respect and unjust in another
(4) he thought it was neither just nor unjust.

Position (1), which has come to be known as the Tucker–Wood thesis,[1] relies on a number of very telling passages. In *The Critique of the Gotha Programme*, in response to the Lasallean demand for 'a fair distribution of the proceeds of labour', Marx asks:

Do not the bourgeois assert that the present-day distribution is 'fair'? And is it not, in fact, the only 'fair' distribution on the basis of the present-day mode of production? Are economic relations regulated by legal conceptions or do not, on the contrary, legal relations arise from economic ones?[2]

More specifically, he wrote that the capitalist's extraction of surplus value from the worker was 'by no means an injustice (*Unrecht*)' to the latter:

Steven Lukes, 'Justice and Rights', ch. 4 of *Marxism and Morality* (Oxford University Press: Oxford, 1985), © Steven Lukes 1985. Reprinted by permission of Oxford University Press.

[1] See R. C. Tucker, *The Marxian Revolutionary Idea* (W. W. Norton: New York, 1969). Also A. Wood, 'The Marxian Critique of Justice:', *Philosophy and Public Affairs*, 1/3 (Spring 1972); 'Marx on Right and Justice: A Reply to Husami', *Philosophy and Public Affairs*, 8/3 (Spring 1979); *Karl Marx* (Routledge and Kegan Paul: London, 1981).

[2] Karl Marx, *Critique of the Gotha Programme* (1875), *Selected Works* (Foreign Languages Publishing House: Moscow, 1962), vol. ii.

The circumstance, that on the one hand the daily sustenance of labour power costs only half a day's labour, while on the other hand the very same labour-power can work during a whole day, that consequently the value which its use during one day creates is double what [the capitalist] pays for that use, this circumstance is, without doubt, a piece of good luck for the buyer and by no means an injustice to the seller.[3]

And in rebuttal of Adolph Wagner's suggestion that he, Marx, thought that the capitalist robs the worker, he wrote:

The obscurantist falsely attributes to me [the view] that 'the *surplus value* produced by the labourers *alone*, was left to the capitalist employers in an *improper way*'. Well, I say the direct opposite, namely, that commodity-production is necessarily, at a certain point, turned into 'capitalistic' commodity production, and that according to the *law of value* governing it, 'surplus value' is properly due to the capitalist and not to the labourer. . . .

. . . in my presentation, profit is *not* [as Wagner alleged] 'merely *deduction* or "robbery" on the labourer'. On the contrary, I present the capitalist as the necessary functionary of capitalist production and show very extensively that he does not only 'deduct' or '*rob*', but forces the *production of surplus value*, therefore the deducting only helps to produce; furthermore, I show in detail that even if in the exchange of commodities *only equivalents* were exchanged, the capitalist—as soon as he pays the labourer the real value of his labour power—would secure with full rights, i.e. the rights corresponding to that mode of production, *surplus-value*.[4]

In accordance with this last thought, Marx stated his more general position about the issue as follows:

The justice of the transactions between agents of production rests on the fact that these arise as natural consequences out of the production relationships. The juristic forms in which these economic transactions appear as wilful acts of the parties concerned, as expressions of their common will and as contracts that may be enforced by law against some individual party, cannot, being mere forms, determine their content. They merely express it. This content is just whenever it corresponds, is appropriate, to the mode of production. It is unjust whenever it contradicts that mode. Slavery on the basis of capitalist production is unjust; likewise fraud in the quality of commodities.[5]

And finally, he stated this position even more clearly in *Wages, Prices and Profit*:

To clamour for *equal or even equitable retribution* on the basis of the wages system is the same as to clamour for *freedom* on the basis of the slavery

[3] *Capital* (1867), tr. Moore and Aveling (Foreign Languages Publishing House: Moscow, 1959), i. 194; translation amended.
[4] 'Notes on Adolph Wagner' (1879–80), tr. in Terrell Carver (ed.), *Karl Marx: Texts on Method* (Blackwell: Oxford, 1975), 186.
[5] *Capital* (1861–79), ed. Engels (Foreign Languages Publishing House: Moscow, 1962), iii. 333–4.

system. What you think just or equitable is irrelevant. The question is: what is necessary and unavoidable within a given system of production?[6]

On the basis of passages such as these (all of which but the last he cites) Wood argues that transactions are just if they correspond or are appropriate to, or are functional to, the prevailing mode of production: judgements about justice are not made by reference to abstract or formal principles independent of the existing mode of production, indicating some ideal to which social reality could be adjusted; rather they are 'rational assessments of the justice of specific acts and institutions, based on their concrete functions within a specific mode of production'.[7] Thus, since the exploitation of wage labour by capital is essential to the capitalist mode of production, there is nothing unjust about the transaction through which capital exploits labour; the worker is paid the full value of his labour power (unless, of course, he is defrauded), and the capitalist, in subsequently appropriating surplus value, is not required to pay the worker an equivalent for it, since under capitalism the worker has no right to the full value created by his labour. He did have such a right under the petty-bourgeois system of 'individual private property', but the very productive success of capitalism required its abolition. So, in short, according to Wood,

as Marx interprets it, the justice of capitalist transactions consists merely in their being essentially capitalist, in the correspondence of capitalist appropriation and distribution to those standards of justice which serve the system itself.[8]

Capitalist exploitation 'alienates, dehumanises and degrades wage labourers', but 'it does not violate any of their rights, and there is nothing about it which is wrongful or unjust'.[9]

Position (2), held by Husami, Cohen, and others relies on a variety of no less telling passages in which Marx plainly does speak of exploitation as 'robbery', 'usurpation', 'embezzlement', 'plunder', 'booty', 'theft', 'snatching', and 'swindling'.[10] Thus, the 'yearly accruing surplus product [is] embezzled, because extracted without return of an equivalent, from the English labourer'.[11] So for example in the *Grundrisse* Marx wrote of 'the theft of alien labour time [i.e. of surplus value or surplus labour] on which the present wealth is

---

[6] *Wages, Prices and Profit* (1865), *Selected Works*, i. 426; translation amended.

[7] Wood, 'The Marxian Critique of Justice', 16.

[8] 'Marx on Right and Justice', 108.

[9] Wood, *Karl Marx*, 43.

[10] Z. I. Husami, 'Marx on Distributive Justice', *Philosophy and Public Affairs*, 8/1 (Autumn 1978), 43–5.

[11] *Capital*, i. 611; translation amended.

based'.[12] And in *Capital* he wrote of the surplus product as

the tribute annually exacted from the working-class by the capitalist class. Though the latter with a portion of that tribute purchases the additional labour-power even at its full price, so that equivalent is exchanged for equivalent, yet the transaction is for all that only the old dodge of every conqueror who buys commodities from the conquered with the money he has robbed them of.[13]

In the light of passages such as these, Cohen maintains that

since, as Wood will agree, Marx did not think that by capitalist criteria the capitalist steals, and since he did think he steals, he must have meant that he steals in some appropriately non-relativist sense. And since to steal is, in general, wrongly to take what rightly belongs to another, to steal is to commit an injustice, and a system which is 'based on theft' is based on injustice.[14]

And Husami argues that those who defend Position (1) miss the satirical and ironic tone of the passages they cite in its defence, and that, by arguing that the only applicable standard of justice is that appropriate to the existing economic system, they make it 'impossible for the oppressed to criticise the injustice of their life situations'.[15] According to Husami, Marx 'evaluates pre-communist systems from the standpoint of a communist society' (ibid. 50): far from adopting capitalism's self-evaluation, he 'regarded capitalism as unjust precisely because, as an exploitative system, it does not proportion reward to labour contribution, and because it is not oriented to satisfy human needs' (ibid. 78). This judgement, Husami insists, 'is made from the Marxian ethical standpoint which, Marx held, was a proletarian standpoint' (ibid. 77).

The defenders of Position (1) must somehow explain away the

---

[12] *Grundrisse der Kritik der politischen Ökonomie* (1857–8); tr. as *Foundations of the Critique of Political Economy (Rough Draft)* by Martin Nicolaus (Penguin: Harmondsworth, 1973), 705.

[13] *Capital*, i. 582. There is a further passage which tells heavily in favour of Position (2). In the *Grundrisse* Marx writes: 'The recognition [by labour] of the products as its own, and the judgment that its separation from the conditions of its realization is improper (*ungehörg*)—forcibly imposed—is an enormous awareness (*enormes Bewusstsein*), itself the product of the mode of production resting on capital, and as much the knell to its doom as, with the slave's awareness that he *cannot be the property of another*, with his consciousness of himself as a person, the existence of slavery becomes a merely artificial, vegetative existence and ceases to be able to prevail as the basis of production' (463). Highly interestingly, in the 1861–3 *Critique*, Marx reproduces this passage but replaces 'ungehörig' (improper) by 'ein Unrecht' (an injustice) (*Zur Kritik der politischen Oekonomie*, MS 1861–3, *Marx–Engels Gesamtausgabe* (Dietz: Berlin, 1982), 6, 2287). I am grateful to Jon Elster for drawing this significant piece of evidence to my attention.

[14] G. A. Cohen, review of Wood, *Karl Marx*, *Mind*, 92/367 (July 1983), 443.

[15] 'Marx on Distributive Justice', 52.

passages supporting Position (2), and vice versa. So it is no surprise to find Wood suggesting that Marx there uses 'robbery' in a special sense that does not imply injustice; and to find Husami stressing the 'ironic tone' of the cited passages concerning the justice of the capitalist wage relation. And indeed it *is* the case that the 'robbery' involved in capitalist exploitation has some special features, of which three are worth noting. First, as Marx himself observes, what the capitalist steals he himself 'helps create' by 'forcing the production of surplus value': if it were not for the capitalist, there would be nothing to rob the workers of. Second, as Marx elsewhere notes in criticism of Proudhon, their robbery is robbery according to bourgeois property rights, not necessarily according to other criteria. And third, as Wood points out, if the robbery relation is like that of conqueror to conquered, 'it is not so clear that robbery has to be unjust' (*Karl Marx*, 137–8), since it constitutes a regular production relation sanctioned by prevailing norms of justice. And it is also the case that some of the passages about the alleged justice of the capitalist's relation to the worker are highly satirical and ironic. On the other hand, Marx does plainly and frequently say that the relation is one of robbery, and he also plainly and occasionally says, sometimes that it is just, and sometimes that it is not unjust.

Position (3), which has been ably defended by Gary Young,[16] relies upon drawing a distinction, much favoured by Marx, between the sphere of exchange or circulation and that of direct production, and the correlative distinction between the worker as owner and seller of labour power, and the worker as 'a living component of capital', owned by the capitalist. Consider the following passages:

the transformation of money into capital breaks down into two wholly distinct, autonomous spheres, two entirely separate processes. The first belongs to the realm of the *circulation of commodities* and is acted out in the *market-place*. It is the *sale and purchase of labour-power*. The second is the *consumption of the labour-power that has been acquired*, i.e. the process of production itself. . . . In order to *demonstrate* therefore, that the relationship between capitalist and worker is nothing but a relationship between commodity owners who exchange money and commodities with a free contract and to their mutual advantage, it suffices to isolate the first process and to cleave to its formal character. This simple device is no sorcery, but it contains the entire riddle of the vulgar economists.[17]

Secondly, the sphere of circulation or the exchange of commodities,

---

[16] G. Young, 'The Fundamental Contradiction of Capitalist Production', *Philosophy and Public Affairs*, 5 (1975–6); 'Justice and Capitalist Production: Marx and Bourgeois Ideology', *Canadian Journal of Philosophy*, 8 (1978); 'Doing Marx Justice', in K. Neilson and S. C. Patten (eds.), *Marx and Morality* (Canadian Assoc. for Publishing in Philosophy: Guelph, Ontario, 1981).

[17] Marx, 'Results of the Immediate Process of Production' (1863–4); tr. in *Capital*, i (Penguin: Harmondsworth, 1976), 1002.

within whose boundaries the sale and purchase of labour-power goes on, is in fact a very Eden of the innate rights of man. There alone rule Freedom, Equality, Property and Bentham. . . . Equality, because each enters into relation with the other, as with a simple owner of commodities, and they exchange equivalent for equivalent. . . . On leaving this sphere of simple circulation or of exchange of commodities . . . we think we can perceive a change in the physiognomy of our dramatis personae. He, who before was the money-owner, now strides in front as capitalist; the possessor of labour-power follows as his labourer. The one with an air of importance, smirking, intent on business; the other, timid and holding back, like one who is bringing his own hide to market and has nothing to expect but—a hiding. (Marx, *Capital*, i. 176.)

And finally,

It must be acknowledged that our labourer comes out of the process of production other than he entered. In the market he stood as the owner of the commodity 'labour power' face to face with other owners of commodities, dealer against dealer. . . . The bargain concluded, it is discovered that he was no 'free agent', that the time for which he is free to sell his labour-power is the time for which he is forced to sell it, that in fact the vampire will not loose its hold on him 'so long as there is a muscle, a nerve, a drop of blood to be exploited' [the quotation is from Engels]. (Ibid. 301–2.)

Young criticizes Position (1) for failing to see the import of the distinction between worker as seller and worker as producer of surplus value, and insists that Marx thought both that the worker was treated justly (according to the laws of commodity exchange, specifying 'market rights'), and that the extraction of surplus value from him in the production process was robbery ('in the ordinary sense in which robbery is unjust'[18]). In short, 'on Marx's view, the worker is treated justly as seller in the exchange of labour power for wages, but is then robbed in the production process, during which the capitalist extracts surplus value from the worker' (ibid. 252). And Young further argues that, for Marx, only the latter is 'real', the former being merely ideological appearance, veiling and mystifying the transfer of surplus value, which is the essence of capitalist production.

Finally, Position (4), argued for by Richard Miller, relies on the observation that the passages on which Position (1) relies do not unambiguously support it. With regard to the wage relation, on the one hand their thrust is to deny that injustice is done, and on the other to insist that equivalents are exchanged. In these passages, the vocabulary of justice is used in a way that relativizes it to a mode of production and is, as we have seen, satirical, even ironic. ('Admire',

[18] Young, 'Doing Marx Justice', 260.

he writes, 'this capitalistic justice!' (Marx, *Capital*, i 660)). Nowhere, as Miller writes, 'is there a non-relativized, unequivocal statement that capitalism is just. That is what one would expect if Marx does not regard justice as a fit category either for political recommendations or for scientific analysis'.[19]

In other words, Position (4) focuses on Marx's view . . . that justice is an archaic, scientifically irrelevant category, comparable to medieval theological notions; and on the view, which Marx also held, that its invocation is futile, and even dangerous, in social criticism and political action, in so far as it suggests objectively based and universally applicable standards for judging distributive arrangements and social institutions. Given this, 'the normal function of the term in criticism and justification should rationally be abandoned' (ibid. 81). Appraising the relations of capitalism for their justice or injustice was scientifically anachronistic and politically fruitless.

What is one to make of this cacophony of interpretations? Some partial resolutions have been offered of some of the conflicting views we have sketched here. For example, Cohen (who adopts Position (2)) suggests that 'perhaps Marx did not always realise that he thought capitalism was unjust'.[20] More generally, Cohen has argued that:

Revolutionary marxist belief often misdescribes itself, out of lack of clear awareness of its own nature, and marxist disparagement of the idea of justice is a good example of that deficient self-understanding.[21]

Similarly, Jon Elster (who also adopts a version of Position (2)) suggests that 'both the theory of exploitation in *Capital* and the theory of distribution in *Critique of the Gotha Programme* embody principles of justice', but that 'like M. Jourdain, he did not know how to describe correctly what he was doing; unlike M. Jourdain, he actually went out of his way to deny that the correct description was appropriate'.[22] And Elster further suggests that 'the best way of making sense *both* of Marx's critique of capitalism and of the remarks on communism in the *Critique of the Gotha Programme* is by imputing to him a hierarchical theory of justice in which the contribution principle (to each according to his contribution) provides a second-best criterion when the needs principle (from each

---

[19] R. Miller, *Analyzing Marx* (Princeton University Press: Princeton, NJ, 1984), 80.
[20] Cohen, review of Wood, *Karl Marx*, 444.
[21] G. A. Cohen, 'Freedom, Justice and Capitalism', *New Left Review*, 126 (Mar.–Apr. 1981), 12.
[22] J. Elster, *Making Sense of Marx* (Cambridge University Press: Cambridge, 1985).

according to his ability, to each according to his needs) is not yet historically ripe for application' (ibid.).

Let us, then, look at what Marx explicitly says in the *Critique of the Gotha Programme* about the distributive arrangements of the future. Here if anywhere we should hope to find a clue to his positive thoughts about justice.

In communism's lower phase, he writes, 'still stamped with the birth marks of the old society from whose womb it emerges', each producer receives back from society means of consumption costing the same as the labour he has expended (minus various deductions for future investment, public services, and funds for those unable to work, etc.): '*equal right* here is still in principle—*bourgeois right*, although principle and practice are no longer at loggerheads'.[23] But

this *equal right* is still constantly stigmatized by a bourgeois limitation. The right of the producers is *proportional* to the labour they supply; the equality consists in the fact that measurement is made with an *equal standard*, labour.

But one man is superior to another physically or mentally and so supplies more labour in the same time, or can labour for a longer time; and labour, to serve as a measure, must be defined by its duration or intensity, otherwise it ceases to be a standard of measurement. This *equal* right is an unequal right for unequal labour. It recognises no class differences, because everyone is only a worker like everyone else; but it tacitly recognises unequal individual endowment and thus productive capacity as natural privileges. *It is, therefore, a right of inequality, in its content, like every right. Right by its very nature can consist only in the application of an equal standard; but unequal individuals (and they would not be different individuals if they were not unequal) are measurable only by an equal standard in so far as they are brought under an equal point of view, are considered in one particular aspect only, for instance, as in the present case, are regarded only as workers and nothing more is seen in them, everything else being ignored.* Further, one worker is married, another not; one has more children than another, and so on and so forth. Thus, with an equal contribution of labour, and hence an equal share in the social consumption fund, one will in fact receive more than another, one will be richer than another, and so on. To avoid all these defects, right instead of being equal would have to be unequal. (Ibid. translation amended, italics added.)

But what exactly are the defects? The first is simply that workers with higher productive capacities benefit by higher incomes. But this defect would simply be rectified by paying them all the same. Another is that some workers have dependents—members of their families—who do not work. But in an earlier paragraph of the *Critique* Marx has already allowed taxes to provide funds for those unable to work; and there seems to be no reason in principle why socialism could not provide non-working members of families with adequate incomes.

[23] Marx, *Critique of the Gotha Programme*, 23.

Aside from these particular and remediable defects, it is, however, the third defect, indicated by the passage in italics, which takes us to the heart of the matter. For here the objection is not that a particular principle of distribution is unfair, but rather that *any* system of rules specifying justifiable claims (*Recht*) treats people unequally, since, *by its very nature*, it applies a common standard to them, considering them in one particular aspect only. But, as Moore has pointed out, this amounts to a general argument that any social system is inequitable to the extent that it operates through general rules. According to this argument, 'no system of general rules, however complicated, can consider all the aspects in which individuals differ from one another. To apply such rules entails applying the same standard to different cases'.[24] Marx would clearly not be satisfied by increasing the number of aspects in which people are considered, since his view appears to be that every respect in which individuals differ from one another could in principle be relevant; accordingly, no common standard could ever fit the bill. In short, he seems here to be taking all too seriously his doctrine of the 'universality of individual need, capacities . . . ', etc. and 'rich individuality that is as all-sided in its production as in its consumption'. He seems to have supposed that any rule of law or morals, which by its very nature singles out certain differences between people as grounds for differential treatment, is for that very reason 'abstract' and 'one-sided'. In the higher phase of communism, which the *Critique* goes on to describe,

after the enslaving subordination of the individual to the division of labour, and therewith also the antithesis between mental and physical labour, has vanished; after labour has become not only a means of life but life's prime want; after the productive forces have also increased with the all-round development of the individual, and all the springs of co-operative wealth flow more abundantly—only then can the narrow horizon of bourgeois right be crossed in its entirety. (Ibid. 24.)

I take this to mean, not merely that there will no longer be *bourgeois* right, but that there will be no more *Recht*, no more legal and moral rules: the horizon is a limit to thought and action set by bourgeois *Recht*; beyond it, there will be no bourgeoisie, and no *Recht*. The principle that such a society would inscribe on its banners—'From each according to his ability, to each according to his needs'—would not be such a rule, since (1) those abilities and needs would be infinite, that is, unlimitable in advance, and unspecifiable by any rule; (2) the former would be harnessed to 'the common interest of

[24] S. Moore, *Marx on the Choice between Socialism and Communism* (Harvard University Press, Cambridge, Mass., 1980), 48–9.

all individuals who have intercourse with one another' through what Marx called *gemeinschaftlich* relations (and Lenin 'a new and higher social bond'); and (3) the latter would all be satisfiable without conflicting claims because of those relations and because of material abundance.

I am now in a position to offer my own suggestion about how the dispute about Marx's views about capitalism's justice might be resolved. It starts from the observation that all four positions considered above are plausibly Marx's and are supported by textual evidence. Now, Cohen and Elster may be right in suggesting that Marx may, like M. Jourdain, have just failed to understand his own view of justice: I myself have suggested . . . that he did not adequately reflect upon his own moral position. But I think we can go further in explicating the problem.

My suggestion is that Marx's view of capitalism's justice was both internally complex and hierarchically organized. In the first place, he did offer a functional account of the norms by which capitalist exploitation is judged just: the capitalist wage relation is judged just (on average, and apart from fraud, etc.) according to prevailing norms, viz. juridical norms of contract law, backed by conventions specifying the minimum socially necessary wage from the perspective of the vulgar economists, who 'translate the singular concepts of the capitalists, who are in the thrall of competition, into a seemingly more theoretical and generalised language, and attempt to substantiate the justice of those conceptions'.[25] These norms and the perspective prevail because they sanction and stabilize capitalist exploitation and thus the capitalist system. This is the truth in Position (1). Secondly, however, Marx also offered an 'internal' or 'immanent' critique of those norms and that perspective, as registering the mere appearance of an equivalent exchange of commodities. As Holmstrom has observed, it 'views the exchange between capitalist and worker too narrowly, abstracted from its background',[26] failing to see that the worker is not free but 'forced' to sell his labour to (some) capitalist and thereafter under (that capitalist's) control. This is the truth in Position (3). But thirdly, Marx also offered an 'external' critique of capitalist exploitation and of the norms and perspective from which it appears just. That critique is in turn made from the perspective of communism's lower phase: capitalist exploitation is from this standpoint unjust because it violates the principle 'To each according to his labour contribution' (minus the appropriate deductions). This is the truth

[25] Marx, *Capital*, ii. 226.
[26] N. Holmstrom, 'Exploitation', *Canadian Journal of Philosophy*, 7/2 (1977), 366–7.

in Position (2). And finally, Marx offered a radical critique of capitalist exploitation, of the norms and perspective justifying it *and* of the critical perspective from which it appears unjust, from the perspective of communism's higher phase. From that standpoint, the very attribution of justice and injustice is a mark of class society, a sign that society is still in a prehistorical phase, an archaism eventually to be transcended. This is the truth in Position (4).

This solution to our interpretative puzzle may cause discomfort to someone who wants to know what, in the end, Marx actually believed *in propria persona*. Did he think capitalism unjust, or didn't he? But the answer, I believe, is that Marx maintained all these positions and that he brought all these perspectives to bear at once. So I disagree with Cohen's suggestion that Marx 'must have meant that the capitalist steals in some appropriately non-relativist sense', since, for Marx, there was no such sense: all such judgements are perspective-relative. Objectivity, in the sense of perspective-neutrality, was, for him, an illusion, indeed an ideological illusion.

I further disagree, as the whole argument of this book should make clear, with Elster's suggestion that the best way of making sense of both Marx's critique of capitalism and his vision of communism is to impute to him 'a hierarchical theory of justice', with the needs principle taking priority over the contribution principle. In my view, there is in Marx and Marxism a hierarchy, but not a hierarchy of justice. I take a principle of justice to be one which is needed for 'assigning basic rights and duties and for determining . . . the proper distribution of the benefits and burdens of social co-operation', such that 'institutions are just when no arbitrary distinctions are made between persons in the assigning of basic rights and when the rules determine a proper balance between competing claims to the advantages of social life'.[27] What Marx offers is a multi-perspectival analysis in which capitalism's self-justifications are portrayed, undermined from within, and criticized from without, and then both justification and criticism are in turn criticized from a standpoint that is held to be beyond justice.

EXPLOITATION

This way of interpreting Marx makes the best sense, I believe, of the Marxist concept of exploitation, which, on this account, is internally complex and multi-perspectival, in exactly the way I have indicated. (I shall comment here only on capitalist exploitation.)

[27] J. Rawls, *A Theory of Justice* (Clarendon Press: Oxford, 1972), 5.

What, after all, are the defining features of capitalist exploitation, according to Marx? First, it is a market phenomenon. It is that form of surplus labour extraction which, formally speaking, at the level of 'appearances', equivalent (labour power) is 'voluntarily' exchanged for equivalent (wages). Second, that extraction is achieved through the *power* of the exploiters (backed by that of the state): wage labour is forced labour, in which, under the 'dull compulsion of economic relations' (Marx, *Capital*, i. 737)—as opposed to direct coercion—the labourer is, first, compelled to sell his labour power (though not to any given capitalist) and, second, then compelled to engage in the labour process under his master's supervision and control. The former compulsion is compatible with, what Marx called 'formal freedom' (for instance, of whom to work for and what to purchase): it consists in the impersonal, anonymous constraints of the labour market, given the differential resources and organizational capacities of the agents of production, which render wage labour his only real option. The latter consists in the capitalist's legally backed control—based on ownership of the means of production—over the labour process. Third, surplus value is extracted from the labourer *unfairly* or unjustly, when judged against the contribution principle: 'the greater part of the yearly accruing surplus product [is] embezzled, because abstracted without return of an equivalent' (ibid.: 611). Of course, as stated before, Marx recognized that the employer helps create what he embezzles, and indeed would probably not have done so but for the prospect of such embezzlement. This last fact, and the workers' acceptance of it as inevitable and of their rewards as just, result from the general capitalist mentality internalized by capitalists and workers alike. Marxian exploitation counts as such only when set against the external standard of justice as fairness provided by the contribution principle.

Finally, exploitation involves the inhuman character of the capitalist–worker relationship itself—and exchange relationships in general (this being Marx's earliest view of the matter): its calculative, instrumental nature, based upon the pursuit of conflicting interests by the parties to it, who view and treat one another and themselves in a manner incompatible with truly human relationships. This aspect of exploitation is well brought out in a striking passage from the *German Ideology*, where Marx writes of exploitation as a 'utility relation' in which

I derive benefit for myself by doing harm to someone else (*exploitation de l'homme par l'homme*): in this case moreover the use that I derive from some relation is entirely extraneous to this relation. . . . All this is actually the case with the bourgeois. For him only one relation is valid on its own account—the relation of exploitation; all other relations have validity for him only insofar as he can include them under this one relation, and even where he encounters relations which cannot be directly subordinated to the relation of exploitation, he subordinates them to it at least in his imagination. The material expression of this use is money which represents the value of all things, people and social relations.[28]

And an early note, dating from 1844, makes even clearer how Marx saw this, the most general aspect of exploitation:

I have produced for myself and not for you, just as you have produced for yourself and not for me . . . [our production] is not *social* production. . . . Each of us sees in his product only the objectification of his *own* selfish need, and therefore in the product of the other the objectification of a *different* selfish need, independent of him and alien to him.

As a man you have, of course, a human relation to my product: you *need* of my product. Hence it exists for you as an object of your desire and your will. But your need, your desire, your will are powerless as regards my product. . . . The *social* relation in which I stand to you, my labour for your need, is therefore also a mere *semblance*, the basis of which is mutual plundering.[29]

In short, this aspect of exploitation is identified from the perspective of human emancipation, to which the next chapter is devoted.

RIGHTS

Finally, we must ask: how do rights fit into the framework of Marx's and Marxist thought? And, more particularly, can a Marxist believe in human rights?

Plainly, Marx defended various particular rights in the course of his life, such as the right to a free press, the right to vote, workers' rights to decent factory conditions, and so on. The same goes for countless Marxists ever since. Indeed, Marxists across the world, especially since the Resistance to the Nazis, have been in the forefront of struggles against tyranny and oppression in many countries, often in the name of human rights, especially since the Helsinki Accords. In fact, I would argue that the establishment and protection of basic civil rights often depends on the existence of a strong and well-organized labour movement, and that Marxist parties and groups have played an important role in achieving this.

[28] K. Marx and F. Engels, *The German Ideology* (1845–6), *Collected Works of Marx and Engels* (Lawrence and Wishart: London, 1975), v. 409–10.
[29] Marx, 'Comments on James Mill, *Éléments d'économie politique*' (1844), *Collected Works of Marx and Engels*, iii. 225–6.

Nevertheless, Marxism as a body of thought has generally been inhospitable to rights. For instance, as Claude Lefort has remarked,

The expansion of marxism throughout the entire French left has for a long time gone along with a deprecation of law (*droit*) in general and the vehement condemnation, ironic or 'scientific', of the bourgeois notion of the rights of man.[30]

Rights are central to the theoretical tradition of liberalism (apart from its utilitarian strand), so that when they are violated in its name, this goes against the grain, so to speak, even if the violations are fully justified. Marxism, by contrast, displays no such tension. It is . . . from its origins committed to an ideal of freedom whose coming realization it labels human emancipation. It has never been similarly committed, as a matter of principle, to the promulgation and protection of *rights* that, when respected, serve to guarantee freedoms. For one thing, it has always tended to see rights as arising from and expressing the individualism and the contradictions of bourgeois society. For another, it is often ambivalent at best about the reality of bourgeois freedoms. And finally, it looks towards a future ideal society in which the freedoms it proclaims will require no guarantees.

A depressing illustration of what this way of thinking can lead to in practice is provided by the story of the early Soviet jurists Reisner, Stuchka, and Pashukanis. Accepting Lenin's view of the dictatorship of the proletariat as not supported by any laws, they used 'all their energy in order to prove the conservative function of the ideology of law', attacking law as such as conservative, ideological, tied to the 'commodity form', and as the 'opium of the people', and they justified the full subordination of law to politics in terms of 'revolutionary purposefulness' and 'political flexibility'. Pashukanis summed up this position when he wrote that 'revolutionary law' was 'ninety nine per cent a political task'.[31] As the Yugoslav *Praxis* philosopher Tadic has observed,

After the critical year of 1921, the dominant point of view in the Bolshevik party leadership theoretically advocated by Bukharin was that 'the party mechanism in the dictatorship of the proletariat can secure its leading position only under the condition of a monolithic unity. . . . This point of view led to the conclusion that the dictatorship of the proletariat was incompatible with political democracy . . . 'revolutionary purposefulness' soon turned into an arbitrary, despotic practice of 'state reason'. (Ibid. 425.)

[30] C. Lefort, *L'Invention démocratique: les limites de la domination totalitaire* (Fayard: Paris, 1981), 46.
[31] L. Tadic, 'The Marxist Critique of Right in the Philosophy of Ernst Bloch', *Praxis International*, 1/4 (1982), 424–5.

The roots of the Marxist view of rights (and human rights) can be found in Marx's early essay 'On the Jewish Question'. There Marx made it plain that he saw rights—the rights of man of the American Constitution and of the French Declarations of 1789 and 1793—in one perspective only: 'nothing but the rights of a *member of civil society*, i.e. the rights of egoistic man, of man separated from other men and from the community'.[32] He saw them as securing the 'right of self-interest' of a monadic and 'restricted individual, withdrawn into himself and separated from the community' (ibid. 163), and as basically reducing to the protection of private property; and as enshrining the illusory notion of a separate sphere of political emancipation (in which men *appear* free and equal) as a surrogate for (and precursor of) general human emancipation. In *The Holy Family*, he summarized his view even more extremely: 'It was shown', he wrote, 'that the *recognition of the rights of man* by the *modern state* has no other meaning than the *recognition of slavery* by the *state of antiquity* had'.[33]

It must be said that Marx's was a narrow and impoverished view of the meaning of the rights of man, even in their late eighteenth-century forms: it treated them *only* as symptomatic of the individualism and contradictions of bourgeois life. Consider only some of the rights included in the 1789 Declaration (which became the Preface to the Constitution of 1791). Articles 10 and 11, for example, state:

No-one may be harassed for his opinions, even his religious opinions, provided that their expression does not disturb public order established by law.

and

The free communication of thoughts and of opinions is one of the most precious rights of man; every citizen can therefore speak, write and print freely, except that he may be prosecuted for the abuse of that liberty in cases determined by the law.

These rights cannot easily bear Marx's interpretation, even if opinion is seen as the private property of the individual. As Lefort has written, the second of these two articles makes it clear that it is

the right of man, one of his most precious rights, to go beyond himself and relate to others, by speech, writing and thought. In other words, it makes clear that man could not be legitimately confined to the limits of his private wants, when he has the right to public speech and thought. Or in yet other words, for these last expressions risk reducing communication to the

---

[32] 'On the Jewish Question' (1843), *Collected Works of Marx and Engels*, iii. 162.
[33] Marx and Engels, *The Holy Family* (1845), *Collected Works*, iv. 133.

operations of its agents, individuals, defined one by one as examples of man as such, let us say that the article makes clear that there is a communication, a circulation of thoughts and opinions, of words and writing, which escapes in principle, except in cases specified by the law, the authority of power. The affirmation of the rights of man concerns the independence of thought and opinion in the face of power, and the cleavage between power and knowledge, not only and not essentially the divorce between bourgeois and citizen, between private property and politics.[34]

Or consider articles 7, 8, and 9:

No man can be accused, arrested or detained except in cases determined by law and according to the form it has prescribed. Those who solicit, expedite, execute or have executed arbitrary orders must be punished; but every citizen called or seized by virtue of the law must obey at once: he renders himself guilty by resistance.

and

The law can only establish punishments that are strictly and evidently necessary and no-one can be punished except by virtue of a law established and promulgated prior to the offence and applied legally.

and

Every man being presumed innocent until declared guilty, if it is judged indispensable to arrest him, every act of force that is not necessary to apprehend him must be severely punished by law.

These articles, all in the text Marx discusses, are passed over in silence. They do not lend themselves to his interpretation; and he failed to consider their positive, world-historical significance, their applicability to non-egoistic, non-bourgeois forms of social life, and their consequent relevance to the struggle for socialism, because his mind was so exclusively fixed upon the critique of the egoism of bourgeois society and the mystifying ideology that pervaded it, from the perspective of a future he imagined as emancipated from both.

There is, of course, much to be said for that critique. It is full of insight and is still pertinent. In particular, it *is* probably true that the very concept of 'rights' is, in a sense, individualistic: property rights are centrally important in the contemporary liberal tradition and form a kind of paradigm for both its Lockean and Kantian variants. Rights are typically the basis for claims by individuals to be treated in certain ways: rights offer the *interests* of these individuals as sufficient grounds for holding another or others to be under an obligation to treat them in certain ways. It is probably true that an exclusively rights-based morality would be an impoverished

[34] Lefort, *L'Invention démocratique*, 58–9.

one, unable to accommodate collective goods and the role of virtue in moral life: these are hard to capture in the form of individuated interests generating obligation.[35] But, as the passage quoted from Lefort eloquently shows, taking some rights seriously is positively to demand a certain form of social life in which social relationships flourish free of arbitrary political power. To think of them merely as expressing the egoism of civil society and the contradictions between civil society and the state is precisely to fail to take them seriously.

Moreover, the underlying thesis that we have attributed to Marx, that it is only the conflicting interests of class society that render rights necessary, is hard to believe in, in the face both of the historical record and of theoretical considerations. It is, after all, not only conflicting class interests that generate the need for the protections and guarantees that rights afford. As Buchanan has convincingly shown,[36] such protections and guarantees may be needed in at least the following circumstances: where minorities are disfavoured by democratic procedures, where paternalist policies interfere with individual liberties, where disagreements exist about what constitutes welfare or the common good, where coercion is required for the provision of public goods, and where guidelines and limits must be set to the provision for future generations. Why should we believe that any feasible form of social life, albeit abundant and free of class antagonisms, could be beyond circumstances such as these? Nor would the practice of altruism (which, as we have seen, Marx did not envisage) render such rights unnecessary. Even under altruism, there will be a need to protect people from others' mistakes about what altruism requires. Indeed, the more altruistic a society claims to be, the more important such protections and guarantees will be in case such claims are spurious, since only where they exist can the claims be tested.

My argument has been that Marxism has inherited too narrow an account of the significance of rights and too narrow a view of circumstances that render them necessary. The former narrowness has made them seem unimportant, the latter potentially dispensable. But are there resources within the Marxist tradition for overcoming this double narrowness? More specifically, can a Marxist believe in human rights?

I have already said that countless Marxists have in fact believed in and fought for human rights. So the question is not whether those whose beliefs and affiliations are Marxist in fact believe in human rights. It is rather whether they can *consistently* do so. But the

[35] J. Raz, 'On the Nature of Rights', *Mind*, 93/370 (Apr. 1984).
[36] A. E. Buchanan, *Marx and Justice: The Radical Critique of Liberalism* (Methuen: London, 1982).

question thus formulated is still not adequate. For I am certain that many of those who are called, and call themselves, Marxists and who believe in human rights hold a consistent set of beliefs that do not contradict their belief in and actions for human rights. The question, therefore, should be reformulated thus: can those whose beliefs and affiliations are Marxist believe in human rights and remain consistent with central doctrines essential to the Marxist canon?

To 'believe' in human rights, I shall assume, is, precisely, to take them seriously: to give priority to the interests they presuppose and the obligations they impose, and to be prepared to act accordingly when the occasion arises. Indeed, one test of such a belief is being prepared so to act.

Here I shall follow Feinberg in defining 'human rights' as 'generically moral rights of a fundamentally important kind held equally by all human beings, unconditionally and unalterably'.[37] They are sometimes understood to be 'ideal rights', or rights that are not necessarily actually recognized, but which ought to be; that is, they ought to be positive rights and would be so in a better or ideal legal system. Sometimes, they are understood to be 'conscientious rights', that is, the claim is to recognize them as valid by reference to the principles of an enlightened conscience. Are they absolute?

To be absolute in the strongest sense, they would have to be absolutely exceptionless in all circumstances: given that the possessor of the right has the appropriate interests, the obligation the right imposes on appropriate others to protect or promote those interests would be categorical and absolute, admitting of no exceptions. But this is an impossibly strong requirement. For in the first place, the obligation, and thus the right, may be unfulfillable. This is the case with many of the rights specified in the United Nations Universal Declaration of Human Rights, especially the positive rights (rights to be treated in certain ways). These—for instance, the so-called 'social and economic rights', and in general rights to be given the means of living a decent life, or even a life at all—depend for their implementation on the availability of resources, and therefore, since ought implies can, they cannot be absolute in this sense. But second, and more fundamentally, the obligation, and thus the right, can always be legitimately overridden, in certain circumstances. Consider some promising candidates for absolute status. Take, first, the right not to be tortured. Suppose you have captured someone who knows where the bomb is that will blow up a crowded airport which there is no time to clear. The putatively

---

[37] J. Feinberg, *Social Philosophy* (Prentice-Hall: Englewood Cliffs, NJ, 1973), 85.

absolute right not to be degraded or exploited falls to a similar objection. What of the more general rights to liberty, or to be treated with equal concern and respect? But what these mean in practice is unspecifiable in uncontestable terms; and in each case, it is not hard to think up non-eccentric situations in which they may be overridden for the sake of some greater good.

It is therefore perhaps better to say that human rights are strongly prima-facie rights which, in general, are justified in defending people's vital interests and which, in general, override all other considerations bearing upon some policy or action, whether these concern goals and purposes or the protection of other, less central rights. They thus have a 'trumping' aspect:[38] to believe in them is to be committed to defending them, even (or rather especially) when one's goals or strategies are not to be served, and indeed may be disserved, by doing so.

To put this another way (which shows the connection between justice and rights), talk of rights is a way of asserting the requirements of a relationship of justice, from the viewpoint of the persons benefiting from it. It involves adopting 'the viewpoint of the "other(s)"' to whom something (including, inter alia, freedom of choice) is owed or due, and who would be wronged if denied that something'.[39] Talk of human rights is to do this, while emphasizing the fundamental and prima-facie overriding status of this viewpoint with respect to certain matters, specifically those central to the flourishing of human beings. Proof that such talk is serious is being prepared to abandon goals and policies and strategies, except in rare and extreme cases, where to recognize such rights conflicts with their implementation.

On a narrower and more extreme view, rights might, following Robert Nozick, be seen as 'side constraints'—moral constraints upon goal-directed behaviour. This way of viewing rights (rather than building the minimization of the violation of rights into one's goals) is a strictly deontological position: the constraints must not be violated even if such violations would lead to better consequences (even if these consist in the minimizing of rights violations). Individuals, as Nozick puts it, 'have rights, and there are things no person or group may do to them (without violating their rights)'; their rights 'set the constraints within which a social choice is to be made, by excluding certain alternatives, fixing others, and so on'.[40] This view of rights, according to Nozick, reflects the basic Kantian position of treating persons as ends and not merely as means, of

---

[38] R. Dworkin, *Taking Rights Seriously* (Duckworth: London, 1977).
[39] J. Finnis, *Natural Law and Natural Rights* (Clarendon Press: Oxford, 1980), 205.
[40] R. Nozick, *Anarchy, State and Utopia* (Blackwell: Oxford, 1974), pp. ix, 166.

ruling out certain ways in which persons (or the Party or the State) may use others. On this view, their basis is that they

express the inviolability of other persons. But why may one not violate persons for the greater social good? Individually, we each sometimes choose to undergo some pain or sacrifice for a greater benefit or to avoid a greater harm: we go to the dentist to avoid worse suffering later: we do some unpleasant work for its results; some persons diet to improve their health or looks; some save money to support themselves when older. In each case, some cost is borne for the sake of the overall good. Why not, *similarly*, hold that some persons have to bear some costs that benefit other persons more, for the sake of the overall social good? But there is no *social entity* with a good that undergoes some sacrifice for its own good. There are only individual people, with their own individual lives. Using one of these people for the benefit of others uses him and benefits the others. Nothing more. What happens is that something is done to him for the sake of the others. Talk of an overall social good covers this up. (Intentionally?) To use a person in this way does not sufficiently respect and take account of the fact that he is a separate person, that his is the only life that he has. He does not get some overbalancing good from his sacrifice. . . . (Ibid. 32–3.)

But the trouble is that, for reasons stated above, it is not clear that any rights can be absolute. Perhaps, then, the constraints can be held to be unconstraining under certain circumstances? Nozick himself allows for this possibility when he writes in a concessionary footnote that 'the question of whether these side-constraints are absolute, or whether they may be violated to avoid catastrophic moral horror, and if the latter what the ensuing structure [of justification] might look like, is one I hope largely to avoid' (ibid. 29–30 n.). This 'threshold' approach requires some account of the conditions under which strongly prima-facie rights, seen as constraints, may be overridden, and indeed of how rights differ in this regard; and this in turn would seem to require an analysis that is, in Sen's phrase, 'consequence-sensitive',[41] comparing the consequences of obeying the constraint with those of violating it. Presumably such an analysis of *human* rights will set the threshold for such rights especially high.

Accordingly, Sen has proposed a consequence-sensitive approach to rights, building the fulfilment and non-realization of rights into the goals of action which is evaluated in terms of its consequences. This approach addresses directly the strength of rights claims against other considerations, especially where rights clash (e.g. where one right cannot be defended without another being violated). According to Sen, some rights are much more 'serious' than others, and these relate persons to basic capabilities to which they have a

---

[41] A. K. Sen, 'Rights and Agency', *Philosophy and Public Affairs*, 11/1 (1981).

right (e.g. the general right not to be beaten up relates to the capability to 'move about without harm' [ibid. 18–19]). So on this account too, rights set limits to other social policies and to the individual pursuit of goals (including the attainment of less important rights). *Human* rights, presumably, set maximally narrow limits.

Our question, then, reduces to this: has Marxism any interest in taking such limits seriously, or is to do so not to take Marxism seriously? My argument so far has tended to suggest the latter, first, because Marxism sees them as expressive of the egoism of bourgeois society and, second, because it sees them as answering to a (pre-human) condition that must itself be transcended; *human* rights it tends to oppose as unwarrantably abstract and decontextualized. And yet at least one great Marxist thinker has argued eloquently for a rights-based utopian perspective, namely Ernst Bloch, and the question inevitably arises: is not the future ideal of freedom to which Marxism is committed unapproachable through the violation in the present and in the future of the limits that basic or human rights impose?

NOTES ON CONTRIBUTORS

ARISTOTLE was born in 384 BC in Macedonia; he joined the Academy in 367, was tutor to the young Alexander the Great from 343, and founded his own school, the Lyceum, in 335. He died at Chalcis in 322.

CICERO was born in 106 BC. He combined a career in Roman politics with literary and philosophical pursuits; in 79 he visited Athens to study philosophy, in 63 he was Consul. He sided with the losing forces in the civil war, was proscribed by Mark Anthony, and was killed in 43 BC.

FRIEDRICH VON HAYEK was born in 1899 and died in 1992; he taught economics at Universities of Vienna, London and Chicago, and was awarded the Nobel Prize for Economics in 1974. His most famous book was, perhaps, *The Road to Serfdom* (1944).

DAVID HUME was born in 1711 and died in 1776; apart from a brief appointment as tutor to the Marquis of Annandale and two years in diplomatic service, he lived as an independent man of letters in England, Scotland and France.

STEVEN LUKES is Professor of Politics at the European University in Florence; he is the author of *Emile Durkheim*, *Individualism*, and *Moral and Political Conflict* as well as many shorter essays.

KARL MARX was born in Trier in 1818 and died in London in 1883; his most substantial, but not most widely read work was *Das Kapital*.

JOHN STUART MILL was born in London in 1806 and died in Avignon in 1873; he was the author of *A System of Logic*, *The Principles of Political Economy*, and *On Liberty*, in addition to innumerable shorter essays.

ROBERT NOZICK is Professor of Philosophy at Harvard University; he is the author of *Philosophical Explanation* and *The Examined Life*, as well as *Anarchy, State and Utopia*.

PLATO was born in Athens in 428 BC; after the death of Socrates in 399, he withdrew from politics into the life of the Academy, and died in Athens in 348 or 347.

JOHN RAWLS is Professor Emeritus of Philosophy at Harvard University, from which he retired in 1991. He is the author of *A Theory of Justice* and many essays in ethics.

FURTHER READING

This list is a very small selection from the enormous literature on justice, narrowly confined to books and articles that follow up the passages selected above. Collections and sources with extensive bibliographies are indicated with an asterisk.

HISTORICAL TEXTS AND COMMENTARIES

Plato, Aristotle, Cicero

ANNAS, JULIA, *An Introduction to Plato's Republic* (Clarendon Press: Oxford, 1982).
CROMBIE, I. M., 'A Dream of Socrates', *Philosophy* (1989), 29–38.
HALL, I. W., *Plato* (Allen and Unwin: London, 1981).
IRWIN, T. H., 'Aristotle on the Human Good,' *Ethics*, 101/2 (1990–1) 382–91.
JOHNSON, CURTIS, 'Socrates on Obedience and Justice', *Western Political Quarterly* (1990), 719–40.
LEYDEN, W. VON, *Aristotle on Equality and Justice* (Macmillan: London, 1985).
LYCOS, KIMON, *Plato, Justice and Power* (Macmillan: London, 1987).
MULGAN, RICHARD, *Aristotle's Politics* (Allen and Unwin: London, 1981).
PLATO, *The Laws*, tr. Thomas Pangle (Basic Books: New York, 1980).
POPPER, KARL, *The Open Society and its Enemies*, vol. i (Routledge: London, 1945).
WOOD, NEAL, *Cicero's Social and Political Thought* (University of California Press: Berkeley, Calif., 1988).
YACK, BERNARD, 'Natural Right and Aristotle's Understanding of Justice', *Political Theory* (1990), 216–27.

Hume, Kant, Utilitarian Justice, Mill

BERGER, FRED, *Happiness, Justice and Freedom* (University of California Press: Berkeley, Calif., 1985).
GODWIN, WILLIAM, *Political Justice*, ed. K. Codell Carter (Oxford University Press: Oxford, 1974).
GRAY, JOHN, *Mill on Liberty: A Defence* (Routledge and Kegan Paul: London, 1983).
HARRISON, JONATHAN, *Hume's Theory of Justice* (Oxford University Press: Oxford, 1984).
HUBIN, D. CLAYTON, 'The Scope of Justice', *Philosophy and Public Affairs*, 9 (1979), 3–24.
KANT, IMMANUEL, *Metaphysical Elements of Justice* (Library of Liberal Arts, Macmillan: New York, 1965).

KANT, IMMANUEL, *Political Writings*, ed. Hans Reiss (Cambridge University Press: Cambridge, 1992).

NORTON, DAVID FATE, *Hume* (Princeton University Press: Princeton, NJ, 1982).

O'NEILL, ONORA, 'Kantian Politics I: The Public Use of Reason', *Political Theory* 14/4 (1986), 523–51.

——*Constructions of Reason* (Cambridge University Press: Cambridge, 1989).

PHILP, MARK, *Godwin's Political Justice* (Duckworth: London, 1989).

POGGE, T. W., 'Kant's Theory of Justice', *Kant Studien*, 79 (1988), 407–33.

RYAN, ALAN, *J. S. Mill* (Routledge and Kegan Paul: London, 1974).

SKORUPSKI, JOHN, *John Stuart Mill* (Routledge and Kegan Paul: London, 1990).

SORELL, TOM, 'Self, Society, and Kantian Impersonality', *Monist*, 74 (1991), 30–42.

WHELAN, F. G., *Order and Artifice in Hume's Political Philosophy* (Princeton University Press: Princeton, NJ, 1987).

WILLIAMS, HOWARD, *Kant's Political Philosophy* (Blackwell: Oxford, 1983).

CONTEMPORARY DISCUSSIONS

'Social Justice'

ACKERMAN, BRUCE, *Social Justice and the Liberal State* (Yale University Press: New Haven, Conn., 1980).

LUCAS, JOHN, *On Justice* (Clarendon Press: Oxford, 1989).

MACPHERSON, C. B., *The Rise and Fall of Economic Justice*, (Oxford University Press: Oxford, 1987).

MAPEL, DAVID, *Social Justice Reconsidered* (University of Illinois Press: Champaign, 1989).

MILLER, DAVID, *Social Justice* (Clarendon Press: Oxford, 1978).

NAGEL, THOMAS, *Equality and Partiality* (Oxford University Press: Oxford, 1991).

SEN, AMARTYA, 'Justice: Means vs Freedom', *Philosophy and Public Affairs*, 19 (1990), 111–21.

WALZER, MICHAEL, *Spheres of Justice* (Martin Robertson: Oxford, 1983).

Rawls and his Critics

ARNESON, RICHARD, *et al.*, 'Symposium on the Later Work of John Rawls: Introduction', *Ethics*, 99/4 (1989), 695–710.

BAIER, ANNETTE, '*A Theory of Justice*', *Ethics*, 99/4 (1989), 771–90.

BARBER, BENJAMIN, 'Justifying Justice: Problems of Psychology, Politics and Measurement', in Daniels, *Reading Rawls*, 292–316.

BARRY, BRIAN, *The Liberal Theory of Justice* (Clarendon Press: Oxford, 1973).

BLOOM, ALLAN, 'Justice: John Rawls vs The Tradition of Political Philosophy', *American Political Science Review*, 69 (1975), 648–62.

COHEN, G. A., 'On the Currency of Egalitarian Justice', *Ethics*, 99/4 (1989), 906–44.

DANIELS, NORMAN (ed.), *Reading Rawls: Critical Studies on Rawls's 'A Theory of Justice'* (Blackwell: Oxford, 1976*).

DWORKIN, RONALD, 'The Original Position' in Daniels, *Reading Rawls*, 16–53.

GALSTON, WILLIAM, *Justice and the Human Good* (University of Chicago Press: Chicago, 1980).

HART, H. L. A., 'Between Utility and Rights', in Alan Ryan, ed., *The Idea of Freedom* (Oxford University Press: Oxford, 1979).

KUKATHAS, CHANDRAN, and PETTIT, PHILIP, *Rawls's A Theory of Justice and its Critics* (Polity Press: Oxford, 1990).

MILLER, RICHARD, 'Rawls and Marxism', in Daniels, *Reading Rawls*, 206–30.

NAGEL, THOMAS, 'Rawls on Justice', in Daniels, *Reading Rawls*, 1–16.

POGGE, THOMAS, *Realizing Rawls* (Cornell University Press: Ithaca, NY, 1989).

RAWLS, JOHN, *A Theory of Justice* (Harvard University Press: Cambridge, Mass., 1971).

——'Justice as Fairness: Political not Metaphysical', *Philosophy and Public Affairs*, 14 (1985), 223–51.

RAZ, JOSEPH, 'Facing Diversity: The Case of Epistemic Abstinence', *Philosophy and Public Affairs*, 19/1 (1990), 3–46.

RORTY, RICHARD, 'The Priority of Democracy to Philosophy', in Merrill Peterson and Robert Vaughan (eds.), *The Virginia Statute for Religious Freedom* (Cambridge University Press,: Cambridge, 1988).

SCANLON, T. M., 'Rawls' Theory of Justice', in Daniels, *Reading Rawls*, 169–205.

SEN, A. K., 'Rawls versus Bentham: An Axiomatic Examination of the Pure Distribution Problem', in Daniels, *Reading Rawls*, 283–92.

Hayek and Nozick

BARRY, NORMAN, *Hayek's Social and Economic Philosophy* (Macmillan: London 1979).

GRAY, JOHN, 'Hayek on Liberty, Rights, and Justice', *Ethics*, 92/1 (1982), 73–84.

——*Hayek on Liberty* (Routledge: London, 1983).

KUKATHAS, CHANDRAN, *Hayek and Modern Liberalism* (Clarendon Press: Oxford, 1990).

LYONS, DAVID, 'The New Indian Claims and Original Rights to Land', in Daniels, *Reading Rawls*, 355–79.

O'NEILL, ONORA, 'Nozick's Entitlements', in Paul, *Reading Nozick*, 305–22

PAUL, JEFFREY, *Reading Nozick* (Blackwell: Oxford, 1982*).

SCANLON, THOMAS, 'Nozick on Rights, Liberty and Property', in Paul, *Reading Nozick*, 107–29.

STEINER, HILLEL, 'Justice and Entitlement', in Daniels, *Reading Rawls*, 380–2.

VAN DER VEEN, R., and VAN PARIJS, P., 'Entitlement Theories of Justice: From Nozick to Roemer and beyond', *Economics and Philosophy*, 1 (1985), 69–81.

VARIAN, HAL, 'Distributive Justice, Welfare Economics, and the Theory of Fairness', *Philosophy and Public Affairs*, 4 (1974), 223–47.

WOLFF, JONATHAN, *Robert Nozick* (Polity Press: Oxford, 1991).

Marxian Justice

BUCHANAN, ALLEN E., *Marx and Justice: The Radical Critique of Individualism* (Methuen: London, 1982).

CAMPBELL, TOM, *The Left and Rights* (Routledge: London, 1983).

COHEN, G. A., 'Freedom, Justice, and Capitalism', *New Left Review*, 126 (1981), 3–16.

COHEN, MARSHALL, NAGEL, THOMAS, and SCANLON, THOMAS (eds.), *Marx, Justice and History* (Princeton University Press: Princeton, NJ, 1980).

ELSTER, JON, *Making Sense of Marx* (Cambridge University Press: Cambridge, 1985).

GERAS, NORMAN, 'On Marxism and Justice', *New Left Review*, 150 (1988), 47–89.

HELLER, AGNES, *Beyond Justice* (Basil Blackwell: Oxford, 1987).

LUKES, STEVEN, *Marxism and Morality* (Oxford University Press: Oxford, 1985).

NIELSEN, KAI, 'Arguing about Justice: Marxist Immoralism and Marxist Moralism', *Philosophy and Public Affairs* 17 (1988), 212–34.

NORMAN, RICHARD, *The Moral Philosophers* (Oxford University Press: Oxford, 1985).

RYAN, ALAN, 'Justice, Exploitation, and the End of Morality', in J. D. G. Evans (ed.), *Moral Philosophy and Contemporary Problems* (Cambridge University Press: Cambridge, 1987).

Communitarianism and Justice

BUCHANAN, ALLEN E., 'Assessing the Communitarian Critique of Liberalism', *Ethics*, 99/4 (1989), 852–82.

CARNEY, SIMON, 'Sandel's Critique of the Primacy of Justice', *British Journal of Political Science*, 21/4 (1991), 511–21.

KYMLICKA, W. F., *Liberalism, Community, and Culture* (Clarendon Press: Oxford, 1989).

MACINTYRE, ALASDAIR, *Whose Justice? Which Rationality?* (Duckworth: London, 1989).

SANDEL, MICHAEL, *Liberalism and the Limits of Justice* (Cambridge University Press: Cambridge, 1982).

SHARP, ANDREW R., 'Liberty, Community, and Justice', *Political Theory*, 17/2 (1989), 333–8.
SWIFT, ADAM, and MULHALL, STEPHEN, *Liberals and Communitarians* (Blackwell: Oxford, 1992).

Methodological Issues

ARROW, KENNETH, *Social Choice and Justice* (Blackwell: Oxford, 1984).
BARRY, BRIAN, 'Justice as Reciprocity', in Eugene Kamenka and Alive Erhsoon Tay (eds.), *Justice* (Edward Arnold: London 1979*).
——*Therories of Justice*, vol. i (Harvester Press: Brighton, 1989).
CAMPBELL, TOM, *Justice* (Macmillan: London, 1988).
CHAPMAN, JOHN W., and PENNOCK, ROLAND (eds.), *Justice: Nomos VI* (Atherton Press: New York, 1963*).
GIBBARD, ALLAN, 'Constructing Justice', *Philosophy and Public Affairs*, 20/2 (1991), 101–33.
GOODIN, ROBERT E., *The Politics of Rational Man* (Wiley: Chichester, England, 1976).
LADEN, ANTHONY, 'Games, Fairness, and Rawls's *Theory of Justice*', *Philosophy and Public Affairs*, 20 (1991), 189–222.
OKIN, SUSAN, 'Reason and Feeling in Thinking about Justice' *Ethics*, 99/2 (1989), 229–49.
——*Justice, Gender and the Family*, (Basic Books: New York, 1990).
RAPHAEL, D. D., *Justice and Liberty* (Athlone Press: London, 1980*).
RAWLS, JOHN, 'Kantian Constructivism in Moral Theory', *Journal of Philosophy*, 77 (1980), 515–72.

INDEX

distribution (*cont.*):
  fair 159, 162, 164
  income 81, 92, 93, 121, 144; just 85
  theory of 170
  wealth 81, 86, 90; just 85, 121
distributive justice 9, 12, 13–14, 16, 69, 73–116
  see also social justice
Donati, Benevuto 122 n.
duties 54–5, 58, 71, 77, 140, 148
  assignment of 76
  based on personal acquaintance and familiarity 149
  change of, in change of circumstances 43–4
  distasteful 150
  enforced 147
  fundamental 76, 79
  legally enforceable 149
  moral 44, 59, 120, 145
  to those who have wronged us 44–5
  see also obligations
Duverger, M. 144 n.
Dworkin, R. 182 n.

earnings, *see* income; remuneration; rewards
efficiency 80, 84–5, 87, 127, 140
  competitive 93
  concept of 79
  principle of 83, 92
Elster, Jon 167 n., 170, 173, 174
embezzlement 166, 175
emigration 112
Engels, F. 165 n., 169, 176 n., 178 n.
entitlements 3–4, 96–116
envy 103 n.
equality 35–8, 55, 69, 99, 146, 161
  citizenship 74, 84, 94
  expectations 86
  opportunity 80, 81, 84, 86, 93, 142–3
  political 81
  principle of 91, 92
  proportionate 9
  rights 71, 141
ethics 6, 8, 75
  Marxian 15, 167
  utilitarian 72
evil 6, 26, 27, 31, 37, 39, 48
  desert and 54
  evil by 69
  evil for 10, 68
  immunity from 63
  impunity given to justice as 57

lesser/greater 36
punishment to prevent 64
exchange 97, 103–5, 107, 110, 161, 169
  voluntary 38, 95, 96
expectations 77, 79, 80–1, 85, 91–2
  customary 88
  equality of 86
  inequality in 82
  legitimate 90, 151
  long-term 87
expediency 51–3 *passim*, 56, 58, 60, 140
  and inexpediency 63
  social 67, 71
exploitation 15, 166–8, 173, 174–6

faith 42, 54, 59
faults 32
fear 7–8, 42
Feinberg, J. 181
Ferguson, Adam 127 n.
fidelity 45, 46
Finnis, J. 182 n.
Fogarty, M. 132 n.
foreigners 148
forfeiture 53, 54
France 144
Frankena, W. A. 137 n.
fraud 14, 130
free enterprise 131
freedom 13, 67, 68, 81, 84, 147
  formal 175
  ideal of 177
  individual/personal 118, 124, 133, 145, 157, 158
  loss of 74
  social justice and 143–6
French Declarations (1789 and 1793) 178
Friedman, David 115 n.
Friedmann, W. 145 n.

gains 35, 37, 38, 73, 83, 97
Geck, L. H. A. 136 n.
gemeinschaftlich relations 173
geometrical proportion 36–8
George, Henry 113
Geyl, Peter 155 n.
Gibbon, Edward 118 n., 123
Gilbert and Sullivan 2 n.
God 132, 139
good 6–10 *passim*, 27, 37, 39, 53–4, 62–4 *passim*

Index compiled by Frank Pert

CANISIUS COLLEGE LIBRARY

3 5084 00302 6203

JC 578 .J863 1993

Justice

DATE DUE

CANISIUS COLLEGE LIBRARY
BUFFALO, N.Y.